# The Struggle for Mastery in Germany, 1779–1850

Brendan Simms

*Fellow and Director of Studies in History*
*Peterhouse*
*Cambridge University*

St. Martin's Press
New York

THE STRUGGLE FOR MASTERY IN GERMANY, 1779–1850
Copyright © 1998 by Brendan Simms

St. Martin's Press, Scholarly and Reference Division,
175 Fifth Avenue, New York, N.Y. 10010

First published in the United States of America in 1998

This book is printed on paper suitable for recycling and
made from fully managed and sustained forest sources.

Printed in Hong Kong

ISBN 0–312–21309–3 clothbound
ISBN 0–312–21310–7 paperback

Library of Congress Cataloging-in-Publication Data
Simms, Brendan.
The struggle for mastery in Germany, 1779–1850 / Brendan Simms.
p.   cm. — (European history in perspective)
Includes bibliographical references and index.
ISBN 0–312–21309–3. — ISBN 0–312–21310–7 (pbk.)
1. Germany—Politics and government—1740–1806.   2. Germany–
–Politics and government—1806–1848.   3. France—History–
–Revolution, 1789–1799.   4. Conservatism—Germany.   5. Germany–
–Economic conditions—19th century.   6. Political culture—Germany.
7. Nationalism—Germany.   I. Title.   II. Series.
DD197.5.S56  1997
943—dc21                                          97–41113
                                                      CIP

# CONTENTS

# ACKNOWLEDGEMENTS

I dedicate this book to my wife Anita Bunyan, whose intellectual stimulus and moral support were invaluable throughout. She read and commented on countless earlier drafts. I am also extremely grateful to my former supervisor, Tim Blanning, who originally conceived the course of lectures at Cambridge from which this book takes its title, and whose criticisms of the original manuscript were most helpful. Indeed, it has been my good fortune to work in Cambridge at a time when the 'Struggle for Mastery in Germany' united many diverse talents under one roof. Jonathan Steinberg was very kind to me and sharpened my sense of paradox in German history. Chris Clark, the Renaissance man of German history, not only read and improved upon the first draft but has greatly enriched my understanding of innumerable aspects of German social, religious, political and international history. Niall Ferguson first made me aware of the importance of fiscal–political factors. Joachim Voth was kind enough to help me with the social and economic chapters. Maiken Umbach was very generous with her knowledge of the Enlightenment and kindly allowed me to quote from her unpublished thesis. Andreas Fahrmeir greatly improved the nineteenth-century chapters and shared his expertise on migration. My former pupils and erstwhile 'Strugglers', Gidon Katz and Gregory Moreton, read the first draft with a student's critical eye.

I am also very grateful to my mother, Anngret Simms, who read the first draft from a (historical) geographer's perspective and suggested many improvements. Eda Sagarra helped me with aspects of social and cultural history. Last but by no means least, I thank Hamish Scott, who made extremely detailed comments on the eighteenth-century section and saved me from many embarrassing mistakes.

None of these people is in any sense responsible for what I have written, or for any remaining errors, but they can take considerable credit for any merit the book may possess.

Finally, I also owe a broader debt to my colleagues at Peterhouse ·

with whom I have had many interesting discussions on the ambiguities and costs of the modernization process. In particular, I thank Roger Lovatt, my co-director of studies, who unselfishly gave me the necessary time to write. I also thank my other colleagues on the history side – Edward Lipman, John Adamson, Jonathan Shepard, Nicholas Vincent and Mathew Innes – who have made the college such a stimulating place in which to research and teach. Finally, I record my gratitude to those Fellows and friends upon whose support the teaching of history at Peterhouse depends, notably the Master, James Carleton Paget, Roderick Munday, Martin Golding, David Watkin, Andrew Murison, Nick Cumpsty, Graham Ward, Imre Leader, Paul Dupree, Hallard Croft, Dick Plumb and Adrian Dixon.

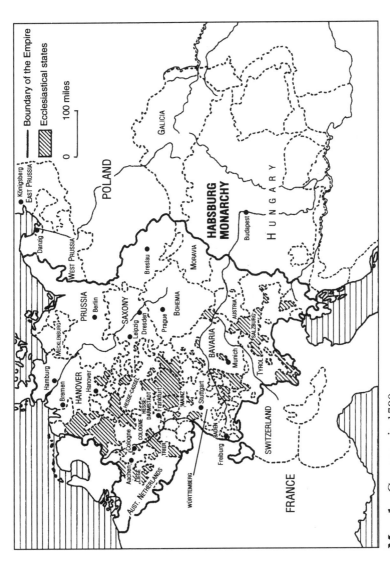

**Map 1** Germany in 1780

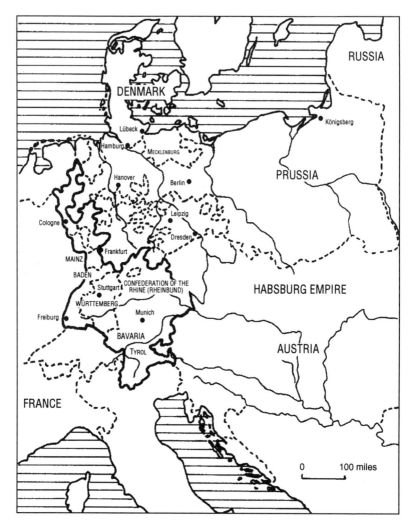

**Map 2**    Germany in 1806 (before the battle of Jena)

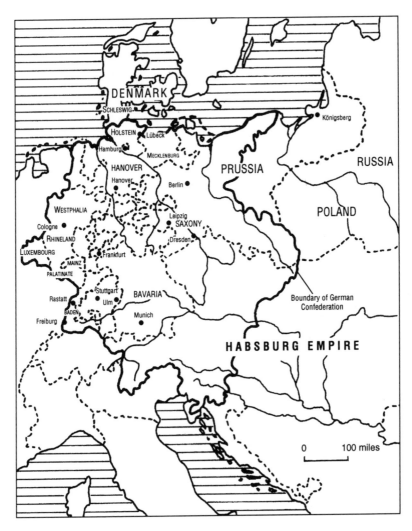

**Map 3**   Germany after 1815

# 1

## INTRODUCTION: GEOPOLITICS, MODERNIZATION THEORY AND THE PRIMACY OF FOREIGN POLICY

Eighteenth-century 'Germany' was not an island. In 1780, the core areas of German settlement were unprotected by major natural boundaries. In the west, German-speakers inhabited both the right and the left bank of the Rhine; to the south, in the Tyrol, they were to be found well beyond the Alpine passes. To the north, in Schleswig-Holstein, German-speaking settlement stretched into Denmark; in the east and south-east there were then no mountains or waterways separating German-speakers from their Slavic neighbours. This geopolitical configuration made Germans particularly sensitive to the overall balance of power in Europe, especially the hegemonic pretensions of France and Russia. 'The [German] empire,' the philosopher Gottfried Wilhelm Leibniz wrote, 'is the main limb, Germany is the centre of Europe . . . Germany is a ball which [the powers] toss to one another . . . Germany is the battlefield on which the struggle for mastery in Europe is fought.'[1] Moreover, around 1780 'Germany' was no *relatively* homogeneous national state on French lines, but a loose agglomeration of independent, semi-independent and dependent territories known as the Holy Roman Empire of German Nationality (*Reich*). At that time, the *Reich* bordered on no fewer than seven states, easily the largest number of neighbours of any state in Europe; this figure had hardly changed by 1850.

By the late eighteenth century, the geopolitical predicament of Germany had been, if anything, aggravated by the completion of the European pentarchy of Austria, Prussia, Russia, France and Great Britain. Whereas Northern Italy, the Rhine, and especially the Low

Countries, had constituted the political 'cockpit of Europe' between 1648 and 1740, the rise of Russian power shifted the centre of gravity eastward so that it straddled Germany as a whole and no longer merely her western border. Perhaps even more important, the German states were *individually* vulnerable and felt it. The Hohenzollern monarchy – Prussia, in short – was well-defended to the south, but wide open to the west and east. It was thus, to quote the seventeenth-century Great Elector of Brandenburg, always in danger of becoming 'the theatre . . . upon which the other powers perform their tragedies'.[2] Similarly, the Habsburg lands – Austria, in short – were protected by mountain ranges to the north, but exposed to the south and east. As for the middling and smaller principalities, many of them geographically dispersed, most of them were not only vulnerable to attack from all sides, but also utterly dependent on the protection of larger sponsors. The Duchy of Baden, a Jackson Pollock smeared along the Upper Rhine valley, was a case in point.

This sense of geopolitical vulnerability ensured that the guiding principle for all, or nearly all, German rulers was the 'primacy of foreign policy'. Events in the *Reich* were profoundly affected, and often simply determined, by developments within the European states' system, in particular the hegemonic threat of France. But the primacy of foreign policy also operated between the German states themselves, in particular among Austria and Prussia whose contest for political supremacy in Germany – 'dualism' – was to set the agenda throughout most of our period, either openly, as in the period from 1780 to 1806, and again after about 1825, or latently, as in the period in between. The use of the term 'primacy of foreign policy' is in no sense normative or prescriptive;[3] it does not applaud, but merely notes the ascendancy of external fears and ambitions not simply in the subjective consciousness of German governments, but also in determining objective developments. Failure to honour the primacy of foreign policy, or even miscalculation, could bring terrible penalties. The dismemberment of Poland and many smaller German states between 1772 and 1806 was an eloquent testimony to this.

If the contest between Austria and Prussia held centre stage, there were also many other struggles for mastery in Germany: between the 'Third [i.e. non-Prussian or Austrian] Germany' of Saxony, Hannover, Württemberg, Bavaria, Baden and, until around 1800, the major ecclesiastical states, and the two great powers for ascendancy in the *Reich*; between the territorial states and the empire as a whole; between princely absolutism and corporate (*ständisch*) liberty; between peasant and lord; between noble and bourgeois; between manufacturer and artisan; between advocates of a militia and proponents of a standing army; mercantilists and free traders; centralists and federalists; nationalists and particularists; Catholics and Protestants; reformed Catholicism and Baroque piety. The list is by no means exhaustive. Many of these struggles corresponded to broader European developments, others were specific to Germany. Yet they were all part of a general process known loosely, but none the less helpfully, as *modernization*.

As conceived by the late nineteenth- and early twentieth-century German sociologist Max Weber, and refined by later generations of mainly German and American theorists, modernization involves parallel developments in society, economy and politics: the replacement of the traditional society of orders by a market-determined and orientated class society; the triumph of capitalism over feudal modes of production; and the emergence of first the rational bureaucratic, and then the national, democratic state. Modernization implies a notable demographic revolution, with exponential population growth; it involves industrialization, mechanization and commercialization; it leads to the division of labour, the decline of the agarian sector, urbanization, increased social and spatial mobility, specialization and professionalization; it replaces the old courtly culture with a bourgeois 'public sphere', and increased literacy; it stimulates a process of secularization and a change in mentalities, away from communal values and traditional piety towards a more rational, individualistic, but often alienated world-view; and it should result in greater popular political participation, reflecting the increased consciousness and self-confidence of society as a whole.[4]

Germany certainly experienced a process of modernization during the late eighteenth and early nineteenth century, though it was far from complete by 1850. German society was now increasingly mobile rather than static; the transformation from imperial estate to sovereign state had been successfully accomplished in almost every German territory; the development of a national as opposed to a regional consciousness was well advanced; agrarian relations had been radically modernized, thanks to a programme of reforms; there was the emergence of a public sphere; authority became less personal and local, more abstract and rational; and Germany had experienced huge demographic growth. But on the other hand, German society at the end of our period was still hierarchic rather than meritocratic; the economy was dominated by agriculture rather than industry; Germany remained disunited; the political system in most German states remained firmly 'pre-modern'; and in East-Elbian Germany the power of the nobility had actually increased.

This perceived gulf between socio-economic and political development – which was to become even more marked after the mid-century – prompted many historians to speak of a German *Sonderweg*, a 'unique path' deviating from the western European norm.[5] Unlike Britain and France, so the argument runs, Germany experienced no 'twin Revolution' (Hobsbawm): her industrial revolution was not followed by a commensurate liberal bourgeois revolution of the political system, or evolution, as in Britain. This lack of 'synchronization' was termed a 'deficit of simultaneity' (*'Die Ungleichzeitigkeit des Gleichzeitigen'*). Indeed, socio-economic development was fostered at the expense of political progress; this became known as 'partial' or 'defensive' modernization.[6]

Over the past two decades, the notion of a *Sonderweg* and modernization theory have been subjected to searching criticism. More detailed studies of French and British history have shown their development to have been more peculiar and less normative than once thought; we are also less confident about the benefits of modernity than we were in the heroic age of modernization theory. A combination of post-modern weariness with all-embracing interpretative frameworks, on the one hand, and empirical research, on the other, has convinced many that the development of Germany before 1850 was more diverse, fragmented and complex than once envisaged by classic modernization theory.[7] Nevertheless, a refined use of modernization models is not merely defensible, but necessary. Like the primacy of foreign policy, modernization theory should be employed descriptively, not normatively; its value lies in explaining what *did* happen, not what *should* have happened. Moreover, modernization theory is essential to an understanding of the domestic implications of the primacy of foreign policy.

Sometimes, the primacy of foreign policy acted as a brake, but more often it was a powerful motor of modernization. For the external demands of the struggle for mastery in Germany provided a strong impetus to the internal processes of rationalization, bureaucratization and other measures aimed at strengthening the power of the state. This *directed modernization*, to adapt the definition of M. R. Lepsius, was 'a process of conscious and planned development to raise the capability of social systems'.[8] This was the motivation behind such developments as the abolition of serfdom, the harmonization of tax systems, and the introduction of religious toleration, to name but a few examples of state-sponsored modernization. But state action could also result in *unintended modernization*. A classic example of this was Austrian support for Czech Slav patriotism in Bohemia after 1815. This was conceived as a short-term manoeuvre against liberal German nationalists in the province, but eventually encouraged full-blown Czech separatism. Finally, there was *self-generated modernization*: population growth, urbanization, the emergence of a European grain market and the consequent transformation of the East-Elbian economy in Prussia, and the creation of mass voluntary associations in the early nineteenth century. Here developments originated either within German society, beyond the direct control of governments, or simply reflected broader European trends.

The main focus of this book is on the state: as an actor within the German and the international states' system; as the sponsor of modernization; as entrepreneur, tax collector, administrator and recruiting sergeant; and as arbitrator between the various strands of society. This involves a quasi-Weberian approach centred on politics, systems of social domination and administration *(Politik – Herrschaft – Verwaltung)*, rather than the classic Weberian model of domination – economy – culture *(Herrschaft – Wirtschaft – Kultur)*. Moreover, our focus will be primarily on the larger and middling German states such as Prussia, Austria, Bavaria, Baden, Saxony and Württemberg, as well as the broader commonwealth of the *Reich* and the German Confederation *(Bund)* after 1815, at the expense of the smaller and smallest principalities. We shall be concerned with the rule, not the exception; the broad contours, not the complexities. It is necessary to note the diversity in German history, but not to fetishize it.

Similarly, because attention is focused on the dynamic role of the state, aspects such as culture, mentalities, the history of everyday life, political thought, gender, generational conflicts, to name but a few, have had to take second place; they are but *patois* to the High German of the cabinets. This is not to minimize the autonomous historical role played by 'ordinary people'. Yet individually and collectively they hardly affected 'high policy'; on the other hand, 'high policy' certainly *did* affect them. Through the medium of taxation, recruitment, bureaucracy and war the state was able to penetrate and transform even the most remote Alpine valley.

The perspective throughout is consciously 'Greater German' *(Grossdeutsch)*. Historically, as parts of the Holy Roman Empire, present-day Austria and Bohemia were as much part of the German common-wealth as East Prussia and Schleswig, which were not. The 'Germany' of this book is essentially bounded by the river Niemen (Memel) in the east, the Leitha in the south-east, and by the Meuse in the west; but the book will also make more than passing reference to Belgium and Alsace, which in 1780 were still very much part of a broader German political commonwealth. We shall start from the premise that there was nothing inevitable about the ultimate resolution of the struggle for mastery in 1866–71 in favour of a Prussian-led unification without Austria *(Kleindeutschland)*: there is no sense in which the events of 1779–1850 were simply a prehistory of Bismarck's Germany, or for that matter of the present Federal Republic of Germany. After all, for much of the 1780s it was Austria, not Prussia, which represented the dynamic element in Germany. On the other hand, the conclusion will be *kleindeutsch*. It will argue that while the outcome was relatively open in 1779, by 1850 it was becoming clear that only Prussia could take control of the national movement; that Prussia was best suited to steer and profit from the tide of socio-economic modernization; and that – perhaps most important of all – Prussia alone could protect Germany against the continued territorial pretensions of France. The triumph of Prussia was certainly not preordained, nor was it necessarily desirable, but the events of 1779 to 1850 made it increasingly likely.

The struggle for mastery in Germany neither began in 1779, nor did it end in 1850. Nevertheless, these dates span a distinct phase in the continuing contest between Austria, Prussia and the Third Germany; they also demarcate approximately the beginning and end of a stage in the modernization of Germany. The treaty of Teschen in 1779 repre-sented both the start of a fresh epoch of Austro-Prussian dualism and the arrival of a new external 'guarantor' of German liberties in the shape of Catherine the Great's Russia. The year 1850, on the other hand, marked both the ruin of German national aspirations with the Prussian 'humiliation' of Olmütz, and the approximate beginning of a fresh stage in German socio-economic development: the 'take-off' into full industrialization, which thus lies outside the scope of this book.

# 2

# GERMANY BEFORE THE FRENCH INVASION, 1779–92

## The Old Reich, 1777–92: Polyocracy, Stasis and Renewal

Our story begins not in 1780, but in 1740, when Frederick II succeeded Frederick William I as king in Prussia. The new monarch was regarded as a sensitive youth who was known to have suffered grievously under the tyranny of his brutal father. Shortly before his accession, Frederick had published *Antimachiavell*, a searing critique of human rapacity and ambition. A year later, he invaded the Habsburg province of Silesia. A new phase in the struggle for mastery in Germany had begun.

In the 1740s, and again between 1756 and 1763, Frederick defied the efforts, albeit sometimes half-hearted, not merely of Germany but almost the whole of Europe to make him both disgorge Silesia and abandon his great-power pretensions. Yet the Holy Roman Empire of the German Nation (*Reich*) managed to absorb the shock; the events of the mid-century did not destroy the *Reich*, though they might have done.

The *Reich* remained the most potent symbol of German political commonwealth in the late eighteenth century. Yet the *Reich* was simultaneously a powerful symbol of German disunity. First, not all Germans lived inside the *Reich*. To the south there were the Swiss Germans, German-speaking and self-governing, yet no longer part of the *Reich*, and then, as now, not considered to belong to a greater German political commonwealth. To the east, millions of Germans in East Prussia,

Poland and the Baltic had never been part of the *Reich*. There were also the Germans of Transylvania, of the Banat and Slovakia, whose ancestors had emigrated to these regions, and who lived not only well outside the confines of the *Reich*, but were separated from their kinsmen by a swathe of Slavic and Magyar peoples. Then there were those areas which were technically part of the *Reich*, but had been under non-German political control for some time. To the west there was Alsace, torn from the *Reich* in the course of the great French drive east at the end of the seventeenth century. Here a process of Frenchification, though far from completed, had already begun. Finally, there were the non-German peoples, the Flemings and Walloons of the Austrian Netherlands, the Slovenes of Carinthia, the Slavs (it is too early to call them Czechs) of Bohemia and Moravia, the Poles and Kaschuben of Eastern Pomerania and Upper Silesia, the Danes of Schleswig, and the much smaller tribe of Sorbs in Lusatia. Taken together, they still constituted only a tiny minority of the overall population of the *Reich*, but their regional concentration was to give some of them a crucial importance in the century to come.

Secondly, the *Reich* was politically divided. Surveying the fragmentation of Germany in 1784, the imperial polemicist Johann Pezzl dubbed the *Reich* a *Polykratie,* a polyocracy of competing power centres.[1] Or to quote the more positive and famous description of its last chancellor, Karl von Dalberg, the noble edifice of the *Reich* resembled a 'sturdy gothic building, which may not have been constructed in accordance with all the wiles of architecture but in which one may live securely'; the nineteenth-century historian, Leopold von Ranke, later extended this image when he compared the old *Reich* to a venerable Gothic cathedral. With its many subsections and innumerable pillars – all so similar and yet at the same time so different and individual – the structure of the old *Reich*, despite its obvious diversity and internal contradictions, unquestionably constituted a harmonic whole. For, underlying the essential political and cultural unity of the *Reich* was an unparalleled variety of independent or semi-independent political existences. The interaction between these entities and the rules governing their relationship to the imperial framework to which they belonged, was known as the *Reichsverfassung*, the imperial constitution.

Four distinct forms of independent, or notionally independent, existence were to be found within the *Reich*. What they all had in common was their 'immediacy' to the emperor; to use the language of the time, they were 'immediate' (*unmittelbar*) to the emperor and thus enjoyed the rank of 'estate of the empire' (*Reichsständisch*). That is to say, there was no intermediate power between them and their imperial overlord. Consequently, these territories enjoyed the coveted politico-legal privilege of *Landeshoheit*, a form of sovereignty curtailed only by a higher obligation towards the *Reich* and its institutions; after 1648 this did not extend much beyond an understanding not to pursue a foreign policy directed against the emperor. This distinguished them from the so-called *Landständisch* nobility ('territorial estates') of the principalities, whose noble status did not derive directly from the emperor and who were therefore subject to the local ruler. In 1780 there were about 1800 different territories within the *Reich* which possessed *Landeshoheit*.

Most important in terms of power and surface area were the larger territorial states, led by Austria and Prussia, followed at a respectful distance by Bavaria, Saxony, Hannover, Württemberg, Baden, Hesse-Darmstadt, Hesse-Cassel and a host of smaller principalities. In second place were the ecclesiastical territories, headed by the three ecclesiastical electors of Mainz, Trier and Cologne but including many other bishoprics and archbishoprics of varying sizes such as Konstanz, Salzburg, Passau and Münster. Given the Roman Catholic rules on clerical celibacy, succession was determined by election through the cathedral chapter. These chapters were bastions of the lesser Roman Catholic nobility, who used their control of the German church, the *Reichskirche*, to compensate for their lack of autonomous political weight. The ecclesiastical princes, though bishops, were essentially secular rulers, not spiritual figures; their religious and pastoral duties were usually delegated to auxiliary suffragan bishops. Apart from the bishops, there were also the imperial monasteries (*Reichsklöster*) such as those at Melk and Kempten. Thirdly, there were the imperial knights (*Reichsritter*) and imperial counts (*Reichsgrafen*); the former had no representation in the imperial Diet (*Reichstag*), while the latter enjoyed several collectively held votes or *Kuriatstimmen*. Together, they ruled about 1600 individual territories, concentrated in the west and south. Fourth and finally there were the fifty-odd imperial cities (*Reichsstädte*), relics of a medieval past: Nuremberg, Rottweil, Rothenburg on the Tauber and Augsburg in the south, and the Hanseatic cities of Bremen, Hamburg and Lübeck in the north.

Two institutions lay at the heart of the common political culture shared to a greater or lesser degree by all German states. These were the imperial Diet (*Reichstag*) and the imperial crown (*Kaisertum*). The *Reichstag* was the supreme legislature of the *Reich*. Theoretically, imperial law overrode territorial law (*Reichsrecht bricht Landesrecht*), but this was short-circuited by *Landeshoheit*, where it existed. The *Reichstag* could only be summoned by the emperor, but had gone into permanent session at Regensburg after 1663. Business was conducted by three separate councils. The Council of Electors (*Kurfürstenrat*) chose the emperor. It was made up of five secular electors – Bohemia (Austria), Brandenburg (Prussia), Saxony, Brunswick-Lüneburg (Hannover) and Bavaria – and three ecclesiastical electors, Mainz, Trier and Cologne. Next came the Council of Princes (*Fürstenrat*), which was divided between secular and ecclesiastical princes. Finally, there was the Council of Cities (*Städterat*); this body was much the least important of the three. The cities voted only on those rare occasions when the first two councils could not agree, in which case it acquired the casting vote. However, adversarial votes were very much the exception. Instead, matters were decided by a process of arbitration known as *Relation*, which was persevered with until a consensus had been reached.

Ever since 1438, the Austrian house of Habsburg – after 1740, strictly speaking, Habsburg-Lorraine – had, with one exception in the 1740s, held the office of German emperor. His main task, apart from leading the resistance to outside aggression, be it Turkish or French, was to act as guardian of the imperial constitution against the depredations of its larger component parts. The fact that the emperor himself might prove the greatest predator of all was to be one of the chief problems in the period around 1780. *De facto*, the emperor drew most of his strength from his Habsburg lands, rather than the powers of his imperial dignity. He had no rights of taxation within the *Reich* and he could not ennoble non-immediate individuals without the consent of the local prince. On the other hand he did enjoy the albeit contingent loyalty of those smaller territories, who were completely dependent on his protection. He could appoint members to the two supreme imperial courts and he could grant or withhold from rulers the right to prevent their subjects from appealing from local territorial courts to imperial courts, the so-called *privilegium de non-appellando*.

Two further pillars of the imperial constitution were the imperial courts (*Reichsgerichte*) and the imperial military constitution (*Reichskriegs-sverfassung*). There were two supreme courts of law: the Imperial Cameral Tribunal (*Reichskammergericht*) and the Imperial Aulic Council (*Reichshofrat*). The *Reichskammergericht* sat in Wetzlar, was staffed by judges nominated on the basis of confessional parity – that is, matching Protestant and Catholic appointees – and dealt with cases arising out of hostile acts between the various estates (*Landfriedensbruch*); it was dominated by the larger territories. The *Reichshofrat* in Vienna dealt with cases involving the rights of the emperor *vis-à-vis* the estates and with criminal matters involving the immediate estates; it was heavily subject to imperial influence. Everything else was open to both courts, which meant that the plaintiffs could choose between them. In so far as the prince in question was unable to invoke the *privilegium de non-appellando* mentioned earlier, these institutions were also the highest court of appeal from territorial courts. This privilege applied mainly to Austria and Prussia; for all the other states the rulings of the imperial courts were more or less binding and had to be reckoned with.

If the *Reichsverfassung* tended to emphasize legislation and deliberation, there was also, in theory, a powerful executive apparatus to assist the emperor. In the *Reichskriegsverfassung* the empire possessed the means by which a common defence could theoretically be rallied, either against external threats, such as the French or the Turks, or against internal transgressors, such as the Prussians in the mid-eighteenth century. In accordance with this arrangement the *Reich* was divided into ten circles or *Kreise*, the Upper and Lower Saxon circles, the Austrian, the Bohemian, the Bavarian, the Westphalian, the Upper Rhenish, the Electoral Rhenish, the Swabian and the Franconian Circles. Each circle had a director, in some cases the office being shared by an ecclesiastical and a secular prince, whose task was to convene the representatives of the circle in time of war. These delegates would then raise the necessary funds and forces to support the military effort of the emperor against the invader. In bygone days the circles had even garrisoned fortresses on the Rhine against the French. The last of these, Philipsburg, was evacuated in 1772. By 1780, the strength and vibrancy of the *Kreise* varied enormously. Whereas the northern and eastern circles had long been moribund, the anterior circles (*vorderen Reichskreise*) of Swabia, Franconia, the Upper and Electoral Rhine, which faced France in the west, the 'front-line circles', still fulfilled a serious defensive function.

To the modern eye, the arcane details of the imperial constitution seem anachronistic, even by eighteenth-century standards. Was the old *Reich* not, in John Gagliardo's neat summary of the standard criticisms a 'feckless political aggregate'?[2] Was it not, in the much-quoted outburst of the seventeenth-century political theorist Samuel von Pufendorf 'an irregular state body, much like a monster'? It is true: at one level, as we shall see, the old *Reich* was becoming increasingly inadequate to face the stresses of the international state system and irrelevant to the needs of the rising socio-political groups; the dynamic forces of the late eighteenth century were undoubtedly the territorial states and the enlightened, reforming bureaucracies within them. It is true: the inefficiency of the *Reich*, especially its sclerotic legal system, was legendary. Nevertheless, the old *Reich* and its constitution, despite all its transparent pretensions and shortcomings, was far from being redundant.

It was the *Reichsverfassung* which enabled Germany to put the religious divisions of the seventeenth century behind her and enable the more or less peaceful coexistence of the component parts of the empire. The *raison d'être* of the old *Reich* was to guarantee the existence of each and every member, however small, of a varied political commonwealth. According to its most distinguished defender, Karl Otmar von Aretin, the *Reich* was not a great power (*Machtstaat*), nor was it meant to be.[3] It was primarily a legal order (a *Rechtsordnung*) or an order designed to maintain the peace (a *Friedensordnung*). Viewed from this perspective, the *Reichsverfassung* was a resounding success. First of all and most obviously, it prevented, or at least hampered, the elimination of the smaller estates by the larger; this was to be proved again after 1780. Secondly, the *Reichsverfassung* provided a role for almost every individual entity, however small. The lesser *Reichsständisch* Roman Catholic nobility, for example, dominated the ecclesiastical states, thus providing an outlet for the energies and ambitions of otherwise insignificant families such as the Schönborns and the Dalbergs; indeed, the imperial church was a system of outdoor relief for the younger sons of the Roman Catholic aristocracy. Though separately of no consequence, the imperial knights and counts were collectively, in their incarnation as ecclesiastical princes, of some value to the emperor on whom they were totally dependent for protection; they provided not only useful votes at the *Reichstag*, but also recruits and loans in times of crisis. Similarly, the imperial cities cultivated a close relationship to the emperor, who exercised a supervisory function over the cities through the *Reichshofrat*. Thirdly, although powerless to intervene in Prussia, the *Reich* was able to curb princely absolutism in Bavaria, Württemberg and elsewhere; of this, more presently.

Perhaps even more important, the confessional struggles which had torn the area apart in the years preceding 1648 were detoxified by the imperial constitution. This was not necessarily because religion had ceased to matter. Rather, religious checks and balances were built into the system. Given the strong Roman Catholic presence in the *Reich*, this was a necessity. Catholics predominated in the two upper chambers of the *Reichstag*, virtually ensuring, among other things, a Catholic emperor. This was compounded by the fact that the emperor was bound to swear a coronation oath to protect the pope and the Roman Catholic church. Catholics also dominated the key offices, such as that of the Imperial Arch-Chancellor (*Reichserzkanzler*) which was held by the Elector of Mainz, and the directory of the *Fürstenrat*, which was held by Austria. So strong was the Catholic grip that one observer referred to the 'catholicity' of the *Reich* and its institutions.

As a result the *Reichstag* was divided into a Protestant and a Roman Catholic section, into the *Corpus Evangelicorum,* encompassing all the Protestant deputies, and the *Corpus Catholicorum*, which embodied all their Roman Catholic counterparts. Instead of counting the votes in the three councils, a decision could be reached by dividing the *Reichstag* on religious lines. The resulting deadlock would then have to be solved by compromise or *Relation*, a process known as *itio in partes*; this procedure had the effect of nullifying the Catholic majorities in the *Fürstenrat* and the *Kurfürstenrat* and was designed to prevent the Protestants from being outvoted on religious matters. By the late eighteenth century, however, nearly all important questions were settled by vote of *corpora* followed by compromise. This reflected the political reality on the ground, which usually saw the smaller Roman Catholic secular and ecclesiastical rulers grouped with the emperor against the larger Protestant territorial states. For the Roman Catholic bishops the strict observance of the constitution was of particular importance, not only because they were princes in their own right, but because it ratified their temporal and ecclesiastical sovereignty.

The religious dimension of the *Reichsverfassung* went beyond the prevention of strife between Catholic and Protestant members. By enforcing a kind of confessional stasis, it also helped to defend the internal balance within the individual states. For example, Saxony retained her membership of the *Corpus Evangelicorum* even after the Elector of Saxony converted to Catholicism in order to ascend the Polish throne. Similar arrangements were made in Protestant Württemberg between Roman Catholic Duke Karl Eugen and his estates and in Hesse-Cassel, where the *Assekurationsakte* ensured the Protestant Succession and membership of the *Corpus Evangelicorum* after the conversion of Prince Frederick to Catholicism;[4] imperial policy was henceforth made by his Lutheran councillors. Now that the *Reichsverfassung* had frozen the confessional order, individual princely conversions no longer had the disruptive effects of the previous two centuries; this was shown by the relatively painless containment of Karl Eugen of Württemberg in the 1760s. Another result was the loss of princely sovereignty induced by the inability to pursue an independent imperial policy. Needless to say, this stability was bought at the expense of religious conviction. Typical of the spirit of compromise and theological indifference underpinning the *Reichsverfassung* was the arrangement in Osnabrück. Here the bishopric was held alternately by a Lutheran and a Catholic incumbent. But anomaly was a small price to pay after the confessional mayhem of the past.

Finally, the institutions of the *Reich* also made no small contribution to the maintenance of social peace. When the occasion demanded, the circles could be activated to mount a concerted response to any serious rural turbulence. But usually force was not applied. Indeed, agrarian unrest could be defused by referring cases to the *Reichshofrat*, which frequently found in favour of the peasants.[5] In this respect, as in so many others, the *Reich* functioned as a mechanism of peaceful conflict resolution.

### Deference, Deviance and Defiance: German Society on the Threshold of Modernity

Imagine yourself travelling from east to west in Germany around 1780. As you started your journey in Prussia you would have been struck by the absence of proper roads: until the 1750s all the highways were *Naturwege*, which turned into mud in the autumn. It was only in the last quarter of the eighteenth century that the Prussian government began a massive programme of road-building. You would also have noted that the predominant crops in the fields on either side of you were rye and potatoes. The peasants you met along the way would have been as likely to be working seigneurial fields as their own; in the worst case they would have spent up to five days a week in the landlord's service. Their relationship to the lord would have been essentially feudal: payments were usually made in kind; freedom of movement was at seigneurial discretion; and most peasants would have been subject to full seigneurial justice. The lord also exercised important cultural control over his peasants through the appointment of pastor and schoolmaster. As you went on your way you would have become increasingly aware that cities were few and far between; that the soil – Brandenburg was the 'sandbox of Europe' – was of poor quality with low yield-ratios; that poverty was widespread, with much of the labour force not having energy for more than a few hours of work; and that despite determined *Peuplierungspolitik* the overall density of population was unusually low.

As you went west, crossing the Elbe, you would have found more and larger towns; you would have encountered free peasants selling their produce in local markets; and you would have found that feudal dues were much more likely to be settled in cash rather than in kind. You would also have seen fewer seigneurs running their estates directly as agrarian entrepreneurs; many more would have been living in the towns as *rentiers* with little or no judicial authority over their peasants. Indeed, if you had wandered south as well as west, you would have found that the spread of strip farming, due to inheritance laws, meant that many peasants had more than one lord. The net result of this was that the socio-political dominance of the nobility became steadily less oppressive as you moved west. But the developmental gap between east and west would have been obvious to you in other ways as well. Communications would have been much better, with a higher density of canals and better roads; of course, a large number of turnpikes and toll stations would have made you pay for the privilege. If you were a merchant you would have been irked, or even deterred, by the huge number of tariff barriers along the way: almost all of the hundreds of sovereign territories levied their own tolls. To make matters worse, there were numerous internal tariff barriers such as those facing trade between the western Prussian enclave of Krefeld and the eastern heartlands of the Hohenzollern monarchy. And if you had attempted to set up an enterprise in one of the towns you would have been hamstrung by the many ancient guild restrictions in place, in the west probably even more so than in the east. Finally, the country you had just traversed had some 16–18 million inhabitants in 1750, rising to about 23–25 million in 1800.

If you had paused for a moment to reflect on your journey, you would immediately have been struck by two things. First of all, the overwhelmingly rural nature of German society: over 70 per cent of the population lived on the land; only in the more highly urbanized south-west and in Saxony would the percentage of townspeople have been significantly higher.[6] Secondly, the hierarchic nature of a society in which inequalities, privileges and discrimination were legally codified and strictly enforced.

The defining element in German rural society was the relationship between peasant and lord. In the east and north, the peasant was not merely socio-economically but legally subordinate. As magistrate, employer and tax-collector, the lord disposed not merely of the labour but also of the person of the peasant and his children; the peasant could not either marry or move without the consent of his master. This bondage was hereditary. As one north German landlord bleakly informed his tenants: 'nothing belongs to you, your soul belongs to God and your bodies, goods and everything you possess belongs to me.'[7] This system was known as *Gutsherrschaft*. In western and southern Germany, on the other hand, the peasant was subject to *Grundherrschaft*, an arrangement by which the lord controlled the land, and sometimes the labour, but not the person of the peasant. Broadly speaking, the dividing line between the two systems ran along the Elbe-Saale rivers, though there were islands of bondage to the west (e.g. Brunswick) and pockets of free peasantry to the east (e.g. the Altmark).[8] In the Habsburg lands, the dividing line ran right through the state, with various forms of 'free' peasantry predominating in the western hereditary lands and bonded peasants in the Slav and Magyar provinces.

It would be wrong, however, to conceive of German agriculture purely in terms of a progressive west and a backward east.[9] Certainly, the western peasant – unlike his bonded eastern counterpart – was much better placed to maximize production for the market. On the other hand, while the fixed rent cash payment made the peasant more independent of the lord, he was consequently more dependent on the market and its contingent price fluctuations.[10] Conversely, in the east it was mainly the lord who produced for the market; and the superiority of river communications there facilitated export via the Baltic to overseas. But this did not mean that the East Elbian peasant was a mere passive object. We now know that the agrarian economy of Prussia was much more advanced than once thought. Wage labour, as opposed to labour service, was important well before the Reform Era,[11] while the peasant was often an entrepreneur in his own right, supervising the work of hired farm-hands. Moreover, in the short and medium term it was the estates of East Elbia rather than the more modest farms of the west which were increasingly the pioneers of commercialized, capitalist, market-oriented agriculture. In short, while agrarian relations in western Germany were undoubtedly *legally* more progressive than in the east, both systems could lay equal claim to *socio-economic* modernity and modernizing potential.

Ironically, the developmental lead of western and southern Germany lay not so much in agriculture, but in rural crafts. Many of these rural artisans had no formal training but were autodidacts who 'learned on the job'; their function was to satisfy local demand.[12] Others were peasants, or peasants' wives and children, who supplemented their earnings by part-time spinning and weaving; often they were part of the 'putting-out' system, by which a market-oriented entrepreneur subcontracted the various stages of the production process to individual households. Not uncommon were manufactories, employing about 10 per cent of all artisans. Here production was centred on workshops owned and tooled by the entrepreneur; technical sophistication was low, sometimes involving the use of water-power. Factories in the modern sense, fuelled by coal or peat, were exceptional until well after the turn of the century. The relative dynamism of cottage industries, which is now widely called 'proto-industrialization', was due to three factors. First of all, the emergence of a supra-regional market for textiles and other products; secondly, the almost total absence of effective guilds in the countryside; and, thirdly, the availability of a cheap and numerous labour force. With the significant exception of Silesia, rural crafts in East Elbia were much less developed, not least because the state enforced guild restrictions in the countryside more strictly.

The immediate social context within which the vast majority of Germans – freeholders, western tenant farmers, bonded peasants and rural artisans alike – acted out their lives was the village community (*Gemeinde*), or its East-Elbian equivalent, the manorial estate (*Rittergut*). It was to the village that the state and the lord looked for the payment of dues and the provision of labour services: the village community was the basic unit of ecclesiastical, military and socio-economic organization. Church services, recruitment, the sale of goods, feasts, festivals and much else were focused on the village. Moreover, the villagers enjoyed a considerable degree of local autonomy, most importantly, the right to regulate the use of common land. In the west the community also controlled the brewing of beer and the village inn; in the east, these privileges were normally reserved to the noble lord.[13]

Each village was made up of individual households ('*Das ganze Haus*'). The presiding figure was the patriarch or *Hausvater,* to whom the various other inhabitants, wife, children, assorted relatives and servants (*Gesinde*), were subordinate; the same phenomenon was to be found in the towns, where many features of the *Ganzes Haus* – servants, maids, apprentices – were replicated.[14] To a considerable extent this community within a community was self-sufficient, growing and making enough to cover its own needs. Here women often made a vital contribution: it was female labour which tended the vegetable garden, helped to bring in the harvest, engaged in domestic or contract crafts, and drew up the family accounts;[15] much the same, *mutatis mutandis*, could be said of children. The size of a household varied. We now know, however, that atomized 'nuclear' families consisting only of two parents and a number of children were more common than the large extended families of romantic and historiographical myth.[16] On the other hand, thanks to high mortality rates, it was not unusual for a household to include not only assorted elderly but also children from earlier marriages, some of them not even necessarily blood relations of either partner.

But the nostalgic picture of a harmonious, autarchic and inclusive household could be deceptive. Doubtless, many, perhaps even most *Hausväter* were conscientious and responsible. But the *Ganzes Haus* was potentially simply another system of exploitation.[17] It was certainly no pre-modern idyll. If the *Hausvater* chose to exercise his traditional right of discipline, familial relations might be characterized as much by violence as affection. Moreover, the household was surprisingly monetarized and materialistic: children were often paid formal wages, while it was quite common for women to keep a watchful eye on the use of their dowry.[18] Above all, the household was often bitterly divided on generational lines. In a society where old age was synonymous with decline and infirmity, fear of old age could be greater than fear of death;[19] it was thus in the interest of the *Hausvater* to delay the handover of the farm until his pension rights (*Altenteil*) had been secured. Hence on your journey across rural Germany you might have met a few wizened and destitute peasants who had rashly thrown themselves on the mercy of their children. You would have been much more likely, however, to have encountered frustrated male Gonerils and Regans engaged in protracted negotiations with crafty patriarchs. Eighteenth-century Germany was no place for young men.

If conflict within the household was endemic, then the same is true of agrarian society as a whole. For a start, the village community was polarized between those who owned land, however little, and those who did not. As a rule, the former dominated. Moreover, the village community was also a system of discipline. Those who fell foul of its norms could be excluded, for example, from use of the commons; they might even be subjected to collective violence. Indeed, gibbets, stocks and other instruments of physical chastisement were routine features of everyday life.[20] Those who offended against communal morality usually suffered ostracism or worse; the stigma attached to illegitimacy is a good example. Furthermore, those at the lower end of the scale were in constant danger of poverty from sickness, old age, injury or even ill-fortune. While the community was prepared to help in the case of genuine hardship, it tried to guard against the strain placed by the 'undeserving poor', primarily work-shy beggars, on the village resources.

Urban life was no less stratified and polarized. Socially and economically, most towns were dominated either by a small patrician elite of *Honoratioren*, the majority of them merchants, or – in the case of the numerous princely residences and garrison towns – by the local court and state bureaucracy. Usually, rights of political participation, where they existed, were strictly limited to the patriciate, whose chief concern was the maintenance of the traditional social order and the control of immigration. Sometimes these rights were extended to prosperous innkeepers and master artisans. Generally excluded were the broad mass of modest craftsmen and small traders who made up the bulk of the urban population. Their livelihoods depended on the guilds, professional associations of the individual crafts: cobblers, bakers, goldsmiths and stonemasons, to name but a few. Ostensibly, the guilds were intended to maintain standards of craftsmanship, but they also served to minimize competition by regulating the admission of new apprentices and preventing rural artisans from entering the urban market; they were not always successful in this. The training and accommodation of unmarried apprentices in the *Ganzes Haus*, the welfare of artisans' widows, and the preservation of a distinctive code of honour – all this was in the hands of the guilds. Of course, there were exceptions. Contrary to popular belief, some towns contained many artisans who were not members of any guild, while a substantial minority of apprentices were married and lived independently.[21] At the very bottom of the scale were the poor who, like their rural counterparts, lived a precarious existence as beggars and day-labourers; they made up about 10 per cent of the population.[22]

The shortest straw in this system of domination and obligation was

drawn by women, servants and the Jews. Here too there were exceptions. Aristocratic women retained their inheritance rights, while
women at court enjoyed influence if not power; Roman Catholic
noblewomen could even become abbesses or hold other positions of
authority within the imperial church.[23] The widows of artisans and
peasants could carry on their husbands' profession unless they remar-
ried. It is even true that divorce was technically possible in Protestant
areas, though highly unusual. But as a rule, women were not supposed
to possess lives or legal identities of their own; they were defined
through subordination to their husbands. Similarly, the lives and
working conditions of the huge servant class were regulated, in theory
at least, by a strict *Gesindeordnung*, with its limitations on movement and
marriage. Finally, approximately 100 000 German Jews – less than 1
per cent of the population – were subject to a complex code of discriminatory regulations concerning movement, clothing, occupation
and financial obligations.[24] In many territories they were granted a
measure of practical toleration, but only in return for special 'Jewish
taxes' or other payments. The legal inferiority of this community,
which ranged from modest rural artisans through wealthy financiers to
a small number of cosmopolitan intellectuals, became a symbolically
important challenge to reformers in the decades ahead.

Socio-legal inequality was thus the defining characteristic of
German society around 1780. But coercion and domination are only
part of the picture; much of the cohesion in German society was provided by deference and cooperation. To this end state, church and
nobility tried to inculcate the peasantry and the urban lower orders
with the values of thrift, obedience and contentment. This ideology of
deference, or 'social control', was aptly summed up by the traditional
injunction: '*Schuster bleib bei deinem Leisten*' – 'Cobbler, stick to your last.'
Indeed, as we have seen, the functioning of rural society required and
received a high level of peasant cooperation, which no amount of
brute force could replace. By assisting in the collection of taxes and
dues, and by organizing seigneurial labour services, the peasantry were
acquiescing in their own subordination.

This does not mean that Germany was merely a society of sub-
servients, an *Untertanengesellschaft*. Far from being uniformly unpolitical
and submissive, many peasants were defiant and subversive. In the
south-east, for example, they showed a particularly litigious streak, frequently bringing their ecclesiastical and minor secular lords to the
imperial courts and winning. This even happened in Brandenburg,

where one might least have expected it. Peasant unrest was thus, to quote its foremost authority, a 'structural characteristic' of the *Reich*;[25] social conflicts were thus 'legalized'. Indeed, the resulting legal judgments and bilateral agreements between peasants and lords became effectively part of the *Reichsverfassung*, and were often guaranteed by the emperor. Admittedly, the majority of German peasants in the larger territorial states had no such recourse. Here peasant defiance manifested itself in the maiming of cattle or the defence of common lands, especially forests, against seigneurial encroachments. In times of dearth there might be the creation of a spontaneous 'moral economy' through the looting and distribution of grain; this happened in Baden in 1770. Finally, one should not exaggerate the extent or success of 'social control'. The classic instance of this is beggary: countless ordinances promulgated throughout the empire reflected legal intent, not necessarily social reality. In practice, the broad mass of beggars seem to have had little difficulty in outwitting the corrupt, underpaid, invalid and overworked guards deployed to contain them.[26] On the whole, beggars were unworried by the panoply of social control – incarceration and physical chastisement. Even measures of the last resort – deportation and execution – were only temporary palliatives for a perennnial and worsening problem.[27]

Moreover, German society around 1780, though overwhelmingly rural, conservative and deferential, was in no sense static. A large proportion of the population, beggars, apprenticed artisans and the rural poor, were highly mobile. By the late eighteenth century, for example, only half of all artisans in Berlin were natives. There was also some social mobility: only half of these artisans were the sons of master artisans. But the most dynamic changes were taking place in the countryside, not in the towns. An important motor of modernization was the huge demographic surge triggered by a decrease in mortality. The relentless increase in population of about 1 per cent per annum – most of it towards the end of the century – forced the repeated subdivision of already modest holdings, put an intolerable pressure on the commons, and led to a disproportionate increase in the number of rural poor.[28] In the course of the eighteenth century the percentage of landless labourers jumped from 12 per cent to 24 per cent of the total population, or about one-third of rural inhabitants.[29] This not only accelerated the process of social differentiation in the countryside but also facilitated the growth of 'proto-industrial' forms of production using cheap and plentiful labour. Simultaneously and relatedly, there was the emergence of a supra-regional demand for grain and textiles. The East-Elbian Junkers, for example, were well placed to produce for the burgeoning British grain market via the Baltic ports: the result was a late eighteenth-century agrarian boom which benefited the lords, who got 'the bulk of the farm production while the tenants are mere servants living on a pittance' (official report from Pomerania). Similarly, by the 1790s about 75 per cent of Silesian linen was being exported, the vast majority of it to western Europe and overseas.[30]

The undoubted flux in rural society and economy had a corrosive effect on legal barriers. Unlike, say, the Westphalian aristocracy, the Junkers proved themselves to be a relatively open elite, assimilating immigrants, new nobles and even middle-class parvenus.[31] By 1800, in fact, some 10 per cent of noble estates in Prussia were in bourgeois hands, despite stringent attempts to stop this. At the same time prosperity led to a surge in aristocratic self-confidence and a renewed vibrancy of their representative institutions, the estates.[32] In south-western Germany it was peasant protest which provided modernizing impulses towards compromise, coexistence and the codification of legal rights: these were not granted from above, but were being wrested from below, long before the French Revolution.

On the other hand, there were few signs that Germany was a society about to cross the threshold to modernity under its own steam; the retardative forces were still too strong. For all its porousness and elasticity, the entrenched socio-legal inequalities of the society of orders acted as a powerful restraint on individual initiative. In the towns, the restrictive guild system limited the chances for entrepreneurial activity. In the countryside, especially in East Elbia, short leases and landlord labour demands inhibited improvements.[33] In the west and south, the traditions of the village community often acted as a brake: the three-field system, the commons and the tendency to prize collective welfare over individual initiative. The peasant mentality was geared to immediate exploitation of marginal resources, not the long-term maximization of his economic potential; he might milk a cow three times a day, thus investing time and energy out of all proportion to the meagre result.[34] Moreover, the festivals and celebrations characteristic of peasant culture may have had their own socio-cultural rationality, but they were a not inconsiderable drain on peasant time and resources. Even proto-industrialization seems to have been something of a false dawn. While some entrepreneurs did use the capital accumulated to fund industrialization after 1800, there seems to have been no general or necessary link between the two developments.[35] In any case, proto-industrialization itself was hardly 'modern': there was no separation of habitation and workplace, it was not capital-intensive and it involved little technological sophistication. Finally, there was no substantial constituency for radical change. A conscious working class did not exist, either objectively or subjectively. The peasant majority, though not docile, was far from revolutionary; their protest was not so much a principled opposition to feudalism as against its abuses.[36] As for the growing rural poor, they were still in a clear minority. Even together with the urban poor they made up no more than about 30 per cent of the population.[37] This meant that at least two-thirds of German society had some stake in the status quo in 1780.

## Reform Absolutism: Modernization under the Primacy of Foreign Policy

If German society showed some capacity for self-generated change before 1800, the most dynamic element in eighteenth-century Germany was undoubtedly the state. According to Landgraf Ludwig IX of Hesse-Darmstadt, the task of the prince was 'to make all endeavours of the good hard-working subject more productive, to make his tasks simpler, his life more joyful, his sky brighter, to make him proud of his Fatherland, content with himself and grateful to his prince'.[38] This definition may seem broad enough as it is. Yet it did not include the most important preoccupation of the absolutist state: security, expansion, international prestige, and the subordination of domestic considerations to this end, in short, the primacy of foreign policy.

There were four ways of conducting the struggle for mastery in Germany: territorial aggrandisement, preventing the aggrandisement of rivals, internal consolidation with the aim of maximizing military strength, and denying such consolidation to rivals. None of these methods were mutually exclusive and most German states pursued the relevant policies either consecutively or concurrently. Thus, if Frederick the Great spent two decades in the mid-century enlarging his realm at the expense of his neighbours, he subsequently became a stout defender of the weak against Austrian expansion; of this more later. And if Prussia strained every nerve to ensure her own internal cohesion, she was no less concerned to hobble her neighbours with the very same retardative structures which she had eliminated at home.

Domestic policy under absolutism, therefore, was largely conditioned by external needs and pressures. In the Prussian case, the extreme geopolitical exposure of the state provided a powerful impulse towards internal cohesion. Prussia, to quote Frederick the Great, was forced 'by the peculiar [geographic] situation of its provinces to be armed and prepared for all eventualities'.[39] Moreover, Prussia was much smaller and more sparsely populated than her European rivals; this made her very survival dependent on the efficient use of limited resources. 'Smaller states,' Frederick asserted in 1775, 'can stand up to the largest states if they achieve order in their internal affairs.' 'The smaller [powers],' the Prussian foreign minister Count Hertzberg echoed in 1782, 'need to mobilize all the strengths which they possess.'[40] But even a large populous state like Austria was concerned to streamline its domestic structure in accordance with the requirements of great power rivalry. When the Austrian chancellor Wenzel Anton von Kaunitz – sometimes seen as an exponent of the primacy of domestic policy – concentrated on long-term internal development (national wealth rather than simply state revenue) over short-term diplomatic gain, this was designed to provide a sounder basis for the projection of external power.[41]

The social and legal inequalities of the society of orders were not God-given, nor did they simply 'happen'. Instead, they had developed and were justified functionally. The classic and most pronounced example of this was Prussia. Here the primacy of foreign policy permeated almost every aspect of society. Ever since the the seventeenth-century governing compromise (*Herrschaftskompromiß*) between prince and estates, the nobility had relinquished all political rights, including consent to taxation, in return for increased control over the peasantry.[42] During the reign of Frederick the Great, this system was further refined to maximize the military potential of the nobility. In return, the nobles provided officers and peasant recruits for the Seven Years' War; this made them, in Frederick's words, 'a breed so valuable as to merit preservation by any means possible'. The state therefore prevented the sale of noble estates to commoners, while rural credit institutes kept struggling Junkers afloat or financed agricultural improvements; nobles also increasingly dominated the bureaucracy. But these privileges were justified functionally, not in terms of custom and tradition.

This structure was enshrined in the General Law Code (*Allgemeines Landrecht*) of 1794, the 'surrogate constitution' (Koselleck) of the Prussian monarchy. If the code guaranteed group rather than individual rights, a startlingly 'modern' ('communitarian') touch, and if it reaffirmed the whole range of aristocratic rights – patrimonial justice, landownership, hunting, entail, legal exemptions – then it did so because the state allotted different roles to the various socio-legal orders. 'As the premier estate (*Stand*) in the state,' the code stipulated, 'the nobility is obliged to ensure the defence of the state, its external honour, and its internal order.'[43] City dwellers, on the other hand, were regarded as a source of steady revenue through the excise tax, which provided about twenty-five percent of Prussian revenue.[44] In return, they were exempt from military service.

The shortest straw in this system of functional inequalities was drawn by the peasantry.[45] Their direct tax, the *Kontribution*, accounted for about a third of state revenue; they were also collectively liable to conscription. The intimate link between social order and military organization was epitomized by the Prussian *Kantonalverfassung*, which divided the monarchy into separate recruiting areas (cantons) each of which was obliged to provide a number of men for military service.[46] After about two years' training, cantonists would return to their village but would be liable for exercises or service at short notice. The officers were provided by the local nobility. For two or three months of the year the rank and file would be sent home to help with the harvest. This system has been aptly described as a 'military-agrarian complex'.[47]

If the functional needs of the state determined the socio-legal inequalities in Prussian society, the same primacy of foreign policy guaranteed the peasantry a basic level of protection. In its determination to safeguard recruitment, the state forbade the absorption of peasant holdings into noble estates (*Bauernschutz*). Collectively, though not individually, the Prussian peasantry was thus cushioned against the rationalizing ambitions of the estate owners. The same protection was extended to the urban guilded artisans: except in Silesia, rural crafts were generally suppressed, and migration into the towns blocked, partly so as to reduce competition for the towns, partly in order to secure the agricultural labour market and partly to ensure a large pool of peasant recruits into the army.[48] Similarly, the state regularly intervened to keep down the price of grain, by buying up surpluses, often cheap Polish grain, and releasing them as appropriate. Indeed, the numerous magazines across the monarchy served a double purpose: to supply the army and to maintain the social peace in times of scarcity.[49] This policy, to quote Frederick II, was a means of 'maintaining the balance between town and countryside'. During the hungry early 1770s and the Oder floods of 1784, state intervention helped to keep the social peace. Lastly, the attitude of the Prussian state to women, children and marriage was heavily influenced by the military and fiscal needs of the state. In the General Code of 1794, marriage was defined as being intended for 'the bearing and rearing of children'; the code also gave some protection to unmarried mothers. Moreover, Frederick II was happy to allow divorce when a marriage was childless. On the other hand, the state was uncompromising in its opposition to infanticide. Here the concern was to protect future taxpayers or recruits from the brutality and despair of their mothers. Geopolitics thus spawned 'biopolitics'; not the least beneficiaries of this were the newborn.[50]

Finally, the whole governmental structure of Prussia was shaped in accordance with the primacy of foreign policy. There were no representative assemblies of the nobility in control of recruitment or taxation. Nor was there an independent imperial church with supra-regional loyalties. Admittedly, the largely Lutheran nobility controlled local church patronage.[51] But despite the fact that the Prussian princely, and later royal, house had been Calvinist for over 150 years, the Lutheran state church, to which a majority of the population, noble and peasant, subscribed, was firmly under the control of the crown. In any case, there was no constraint on royal absolutism in the conduct of foreign affairs. Above all, Frederician Prussia possessed an executive – king, foreign ministry, and cabinet councillors – which facilitated decisive action in the international arena.[52] Of course, the monarch did not rule alone. For the day-to-day running of the state he was dependent on the bureaucracy. Towards the end of the eighteenth century this class of educated administrators – both noble and bourgeois, increasingly developed a sense of their own identity; this was reinforced by the introduction of entrance examinations and security of tenure (*Unabsetzbarkeit*) against arbitrary dismissal by the king.[53] Some observers saw the bureaucracy as the governing class in Prussia; others regarded it merely as an executive committee for the aristocracy. Andreas Kraus, for example, a professor at Königsberg, argued that 'the aristocracy rules the country in the undisguised form of a bureaucracy'. A later generation of historians even spoke of 'bureaucratic absolutism'.[54] It is certainly undeniable that the bureaucracy often sabotaged measures they considered unjust, unrealistic or contrary to their interests. But the political significance of the administration has been exaggerated. The size of the bureaucracy was very small in absolute terms, though large by eighteenth-century standards – a maximum of 14 000 officials around 1780. This was less than a tenth of the army or fewer than 1 per cent of the total population.[55] Besides, when Frederick re-aristocratized the bureaucracy, he did so from a position of strength. His administrators were a functional, not a participatory elite. They executed policy rather than formulated it.

There were superficial similarities between the social, legal and political structures of the Habsburg and Prussian lands around 1780, but the differences were greater. Both states shared a preoccupation with revenue, internal order, secure recruitment and, above all, diplomatic success. In the German provinces of Austria a Prussian-style cantonal system had been in place for about a decade; the Austrian government also protected peasants against seigneurial absorption. Many aristocratic families had a long tradition of service in the army or bureaucracy. As in Prussia, the local nobility was closely involved in the adminstration of taxes and recruitment. As in Prussia, the crown was exclusively responsible for foreign policy. But there the parallels end. Unlike Prussia, the Austrian church enjoyed extra-territorial links to the Pope and the *Reichskirche*; it also controlled education and vast tracts of land, albeit regionally concentrated. Unlike in Prussia, which was largely Protestant and German, the population of the Habsburg lands was linguistically and confessionally highly diverse. It included Catholic and Protestant Hungarians (Magyars) and Czech-speakers, Orthodox Serbs and Romanians, Catholic Belgians, Italians, Croats, Slovak-speakers and Poles. Finally, unlike the Hohenzollerns, the Habsburgs had been only partially successful in eliminating the political power of the estates. Only in the hereditary lands to the west had the aristocracy lost the right to control taxation by 1780.

In Hungary, the representative assemblies of the nobility had survived intact. So far from being neutralized through a Prussian-style *Herrschaftskompromiß*, the Hungarian Diet had ended their last open rebellion against the crown with a compromise peace at Szatmar in 1711. By its terms, the Hungarians agreed to assist in the external defence of the monarchy. In return the Austrians undertook to respect the laws and customs of Hungary and not to introduce any new laws without the consent of the Diet. During the Silesian crisis of the 1740s, they used the distress of Maria Theresa to wrest further concessions; this was not the last time that the struggles for mastery in Germany and Hungary were to interact. The problem in Hungary was not so much the generally sympathetic magnates, such as the Szechenyi, Bathanyi and Esterhazy, as the numerous middling aristocrats, about 20 000 in all, whose representatives dominated the Diet and controlled local government; they were passionate advocates of Hungarian particularism and defenders of the Szatmar settlement. The upshot was that the Austrians were unable to extend conscription to Hungary; all troops raised there, apart from volunteers, required the consent of the Diet, which was usually linked to the stipulation that such levies be deployed only in defence of Hungary itself, rather than serve the monarchy in any number of far-flung theatres.[56] Further representative institutions were to be found in northern Italy, the Austrian Netherlands and a number of other provinces. They posed not merely a fiscal and administrative embarrassment, but a potential political risk. In the 1740s, after all, the estates of Bohemia had wasted no time in paying homage to the Bavarian imperial pretender; similar acts of aristocratic treason could not be ruled out in future.

Nor were the smaller powers exempt from the primacy of foreign policy.[57] Admittedly, the smallest statelets, ecclesiastical and worldly, lacked a critical fiscal-military mass and represented something of a socio-political nature reserve, although they were not totally insulated from the world of international politics.[58] But the aspirant middling powers like Baden, Württemberg, Bavaria and Hesse-Darmstadt were no less concerned than Austria or Prussia to cut a figure on the diplomatic scene; and in their cases the imperative to make up in internal cohesion for what they lacked in military muscle was even more marked. But with the exception of Baden, the lesser German powers were all hamstrung by the survival of the estates. The composition of these representative bodies varied. Mostly, they were made up of nobles and clergy with some peasants and bourgeois; in Württemberg they were entirely bourgeois. But in all cases, they retained control of additional taxation. Of course, the relationship between prince and estates was by no means always antagonistic: for long periods throughout the eighteenth century cooperation and compromise rather than conflict and confrontation were the norm.[59] Nevertheless, while the estates were happy to make regular fixed and relatively modest payments, they were resistant to extraordinary demands.[60]

The failure of the princes to master the estates by 1780 was due to three factors. First of all, there was the remarkable financial power of the estates. Since domestic taxation was largely administered and collected by them, any attempt to raise money unilaterally was politically costly and bureaucratically difficult. Moreover, most princes found it difficult to borrow on the international money markets without the blessing of the estates. When in mid-century, Max Joseph of Bavaria approached Genoese bankers for a loan, they demanded the approval of the estates as collateral.[61] Secondly, in some German territories there was the prolonged absence of the prince; in Hannover and Saxony this left a political void which the estates rapidly filled. Thirdly and finally, the survival of representative institutions in the minor German states was due, paradoxically, to the primacy of foreign policy. For if external pressures and ambitions powered princely assaults on the estates, the determination of the great powers to hobble potential rivals ensured their preservation. Thus in Bavaria, Württemberg and Mecklenburg, the Austrians and Prussians intervened to protect the estates against princely encroachments.[62] For Karl Eugen of Württemberg, the humiliating 'hereditary compromise' (*Erbvergleich*) of 1771 involved a guarantee of estate control over additional taxation, and thus over wartime recruitment, which the impoverished prince could not otherwise finance;[63] in 1780 most lesser German princes still endured similar limits on their sovereignty. The result was a political-fiscal gridlock in the Third Germany which prevented those states from realizing their full potential on the international scene.

An apparent exception to this pattern was Hesse-Cassel. We now know that Landgrave Frederick II was not the cold-blooded provider of mercenary troops, but an enlightened ruler concerned for the welfare of his subjects;[64] to this extent Frederick was unfairly targeted by a transatlantic Anglo-Saxon 'black legend', of which he was not the first or the last victim. In Hesse-Cassel the simple equation, reforms – economic growth – increased revenue – larger army – foreign political activism, did not apply. Instead, the mercenary trade (*Soldatenhandel*) gave the Landgrave the financial flexibility to introduce domestic reforms for their own sake, without corporate consent.[65]

To sum up: all late eighteenth-century German states were based on institutionalized socio-legal inequalities; all, excepting Baden and Prussia, were characterized by the persistence of powerful assemblies at the expense of the central government. But after 1780, these structures were subjected to an increasingly radical challenge by the modernizing state. As we have seen, the assault on the estates was not new, though it was to become ever more intense. Nor was there anything particularly novel about state-sponsored reforms in society and economy. After all, the science of cameralism, according to which generations of German bureaucrats sought to increase population (*Peuplierungspolitik*), maximize revenue, encourage skilled immigration, ensure popular welfare and generally promote a well-ordered police state, was long-established.[66] The new departure lay elsewhere.

It did not come from the Enlightenment as such. Nor did it come from the related 'public sphere' which, as in much of western and southern Europe, began to emerge in Germany from around the middle – some would say the early – eighteenth century;[67] this has been interpreted as a break from the old representational 'courtly' culture.[68] Thanks not least to the educational policies of enlightened reform absolutist rulers, Germany enjoyed a relatively high level of literacy in 1780, about 15 per cent; by 1800, this had risen to 25 per cent.[69] The number of periodicals published between 1770 and 1800 more than doubled; twice as many books were printed after 1750 than before. The number of reading societies tripled from 70 to 200 during the same period, some of them boasting up to 15 000 members. Large numbers also belonged to 'patriotic' and philanthropic societies. *In toto* there were tens of thousands, perhaps even a hundred thousand participants in the enlightened public sphere by the late eighteenth century. Its chief aim was intellectual, moral and material (self-)improvement. 'The public,' as Friedrich Schiller wrote in 1784, 'is now everything to me – my preoccupation, my sovereign and my friend.'

Public discussion was not confined to matters cultural, economic and religious; eighteenth-century Germans were far from 'unpolitical'.[70] After all, the public sphere tended to subvert tradition and the society of orders through the application of reason: in this sense, it could be seen as a middle-class challenge to aristocratic privilege. At the same time, many journals and newspapers took a keen interest in high politics and diplomacy.[71] But any criticism of matters of 'high policy' was frowned upon by the state and subject to intense censorship. Moreover, there were no representative fora through which the enlightened 'bourgeois' public sphere could apply financial pressure on the executive; the estates tended to be dominated by traditional aristocratic concerns. As bureaucrats and counsellors, members of the public sphere could influence and criticize government policy but they could not, as yet, challenge it.

The German Enlightenment (*Aufklärung*) was no pale variant of a French model centred on Paris. Rather, it was a specifically German phenomenon.[72] Philosophers such as Christian Wolff and Immanuel

Kant were not merely French versions of Voltaire, Montesquieu and Rousseau. Where the French Enlightenment tended to be anticlerical, the *Aufklärung* was self-consciously confessional, either Pietist or reformed Catholic. Where the one was metropolitan and centralized, the other was highly regionalized. Above all, where the French public sphere conducted a searing, uncompromising, libellous and often pornographic critique of the political executive and monarchic power, German writers were markedly more sympathetic towards the state.

'Thought precedes action,' the nineteenth-century radical poet Heinrich Heine once said, 'as lightning precedes thunder.' But thought can also replace action. This was certainly the case with many of the radical fringe movements spawned by the growth of the public sphere. The *Sturm und Drang* movement, for example, was a spiritual and mystic critique of pure rationalism. It appealed to lovelorn youths and a growing academic proletariat of frustrated aspirant bureaucrats. But they represented no threat to the established order; their concerns were more aesthetic than political.[73] When the hero of Friedrich Schillers's *Die Räuber* attacked the 'ink-blot century' and the 'limp age of eunuchs',[74] this was a typical case of intellectual denial: it was the state which acted, reformed and legislated while he scribbled. The *Illuminati* – a secret organization of enlightened anticlericalists, which aimed to infiltrate the Bavarian state and overturn the existing order – were taken rather more seriously by the authorities.[75] Yet even they under-took no effective moves until their suppression in 1785–6, after which they disappeared without trace.

These critical voices were exceptional. The German Enlightenment was not a bourgeois manifesto against the aristocracy: the *Aufklärung* actually found disproportionate support among the nobility.[76] Rather, the German Enlightenment created a kind of cultural and functional avant-garde in which aristocrats and bourgeois transcended the con-fines of the society of orders. In any case, the Enlightenment was less a set of beliefs than a method of enquiry.[77] It was certainly not an ideol-ogy, with a coherent view of state and society. Enlightenment, Kant explained in 1784, was 'man's emergence from his self-incurred imma-turity'.[78] But was this to be achieved by the state, by the estates, by a self-motivated public sphere, or by the individual himself, as Kant believed? Opinions differed. This explains why the French Enlightenment produced such a wide spectrum of political attitudes: from the royal despotism of a Voltaire, through the separation of powers of a Montesquieu to the popular sovereignty of a Rousseau.

The *Aufklärung*, on the other hand, was politically less polarized and much more orientated towards monarchic authority: the German public sphere sought to advise princes, not to command them. Indeed, the *Aufklärung* did not subvert the state, it was *part* of the state. In Prussia, for example, less than 5 per cent of the contributors to a leading enlightened journal were *not* civil servants in one form or another.[79] Among German bureaucrats, enlightened ideals blended with traditional cameralism in the quest for a rational, populous, prosperous and well-ordered state.[80] Moreover, many German rulers, Frederick II, Joseph II and numerous lesser potentates, were deeply influenced by the Enlightenment. Yet even here the political impact of the Enlightenment as such was limited. With a few exceptions, such as toleration, the policies of enlightened rulers did not differ much from those of their predecessors. It is therefore not necessarily helpful to speak of enlightened despotism; 'enlightened Reform Absolutism' – as opposed to the pragmatic Reform Absolutism of their parents – best describes the policies of Frederick and Joseph. What had changed was the basis of legitimation, away from divine right and towards a reasoned sense of the common good, rather than the nature of government itself. The link between philosophy and politics was thus complex and attenuated. Certainly, the Enlightenment provided a general intellectual context and princes and bureaucrats were certainly encouraged and influenced by the enlightened public sphere, but they were in no sense either beholden or responsible to it. Frederick famously observed that while he was a *philosophe* in his study he was a king in the cabinet chamber. The much-cited remark attributed to Joseph II that he had made 'philosophy the law-giver' of the Habsburg monarchy, was based on a forgery.[81]

For what matters is not what enlightened rulers thought or said, but what they did. Like the traditional reform absolutists of earlier generations, the enlightened reform absolutists aimed to strengthen the internal cohesion of the state, primarily with a view to external security and expansion. 'All measures,' Frederick said in his Testament of 1752, 'must be well thought out and orient finances, politics, and the military towards a common goal, namely the strengthening of the state and the increase of its power.'[82] Their main concerns were the related areas of finance, population and recruitment. 'Money,' Frederick the Great said, 'is the nerve of the state'; it was, Kaunitz argued, the 'driving force behind everything'.[83] The state sought to maximize revenue by rationalizing the collection and administration of taxes; by fostering indigenous manufactures and shutting out foreign competition; by promoting agricultural improvements and higher yields; and – in Roman Catholic states – by increasing peasant productivity through the abolition of holy days. This was matched by a coordinated *Peuplierungspolitik* which sought to increase the number of taxable and recruitable subjects through the encouragement of economically desirable immigration such as the (French Protestant) Huguenots or the Salzburg Protestants. Where the enlightened reform absolutists broke new ground was in their attitude to religion and toleration. By 1780, the ferocious confessionalism of Maria Theresa of Austria and Frederick William I of Prussia had given way to a policy of active toleration under Joseph II and Frederick the Great; *de facto* toleration had existed in Prussia for some time. Already in mid-century, Frederick had moved to conciliate the Catholic church, most conspicuously by permitting the construction of a Catholic cathedral in the centre of Berlin; imagine a comparable gesture in eighteenth-century London! A similarly tolerant attitude was shown by Joseph to Austrian and Hungarian Protestants. Indeed, his Toleration Edict of 1781 also extended religious freedoms to Jews; at around the same time, the Prussian bureaucrat Christian von Dohm penned his famous pamphlet calling for Jewish emancipation. These policies were clearly influenced by the Enlightenment. Yet they were also decisively motivated by the primacy of foreign policy. For when Frederick the Great conciliated Catholics he did so not merely for its own sake, nor simply to strengthen the state through intra-confessional harmony, but in order to forestall the emergence of a Habsburgist fifth column in largely Catholic Silesia. By and large, this policy was successful, though there were some worries about the loyalty of Catholic Silesians during the War of the Bavarian Succession.

Similarly, Joseph II's policy of toleration was not just a reaction to internal sectarian unrest, a reflection of his enlightened outlook, or to attract and retain skilled Protestants for the sake of economic development. It was all of these things, but it was also an attempt to prevent Prussia from subverting the religious minorities in Hungary, Moravia, Bohemia and Galicia. These fears were justified: under both Frederick and his less enlightened successor, Prussia did not hesitate to support disaffected Roman Catholic clerics, especially Jesuits, Protestant Hungarian nobles, or any other kind of dissident against Joseph. Moreover, Joseph II was concerned not to frighten Protestant opinion in Silesia, or any other areas of potential Habsburg expansion. His *rapprochement* with the Orthodox population in Galicia was intended to prevent them from being sucked into the Russian orbit. Even Jewish emancipation can be seen in some measure, though less so than in the case of the Christian minorities, as a function of the primacy of foreign policy.[84] The Austrians suspected, not entirely unfairly, that many Prussian agents were 'Jews and Jesuits'; they were also concerned to appease the growing power of the Jewish communities in Vienna, Prague and northern Italy. In short, the toleration policy of Joseph II was, at least in part, a direct result of the Austro-Prussian struggle for mastery in Germany.

But the primacy of foreign policy was about to subvert the old society of orders in an even more dramatic way; and it was to do so quite independently of the Enlightenment. For around 1780 the external demands of the Austrian state set in motion a series of processes which prefigured the eventual collapse of the socio-legal *ancien régime* in Germany during the first decades of the next century. It was now that the deeply subversive potential of functional justifications for social inequality became clear. Far from being mere 'rhetoric'[85] the 'functional' as opposed to natural definition of privilege became the lever by which the relationship between state, land and peasant was transformed.

The radical new departure in Austrian policy after the death of Maria Theresa in 1780 was based on a searching analysis of the causes of Habsburg weakness since the mid-century. Her traditional assets – the loyalty of the smaller worldly and ecclesiastical estates, the right of recruitment throughout the *Reich*, favoured access to the south German money markets – had not sufficed to reverse the loss of Silesia. Nor had the programme of reforms initiated by the chief ministers Kaunitz and Frederick William Haugwitz achieved more than an uneasy parity with Prussia. At first sight this was surprising: Austria was not only far more populous than Prussia, she was also much richer in natural resources. Yet, even on paper, she could only field an army one-third larger, a level of militarization which was woefully inadequate for the task of defending the monarchy's extended perimeter line in Bohemia, Galicia, the Balkans, northern Italy and the Austrian Netherlands, let alone any plans for expansion. As Joseph II remarked in 1779: 'Our provinces are impoverished and cannot afford to maintain the present military establishment. Only the improvement of our agriculture, industry, trade and finance will make possible the upkeep and expansion of our military forces to meet future eventualities.'[86]

All larger German states, with the possible exceptions of Württemberg and Saxony, were peasant states. The conventional 'physiocratic' wisdom was that agricultural productivity and rural population were the decisive indicators of economic strength. According to Frederick II the peasantry were a 'class of people . . . who contribute the most to the state, who supply the whole state with food, [and] who supply the army with a large proportion of its recruits'. This opinion was shared by Joseph II, who had written in 1765 that the main task of government was to maximize 'population, that is the conservation and the augmentation of subjects'.[87] 'The peasantry,' Joseph argued,

is the largest class among the state's citizens and therefore it is the foundation and the greatest support of the state. The peasants have to be maintained in such a condition that they can nourish themselves and their families and at the same time be able to contribute to the taxes. The private rights of the manors have to be subordinated to this view.[88]

Hence, as the Prussian chief minister Hertzberg explained in 1779, agriculture was 'the source of prosperity of all states'.[89] There were good reasons for this: most people lived on the land; well over half the gross national product was generated on the land; and land or agricultural produce was much easier to tax than any other form of wealth. Unlike profits from trade, manufactures and crafts, land ownership and land use was difficult to conceal.[90] Indeed, throughout eighteenth-century Germany, the larger part of state income derived from direct land taxes.[91] At the same time, however, the relationship between state and peasantry was determined by a governing compromise between prince and aristocracy: both parties cooperated in extracting as much as possible from the peasantry.

Under this system, state revenue could only be maximized by raising agricultural productivity and increasing peasant population; there was as yet no political will or desire to revise the redistributive process itself. Instead, the reforming bureaucracies concentrated on such improvements as crop rotation, disseminating new theories, technologies and methods. A classic case of agrarian-based reform absolutism was Baden under Karl Friedrich during the 1770s and 1780s.[92] The modernizing effects of these measures should not be underestimated. State demands for cash payments made the peasantry more efficient and helped to commercialize the agrarian economy; on the other hand, it reduced peasant capital formation and limited investment.[93] Most important, in north-western Germany – Hannover, Brunswick, Hesse-Cassel and the western provinces of Prussia – the state-sponsored enclosure of common land had far-reaching effects on peasant society. This process began in the last third of the eighteenth century and was completed during the second quarter of the nineteenth century. The aim of the bureaucrats was to create a 'market-oriented society';[94] this was to be achieved by abolishing all collective claims to the soil and encouraging 'agrarian individualism'. The great beneficiaries of these changes were the nobility and wealthy peasants, who were best placed to exploit subdivision and supply the market; the losers were the rural poor whose livelihoods had depended on the use of common lands.

But in much of northern and eastern Germany, as well as in the Habsburg monarchy, the military-agrarian complex placed a strict ceiling on agricultural productivity. The *Bauernschutz* prevented estate owners from rationalizing and expanding; the institution of serfdom frustrated peasant mobility and improvement. It was a cheap way of ensuring a regular supply of men and taxation, but it was not efficient.

In Prussia, this system 'worked'; in Austria it did not. For when comparing population figures and productivity in both states, one is not comparing like with like. In Austria, the military-agrarian complex supplied the Habsburgs with neither the manpower nor the revenue it required. Throughout the monarchy, the military and administrative cooperation of the aristocracy did not outweigh the loss of revenue from the peasantry. In the Hungarian lands this situation was further aggravated by the power of the Diet to restrict taxation and recruitment. Only about a seventh of the regular army in 1780 was made up of Hungarians; Hungarian taxes did little more than cover the defence of Hungary itself. What mattered was not population *per se* as *taxable* and *recruitable* population. Here Prussia was as fortunate as Austria was hamstrung. One hard-working Lower-Silesian artisan was worth four impoverished Galician peasants; and one cooperative Pomeranian Junker was worth three opinionated Hungarian nobles. No amount of increased taxation in the Austrian and Bohemian lands could compensate for the fact that the Hungarian and Belgian provinces were not pulling their weight. By 1780, therefore, the Kaunitz–Haugwitz reforms were beginning to suffer from the law of diminishing returns.

Joseph's remedy for this impasse was twofold. First of all, he tried to increase peasant productivity; this was in line with traditional reform absolutism. Secondly and more radically, he initiated a radical struggle between state and nobility for the surplus value of the peasantry.[95] Under the traditional system, the lord had taken upward of 70 per cent of peasant production; the rest was shared between peasant and state. Joseph now proposed to reduce the lord's share to about 12 and increase that of the peasant to 70 per cent. His aim was the creation of a populous, largely rural society of prosperous, tax-paying and conscriptable smallholders. Unlike earlier reforms, this involved the fundamental revision of the old governing compromise between state and nobility: in particular the abolition of serfdom, with all its associated labour duties and socio-legal inequalities. Herein lay the radical new departure after 1780, which made Austria temporarily the most dynamic state in Germany. Moreover, the impulse behind Joseph's programme was an explicit primacy of foreign policy. 'Forms of government,' he argued in 1785, 'which have developed are merely contingent and have been shaped only by the national character of the *physical location, by the need to secure protection against outsiders* [my italics] and by the need to promote material progress.'[96] In this instance Joseph was referring explicitly to Hungary, but the principle he was enunciating applied equally throughout the monarchy: the socio-legal inequalities of the old society of orders were sacrosanct only so long as the external geopolitical needs of the state did not dictate otherwise.

Maria Theresa had sponsored a more modest programme of reform at different speeds and with due consideration for the different lands of the monarchy; Joseph attempted radical change everywhere and at once. In 1781 he modified serfdom in the non-Hungarian provinces: peasants were now permitted to marry, move and take up a trade without seigneurial permission. Joseph also abolished compulsory service in the manor house (*Gesindedienst*) though not feudal dues and services. At the same time he strengthened the rights of peasants to appeal to the state against their lords and severely limited patrimonial justice. Simultaneously, Joseph began to reform the church, dissolving 'unproductive' contemplative orders, favouring secular over regular clergy to establish new parishes, attack baroque piety and popular superstition, overturn the church's dominant role in education, and undermine the legal and political autonomy of the hierarchy. In 1783, this culminated in a plan to harmonize the boundaries of Austrian bishoprics with those of the Habsburg state. Instead of allowing his subjects to be supervised from Salzburg, Konstanz, Augsburg and Passau, Joseph created new sees in Budweis, Leoben, St Pölten and elsewhere.

By the mid-1780s Joseph seemed unstoppable. He had shouldered aside clerical and aristocratic objections to introduce obligatory primary education for children aged six to twelve, funded from parish and manorial resources; he inaugurated a frenetic policy of forced economic development; and he equipped his administrators with all the paraphernalia of a modern bureaucracy: training, pensions and promotion by merit. The new spirit of standardization was reflected in the language law of 1784 which stipulated the use of German in government and administration in all lands excepting Italy, Belgium and Galicia. Joseph then turned to deal with the estates. Between 1783 and 1786, the nobility in Lombardy was eliminated as a participatory political force. In 1785, Joseph finally confronted the Magyar nobility by extending the abolition of serfdom into Hungary. Soon afterwards he took on the Belgian estates with a plan to redraw their traditional provincial boundaries. Then in 1789 he mooted his most fundamental reform of all: the introduction of a universal equal land tax, replacing all existing taxes and privileges.

At one level Joseph was remarkably successful. His economic policies certainly contributed to an economic boom during the last decades of the century; some historians have even argued that all the elements for 'modern' economic growth were in place in Austria by 1800.[97] The codification of the law and its publication in German, finally completed in 1811, was begun under Maria Theresa but considerably accelerated by Joseph II.[98] Above all, Joseph ended all vestiges of aristocratic participation in the collection and administration of taxes in Austria.[99] This, combined with increased efficiency in the financial bureaucracy, enabled Joseph to achieve a striking increase in revenue during the early years of his reign;[100] his educational reforms were also reasonably successful. Finally, Joseph inaugurated a *rapprochement* with the peasantry, especially in Galicia, which was to bear fruit many years later.[101] But at another level Joseph was a complete failure. Implementation lagged far behind legislation: many of his later measures, especially the agrarian reforms, were simply ignored.

Joseph regarded society as a kind of *tabula rasa* which he could refashion in accordance with the needs of the state. 'I do not require your permission for doing good,' he told the recalcitrant estates of Brabant, in the Austrian Netherlands, in 1789. But Habsburg society was uniquely well-organized to offer resistance; after all, this is why Joseph embarked on his programme of reforms in the first place. The nobilities of Hungary and the Austrian Netherlands began to obstruct the raising of taxes and troops in protest. At the same time, the clerical casualties of Joseph's religious policies began to conspire against him; here Joseph had the worst of both worlds: Protestant Hungarians were antagonized by his economic policies and his surveillance of the Freemasons while Catholic orders – such as the Jesuits – resented his repressive policies. As if all this were not bad enough, Joseph's agrarian policies had the short-term effect of both bewildering peasants through the introduction of cash payments and encouraging unrealistic expectations of imperial help against their lords.[102] In 1784, inspired with mistaken confidence in imminent emancipation, the largely Romanian Transylvanian peasants rose against their Magyar masters. The suppression of this rebellion by imperial forces and the savage execution of the peasant leader, Horja, defied all norms of enlightened opinion. By the late 1780s this peasant, corporate and confessional resistance had brought the monarchy to the brink of civil war.

To make matters worse, Joseph's domestic problems interacted explosively with foreign political threats. When the estates of Brabant rose in open revolt, Joseph was so preoccupied by his war against the Turks in the Balkans that he could not spare the relatively modest forces needed to put it down. Conversely, the withdrawal of Hungarian cooperation weakened Austria against the Turks after 1787. When it looked as if Prussia would enter the lists against him in 1788–9, all those disaffected by Joseph's policies, from Jesuits to Calvinist Hungarian aristocrats, looked to Berlin for help. Above all, Joseph was now faced with a financial crisis.[103] The Belgian and Hungarian Diets were withholding their taxes; the international money markets were reluctant to lend without collateral from the estates.[104] Even in tranquil provinces of the monarchy the agrarian reforms had the short-term effect of reducing revenue and complicating recruitment. The increased peasant mobility produced by emancipation complicated conscription,[105] while the abolition of labour services threatened the manorial economy with collapse[106] and reduced the tax base.

In the end, it was foreign rather than domestic policy which brought Joseph down. His successor, Leopold II, was forced to withdraw the land tax and halt the distribution of land to the peasantry; the emancipation and toleration decrees remained in force. Yet domestic policy was a powerful contributory factor to the Austrian débâcle of the late 1780s. When Leopold II concluded a compromise treaty with the Turks in 1790, he observed that 'we owe this peace to the bad faith and intrigues of the Hungarians'.[107] Not for the last time, events in

Germany had been decisively influenced by the Hungarian dimension.
Ironically therefore, Joseph's policy of domestic reform, far from providing him with the internal cohesion necessary to defend Austrian
interests abroad, actually turned out to be a liability in the struggle for
mastery in Germany.

Some of the problems facing Joseph – such as Hungary, Belgium
and extensive diplomatic commitments – were specific to Austria,
others were quite common among modernizing states in late eighteenth-century Germany. In Hesse-Darmstadt, for example, the chief
minister, Friedrich Carl von Moser, initiated a programme of reforms
to stave off imminent bankruptcy and re-establish princely authority
against unruly magnates.[108] Moser was quite successful in stabilizing
the finances, raising revenue through rational administration and
restoring confidence among creditors. But in 1780 he was brought
down by an alliance of rival bureaucrats, nobles and patricians; thereafter the modernizing project languished until the Napoleonic period.
In Württemberg, the estates succeeded in having the *Hohe Carlsschule* –
set up in 1771 to train princely bureaucrats and officers – shut down by
1794. Indeed, the estates increasingly constituted a kind of parallel
government with its own foreign and fiscal policy. Similarly, in Bavaria,
the ambitions of Karl Theodor, in particular, the plan to exchange
Bavaria for the Austrian Netherlands and a royal crown, provoked
overt opposition from the estates, who were increasingly coming to
regard themselves as the representatives of a specifically 'Bavarian' as
opposed to a dynastic Wittelsbach interest. In 1785 they openly
demanded that Karl Theodor guarantee the territorial integrity of the
whole of Bavaria. By 1790 the estates were claiming to be not subjects
but representatives of the interests of the whole of Bavaria.[109]

But perhaps the most retardative factor of all among the aspirant
modernizing states of the Third Germany was the *Reich* itself. As
Johann Jacob Moser pointed out in 1769, 'no matter how many taxes
or soldiers any prince, count or prelate may raise . . . once he faces an
appeal to a supreme imperial court, he will soon be made to see that
his sovereignty is very limited.'[110] In Bavaria and Württemberg, it was
the *Reich* which bolstered the estates against the centralizing pretensions of the prince.[111] So long as these mutually reinforcing external
and internal restraints existed, the breakthrough to a fully centralized,
rational state could not take place.

In Prussia, enlightened reform absolutism was both less thorough
and less problematic. Here there were no representative institutions of

the nobility comparable with those in Hungary, Belgium or the Third Germany; here the *Reich* had no power whatsoever to limit the internal sovereignty of the monarch. The divergence between the enlightened reform absolutist agenda in Austria and Prussia thus lay not in any ideological gulf, but in the differing roles of the nobility. This explains both the Josephine assault on aristocratic privilege and the ironic fact that the great process of enlightened legal codification culminating in the Prussian *Allgemeines Landrecht* ended up reinforcing group rights at the expense of the individual. How could it be otherwise, given the crucial role of the nobility in the army and administration? This was the normative power of the successful. On the other hand, the Prussian system had its drawbacks. In return for their cooperation, the nobility were exempt from direct personal taxation. Thanks to serfdom and *Bauernschutz*, the agricultural sector could not reach its full potential as either an economy of independent peasants or one of rationalizing estate owners. Educational reforms were hamstrung by the need for child labour; this was to remain a problem throughout Germany until well into the nineteenth century. Furthermore, in the absence of significant representative institutions, the creditworthiness of the Prussian state was low. This meant that extraordinary expenditure, especially wars, could only be financed through a system of expedients: subsidies, exactions, debased coinage and recourse to a 'war chest' established in times of peace.[112] Finally, the military-agrarian complex, though more efficient than those of Prussia's rivals, left room for improvement. The system of functional inequalities exempted whole groups of the population from military service: sons of offficers, bureaucrats, townspeople, in fact just about everybody except the peasantry and the urban poor, the unemployed, unskilled workers and small artisans. In 1800, about a quarter of the population were exempt for one reason or another; another quarter of the population were politically unreliable Poles. It was thus hardly surprising that half of the army was made up of foreign mercenaries.[113]

Prussian statesmen were aware of these shortcomings but in no hurry to remedy them. To change one element in the equation was impossible; everything would have to change. The abolition of serfdom, for example, would destroy the old governing compromise with the nobility; it would also necessitate the introduction of universal military service in order to compensate for the migration of peasants from their cantons into the towns. In short, the objection to radical social reform was not ideological but practical. As Frederick the Great remarked in 1777, 'if one were to abolish these loathsome practices with one blow, one would thereby endanger the entire agricultural system'.[114] Or, to quote General Rüchel: 'The Prussian military constitution and administration of the state is a venerable original; if one interferes with one of its component parts the whole machine is given a jolt.'[115] For this reason, Frederick drew back when tentative plans for serf emancipation in Pomerania met stiff noble resistance after 1763. In any case, there was no perceived pressing need for reform. The old system had served Prussia well during the crises of the mid-century; more to the point, the army had performed excellently during the invasion of Holland in 1787 and the deterrent mobilizations in eastern Europe two years later.[116] And yet, as we shall see, the primacy of foreign policy was soon to have deeply subversive implications for the seemingly stable socio-political order in Prussia. For the functionally based inequalities reaffirmed by the General Law Code of 1794 could be revoked by a fresh act of positive legislation, as and when necessity of state demanded it.

By itself, enlightened reform absolutism was not enough to transform Germany from a feudal society of orders into a modern capitalist society of citizens. To a considerable extent this was a result of the weakness of the reform impulse and the resilience of the socio-legal *ancien régime*. But it was also a consequence of the ambiguities of the enlightened reform project itself. As we have seen, the Enlightenment was politically neutral: it could serve to legitimate a reform absolutist assault on privilege; it was accompanied by the emergence of a recognizably modern public sphere and literary market; it provided decisive impulses for the development of national feeling through its concern for the vernacular, especially among the Magyars and Slavs of the Habsburg monarchy; and it may even have helped to create a 'communicative cohesion of the German bourgeoisie'.[117] But the Enlightenment also served to legitimate the self-interested resistance of Hungarian Protestants and Freemasons to Josephine modernization, especially the unified, equitable land tax; it was also enthusiastically supported by many craft guilds, whose restrictive practices limited economic modernization; and it was the Enlightenment of Schiller, Herder, Kant and Klopstock which attacked the same mercenary policy which gave the Landgrave of Hesse-Cassel the financial muscle to introduce enlightened policies without the cooperation of his estates.[118]

The role of the state was equally ambiguous. What German princes attempted was a very conditional and directed form of modernization. Joseph, for example, tried to create a rural society of smallholders. The paradox is that had he succeeded, the short-term military and fiscal benefits might have been considerable, but Austria might have been even more backward in the long run. After all, it has been pointed out that the path to agricultural progress lay in emancipating the landowners, not the peasantry.[119] Aspects of Joseph's *Peuplierungspolitik* also had anti-modern implications such as the plan to abolish the succession rights of widows in favour of sons, so as to enable them to found a family sooner; this was a good example of 'biopolitics'.[120] The ambiguity of state-sponsored reform can also been seen in the emancipation of the Jews. Like all emancipatory measures of the time, this was rarely proposed and never undertaken for its own sake, but as a preliminary stage to their assimilation into society. We should not make too much of this: the eighteenth-century state adopted similar standardizing policies towards most minority groups. None the less, it remains a fact that the same Joseph who issued the Toleration Edict demanded that all Jews learn German within two years and upheld discriminatory legislation against the immigration of undesirable impoverished eastern Jews; it was the same Prussian bureaucracy which produced a Christian von Dohm that expelled into rump Poland about 30 per cent of the Jews they inherited in 1772 and issued stern ordinances against begging Jews (*Betteljuden*) in 1780, 1785, 1788 and 1791.[121]

In any case, state-driven modernization was always partial: it was invariably directed towards socio-economic development, not political participation. Indeed, in some ways enlightened reform absolutism was politically regressive. One man's privilege is another man's bondage: when the state granted freedom from socio-legal inequalities with one hand, it took away the traditional political freedoms of the estates with the other. Any thought of broader political participation or of checks on the executive was anathema. 'The highest authority in the state,' Karl Friedrich of Baden argued, 'rests solely upon one [person]. The notion of the system of the balance of powers . . . is a dangerous opinion.'[122] Even Leopold II, who was an enthusiastic supporter of constitutional government and the separation of powers while Grand Duke of Tuscany, forbore to shackle himself with such impediments when he briefly succeeded Joseph as emperor in 1790.

Never ask a question if you mind what the answer is: broader political participation would have retarded, not accelerated, modernization. A hypothetical universal franchise would have reflected the nature of rural society as a whole: suspicious, bigoted, backward and confused. In 1792, Karl von Hardenberg, then the senior Prussian bureaucrat in Franconia, observed that 'an almost universal popular dissatisfaction, which commands extreme circumspection when introducing changes and even requires that prejudices be treated sensitively [was] the main obstacle in the way of the emancipation of the Jews'.[123] The same was true of public debate. As Kant wrote in 1784, 'a lesser degree of civil freedom gives intellectual freedom enough room to expand to its fullest extent'. How right he was: the state was the best guarantor of religious tolerance and free speech against a prejudiced society; the contemporary Gordon riots against Catholics in England – or even a Rushdie affair – would have been unthinkable in Frederician Prussia. In this sense at least, absolutism was thus not just compatible with cultural freedom but actually conducive to it.

The estates have been seen as the progenitors of political modernization in general and nineteenth-century liberalism in particular; the same has also been said for the absolutist state.[124] Both statements are true. On the one hand, the princely assault on estatist freedoms and socio-legal privilege undoubtedly helped to pave the way for later democratization. On the other hand, the preoccupation of the estates with taxation and consent prefigured the concerns of early nineteenth-century liberals. Yet unlike their liberal 'successors', there were clear limits to the modernizing potential of the estates: they were narrowly concerned with 'cheap' government and the preservation of privilege. Nowhere in Germany, except Württemberg during the 1790s, did the estates make a serious bid to take over the running of the state itself.

### Germany of the Cabinets: The Primacy of Foreign Policy, 1777–88

If the guiding principle of the imperial constitution was stasis and continuity, the dynamic for change and upheaval came not only from the reforming imperative in the territorial state, but also from events on the international scene. These events were conditioned by the geopolitical configuration of Germany and Europe as a whole. The *Reich* lay geographically at the centre of a pentarchy of European states of which she herself was not a member. This meant that Germany was inevitably subject to the policies of the great powers, especially France and, increasingly, Russia. Their chief interest was to sustain a power vacuum in the heart of Europe, simultaneously capable of repelling predators and yet incapable of developing hegemonic pretensions of its own. As Jean-Jacques Rousseau observed, the German balance was also the balance of Europe; the imperial German laws forbidding annexations were thus also the public law of Europe. French policy, therefore, sought to extend its informal influence over the *Reich* through the maintenance of the imperial constitution. In practice, as the French diplomat Du Buat pointed out, this involved support for the *forces mortes* in the *Reich*; on no account should France encourage the *forces vives*. This theme was taken up by the French foreign minister Vergennes in 1779. 'Germany,' he argued,

would in general be quite capable of harming France. Being the largest and most populous territory, and able to dispose of the resources of Hungary, it is easy to see what advantage it would have over us if this formidable power were not limited by the form of its constitution . . . We thus owe our superiority and our security to the forces of [German] disunity and to the vices of this constitution.[125]

Twenty years later, the French were to overturn their own advice and thus set free the *forces vives* in Germany.

Austrian policy was shaped by the geopolitical inheritance of 1715. The territorial dispensations of the Treaty of Utrecht, which awarded Austria the southern Netherlands (Belgium), had saddled her with the role of guardian of the gate in the west against France. Subsequently, this role was complicated by the rise of Russia and Prussia in the mid-century and the decline of French power. Unlike the seventeenth century, the main threats to Austria now came from the east and north, whereas her greatest opportunities lay to the west (Bavaria) and southeast (the Balkans); Prussia replaced France as her main rival. As far back as 1706, Joseph I's chief minister, Count Salm, observed that 'The House of Austria fears the power of the king of Prussia more than that of France, which is greater; . . . the king of France only gnaws at the edges of those countries that border on it, but . . . the king of Prussia proceeds directly to the heart.'[126] These suspicions were fully confirmed by the Silesian Wars of 1740–63. From now on, Austria subordinated her general European policy to the dualist struggle with Prussia. As one Habsburg diplomat put it, Austria should be prepared to risk 'such a gain of French power on land and at sea as would make the whole of Europe jealous, if one could thereby secure the complete emasculation of the King in Prussia'.[127] Similarly, towards the end of the century, the Habsburgs were prepared to risk Russian hegemony in eastern Europe as the price of her cooperation against Prussia.

Cumulatively, Austrian commitments in the west, in Germany, in Italy, in eastern Europe and in the Balkans, led to an acute sense of exposure. As Kaunitz observed in 1776,

> [if] that empire which has the most secure borders and which has the least to fear from its neighbours is to be considered the greatest and most powerful, [then Austria] despite its size and internal strengths must be counted among the weaker powers, because it is encircled by three very dangerous neighbours, some more powerful, some equally powerful.[128]

The remedy was a geopolitical reorientation of the monarchy away from her western commitments towards a more consolidated position in central Europe. Belgium in particular came to be regarded as a strategic millstone around Austrian necks: rather than being a barrier against France, the province was now tying the monarchy *to* France and distracting her from more pressing tasks further east. As Kaunitz noted in 1755, the Austrian Netherlands 'involved the archducal house in all wars and whose loss could therefore be accepted'.[129]

Prussian policy was no less motivated by geopolitical considerations. Prussia, as Voltaire remarked, was not so much a state as a 'kingdom of mere border strips'.[130] The Hohenzollerns held scattered lands along the Rhine and in the north, but the centre of gravity of the monarchy lay firmly in the east; this had been confirmed by the first partition of Poland between Austria, Prussia and Russia in 1772 and the annexation of Silesia. As a result, the period after 1780 saw a lively debate between those chief ministers such as Ewald von Hertzberg and later Christian von Haugwitz, who wished for Prussian disengagement in the west, and those such as Karl August von Hardenberg, who were prepared to pursue opportunistic policies directed at gains in western and south-western Germany, especially Franconia.

Overshadowing the policies of both German great powers was the rise of Russia. By reducing the buffer in the east, the partition of Poland had been a geopolitical disaster for Austria and Prussia; this was a large price to pay for the acquisition of West Prussia. Each further partition, motivated by greed and resignation in equal measure, brought the Russian border further west; in this respect, Austria and Prussia were less brutal trenchermen than bulimics, helplessly bolting down slices of Poland. Frederick the Great's fear of Russia was legendary: he described it as 'a terrible power, which will make all Europe tremble'; Austrian anxieties were no less acute.[131] Yet the result was not an Austro-Prussian *rapprochement* to protect the integrity of the *Reich*, or even just to uphold the balance in eastern Europe. Instead, the response was a desperate scramble to appease Russia, or, even better to enlist her support in the struggle for mastery in Germany. 'Russia with us, and we with Russia,' Joseph II commented in 1780, 'can achieve anything we like.'[132]

The middling territorial states, lastly, were also guided by geopolitics and the primacy of foreign policy. Their greatest fear, especially after 1772, was 'polonization': annexation or partition at the hands of the two German great powers. As the British envoy at Munich, who was well placed to judge the fears of the Third Germany, observed, 'the courts of Vienna and Berlin will either prosecute their separate claims by the sword and involve Germany in war, or they will ever extend the same system of partition into the empire that proved so irrestible in Poland'.[133] At the very least, the Third Germany was subject to humiliating intervention: in Mecklenburg, Württemberg and Bavaria, princely attempts at internal consolidation were frustrated by Austro-Prussian support for the estates.[134] Here Prussia was able to kill two birds with one stone: to pose as the champion of the imperial constitution and to preserve her modernizing lead by protecting the *forces mortes* within rival states. The various 'trialist' schemes to unite the Third Germany were a response to this Austro-Prussian tutelage. In 1782, for example, Karl Friedrich of Baden and Karl August of Saxony-Weimar conceived a trialist union for the preservation of the imperial constitution and the integrity of its member states; Prussia was to be the guarantor of the league, but not its leader.[135]

The Third Germany was fearful of Austro-Prussian dualism, and resented the agenda it forced upon them, but they also benefited from it. As Frederick the Great pointed out in his Political Testament of 1768, the Habsburg–Hohenzollern balance served to uphold 'the rights, territories and freedom of this Republic of Princes [the *Reich*] which was in the past frequently in danger of being oppressed by the emperor';[136] and, he might have added, by himself. Similarly, twenty years later, the Württembergian writer and pamphleteer Wilhelm Ludwig Weckhrlin noted that Austro-Prussian rivalry helped to protect smaller states and maintain the peace.[137] Conversely, the Third Germany had no greater fear than an Austro-Prussian *rapprochement* at their expense; such a development promised truly revolutionary consequences in Germany.

Finally, the Third Germany may have been fearful, but it was also ambitious. The task facing smaller princes was threefold. First of all, they wished to keep either German great power at arm's length without submitting to the other. Secondly, they sought to consolidate their domestic power against the estates so as to maximize their external power on the international scene. Thirdly and relatedly, they sought to cast off all external restrictions on their internal sovereignty imposed by the imperial constitution.

Nevertheless, to the superficial observer, there was little in the European and *Reich* scene in 1777 to suggest that a decade of controversy and crisis in Germany lay ahead. The turmoil of mid-century was over. Prussia, fixated largely on retaining possession of Silesia, was manifestly a satiated power; Austria seemed to have lost much of its revanchist fervour. Both powers had come together to share a large slice of Poland with Russia. Neither power had been at war since 1763 and the constitution of the empire continued to be guaranteed, as it had been since 1648, by Sweden and France; after 1779, Russia was to be added to the list of external guarantors.

But beneath this picture of stability were a number of explosive charges which threatened to upset the balance in southern Germany and thus that of the *Reich* itself. The first danger arose out of the fact that neither of the two Wittelsbach princes, Max III of Bavaria and Karl Theodor of the Palatinate, looked like having legitimate heirs. To ensure the succession, both made arrangements to succeed each other. This not only raised the spectre of a united Wittelsbach dynasty for the first time in hundreds of years, it also threatened to weaken Austria's grip on the south by elevating Bavaria to the level of the unquestioned third power in the *Reich*. Furhermore, the new Wittelsbach conglomerate would be strong enough to make another claim to the imperial title, as in 1740–5. The second danger lay in the foreseeable reversion of the two Franconian territories of Ansbach and Bayreuth to Prussian control after the death of the reigning margrave. Quite apart from the overall increase of Prussian territory resulting therefrom, this development was particularly alarming because it would enable her to penetrate southern Germany and dominate the Franconian circle. Thirdly, Joseph II was determined to cast off his geopolitical inheritance and reassert Habsburg dominance over Prussia, even if this meant subverting the whole imperial constitution in the process. Fourthly and finally, an increasingly powerful Russia proved herself willing to compromise her guarantee of the *Reich* in return for substantial gains at the expense of the Ottoman Empire.

All this made future strife in the *Reich* almost inevitable. If Austria was to frustrate a Wittelsbach challenge to the imperial crown, to destroy the danger of trialism with Bavaria as the third German great power and to pre-empt a Prussian eruption into the south, there would have to be some form of intervention. But the pre-programmed conflict became absolutely inescapable when the young Joseph II embraced the geopolitical imperative and launched his state on a decade of aggressive expansionism directed at first against the *Reich* and later against the Ottoman Empire in the Balkans. In fact, Joseph put the *Reich* in double jeopardy, in that he aimed not only to incorporate Bavaria, which was against the spirit if not letter of the imperial constitution, but also, as part of his domestic reforming programme, to overthrow the diocesan order in Germany which was an integral part of that same constitution.

The first crisis to erupt was the Bavarian succession. Joseph's aim was to acquire part of Bavaria through purchase and exchange in order to consolidate his position in southern Germany. By 1777 Habsburg diplomats had worked out a scheme which not only destroyed all prospects of a south German Wittelsbach power concentration, but also promised to start the great geopolitical reorientation necessary to sustain the Habsburg cause in Germany. They secured an agreement with Karl Theodor for a partial exchange of Austrian territories in the west for his new inheritance of Bavaria. No sooner had this been finalized than Max Joseph died and Austrian troops moved to implement the deal. When the Prussians decided to contest this coup, they were joined by Saxony and Mecklenburg. The resulting uneventful war was finally ended by French intervention and Joseph was forced to pull back. At the resulting Treaty of Teschen (1779), Austria made marginal gains, chiefly a slice of eastern Bavaria called the *Innviertel*, which included Braunau on the Inn, where Adolf Hitler was to be born exactly 110 years later. Catherine of Russia gained some prestige by acquiring the status of a guarantor power of the German constitu-

tion; if the guarantee itself was not important, the manifest arrival of Russian influence was. But the real winner was Frederick the Great: he had not only nipped Austrian expansionism in the bud and displayed himself as a protector of the *Reich*, but also retained his claim to the Franconian territories while simultaneously gaining credit as protector of the *Reich*.

Unabashed, Joseph now proceeded to assault another pillar of the imperial constitution: the Roman Catholic church and its diocesan order. It was perhaps not surprising that so anachronistic an institution as the *Reichskirche* should attract the hostile attention of an enlightened despotic reformer like Joseph. In 1780 he moved to reorganize the diocesan boundaries of Austrian bishoprics in order to make them coterminous with his own administrative boundaries. The endeavour was perfectly in keeping with the attempts of absolute rulers to exercise greater control over the church; it also made eminent sense pastorally. The local Austrian episcopate offered no resistance. But very soon Joseph ran up against the furious opposition of bishops in the *Reich* who maintained that his behaviour violated not only his coronation oath to the church, but also the imperial constitution itself, of which the diocesan order was an integral part. The trouble was that nearly all bishoprics covering Austrian territory had their centres outside state borders. This applied to Passau, Salzburg, Freising and Konstanz. Consequently, any attack on them was construed as an attack on the *Reich* as a whole, yet another example of how princely sovereignty was restricted by the imperial constitution.

Josephine expansionism was a calculated break with traditional Habsburg imperial policy. It was symptomatic that Joseph tried to cut expenditure on representation in the *Reich* in the 1780s and even went so far as to plan to reduce funding for the *Reichshofrat*, a major vehicle of imperial influence. But quite apart from gratuitously squandering goodwill in the *Reich*, Joseph's behaviour threatened a main pillar of imperial power. This was the trust of the smaller and smallest ecclesiastical and temporal princes, who were utterly dependent on the emperor for their survival. Though militarily weak, they were often economically sound, making them important allies. Similarly, lack of trust threatened to undermine the advantages that Austria drew from the possession of the imperial title. Individually these rights amounted to little, but cumulatively and well-handled they could greatly enhance Austrian power. Thus the emperor also enjoyed the sole right of recruitment in the *Reich*. It has been estimated that every second

'German', as opposed to Hungarian or Slav, soldier in the Habsburg army came from the *Reich*. The emperor enjoyed the military and economic support of the smaller estates, mobilized through the *Kreise*, in time of war. Indeed, as one Austrian statesman had observed in 1764, Austria was hardly a great power without the imperial dignity.

None of this prevented Joseph from one last attempt at pulling off a coup against the *Reich*. This time Joseph prepared the ground well. A secret alliance with Russia was secured in 1781; the price was Joseph's acquiescence in the Russian annexation of the Crimea in 1783. In return the Russians tolerated his plans in the *Reich*, in spite of the guarantee. Meanwhile, Frederick the Great cast around unsuccessfully for European allies to block Austrian expansionism. By early 1784 Joseph felt strong enough to relaunch his Bavarian exchange plan, a manoeuvre which was as audacious in conception as it was breathtaking in simplicity: an exchange of remote and indefensible Belgium for proximate Bavaria. The Austrians recognized that the deal was economically disadvantageous, but the political benefits were colossal: it would free Vienna from dependence on French goodwill; it would neatly round off Austria's position in southern Germany; it would improve communications with Habsburg lands in Italy; and it would counterbalance any threatened Prussian eruption into Franconia.

At first, the opposition was led by the smaller states led by the Dukes of Anhalt-Dessau and Saxe-Weimar. Originally, their association tried to maintain equidistance between Austria and Prussia, but Joseph's behaviour soon gave the whole project an anti-Austrian spin and before long it had been hijacked by Prussia. The resulting League of Princes (*Fürstenbund*) assembled a formidable coalition of states, including Saxony and Hannover, under Frederick's leadership. Perhaps the cruellest blow came when the Archbishop-Elector of Mainz, the *Reichserzkanzler* and the oldest ally of the emperor in the *Reich*, acceded to the league; Austrian prestige in the *Reich* had collapsed. Yet again, faced with French, Prussian and *Reich* hostility, and insufficiently supported by Russia, Joseph was forced to back down.

The net result of the turbulence of the late 1770s and early to mid-1780s was that Austria and Prussia had reversed roles in the *Reich*. To use T. C. W. Blanning's neat phrase, now that the Austrian gamekeeper had turned poacher, the Prussian poacher turned gamekeeper.[138] Now no longer the pariah of the mid-century, Frederick the Great was reintegrated into the system and soon emerged as a kind of counteremperor to Joseph. Significantly, Prussia did not seize the occasion of the Bavarian succession to partition the *Reich* in conjunction with Austria, but opted instead for the territorial *status quo*, cloaked in conservative *Reich* patriotic rhetoric; frustrated Austrian expansion was Prussian gain. Joseph was thus in a dilemma: reforms directed at achieving parity with Prussia drove the smaller estates into Prussian arms and were thus self-defeating. For each domestic asset realized, Joseph jeopardized an asset among the smaller Austrian client states: recruits, subsidies, access to money markets and political support. What was gained on the swings of reform was lost on the roundabout of the *Reich*.

The consequences of this became increasingly plain as the 1780s wore on. By mid-decade Joseph had lost the proxy *Reichstag* votes of previously friendly estates and lost his grip on the *Fürstenrat*, which fell under Prussian control for the first time. In the end he even succeeded in turning the *Reichshofrat* against him. To make matters worse, Joseph not only managed to antagonize the *Corpus Evangelicorum*, he also wrecked the traditional loyalty of the much less cohesive *Corpus Catholicorum* to the emperor. For the *Fürstenbund* of 1785 was an odd but revealing alliance of Roman Catholic spiritual princes and Protestant territorial states against the Roman Catholic emperor. In this case, religion was merely a cipher for broader political antagonisms. Religious differences between and within the camps were to some extent mapped onto the political sphere, but the driving forces were political rather than confessional. As Kaunitz observed in 1784: 'In my opinion religious differences in Germany have recently become such an object of political pretence and rhetoric that if today the imperial court and the more powerful estates converted to Protestantism, the Protestants would turn Catholic'; this is hardly a sign of the alleged 'reconfessionalization' of imperial politics in the second half of the eighteenth century.[139]

Everything that happened in the *Reich* was under the primacy of European politics. Prussia only hijacked the *Fürstenbund* because she could not assemble the necessary great power coalition against Austria: *ancien régime* France was in terminal decline; Russia was an undisguised ally of Joseph. So it was only for want of a better option that Frederick looked for allies inside the *Reich*. When his successor, Frederick William II, found suitable European partners in the Triple Alliance of 1788, the *Fürstenbund* lost its *raison d'être* and collapsed not long after. Whether, on the other hand, Russia played a stabilizing role as a guarantor power after the Treaty of Teschen, is open to question. It is certainly true that

Catherine II of Russia was herself German and took a keen interest in German affairs. But the direct effect of this seems to have been minimal: Catherine was bribed by Joseph prior to his second exchange project when her help in defending the imperial constitution would have been most needed. Later she was too busy in Poland to assist the hard-pressed western German territories notionally under her protection.

By the late 1780s, therefore, the *Reich* was very far from being on its last legs; instead the *Reich* had shown itself capable of reasserting its natural equilibrium in adversity. It was stabilized rather than torn apart by Austro-Prussian dualism; it had managed, so far, to absorb and neutralize the corrosive modernizing drives of the larger territorial states; and by ensuring the balance of central Europe it made no small contribution to the maintenance of peace on the continent as a whole. Even one of the fiercest critics of the German *ancien régime*, Hans-Ulrich Wehler, was moved to concede that though the *Reich* was 'incapable of developing towards a centralized area state', it was still a precondition for a peaceful Europe by virtue of its status as an internationally guaranteed legal order.[140] The shortcomings and anachronisms of the old *Reich* were a small price to pay for confessional peace and relative political stability.

Indeed, anachronism was *essential* to the success of the *Reich* as a mechanism for the preservation of peaceful coexistence (*Friedensordnung*). The *Reichstag*, for example, may have been a theatre of fruitless intrigue and a platform for the display of arcane knowledge, but at another level it was both a clear expression of the unity in diversity of the *Reich* and a channel for peaceful conflict resolution. Similarly, while the smaller estates blocked the drive of the larger states towards full sovereignty, and thus played an unquestionably anti-modernizing role, they thereby helped to keep the political peace. All attempts to reform the imperial constitution – and there were many – impaled themselves on this fact. Being based on territorial and confessional stasis, the idea of change was as poisonous to the *Reichsverfassung* as it was to the smaller entities dependent on it. If the main benefit conferred by the *Reich* was the preservation of the peace, how was one to introduce reform without causing precisely the kind of trouble one wished to avoid? In short, towards the end of the 1780s, the *Reich* was showing no signs of disintegrating from within, or of conspicuous old age. And yet it was in February 1788 that Joseph took the first in a series of steps which were ultimately to lead to truly revolutionary developments on the German political scene.

# 3

## THE IMPACT OF THE FRENCH WARS, 1792–1815

### The Revolution of 1790 and its Consequences: The German States between Intervention and Accommodation

As far as official Germany was concerned, the events of 1789 in France were something of a non-event. Not even Carl Eugen of Württemberg, who spent the spring of that year in the French capital, showed much interest.[1] All eyes were fixed not on revolutionary Paris, but on the Balkans and the *Reich*. The real watershed in German history is thus not 1789 but either 1788, when Joseph II became embroiled with the Ottoman Empire or, more obviously, 1792/3, when the French revolutionary armies invaded the *Reich*. It was not the French Revolution which changed Europe, T. C. W. Blanning reminds us, but the French Revolutionary Wars.[2]

In February 1788, Joseph II formally joined Russia in a war of conquest against the Ottoman Empire; actual hostilities had already broken out in late 1787. Once again the rest of the *Reich* was forced to readjust to a political scene determined by the direction of Joseph's ambition. The smaller German states breathed a temporary sigh of relief, but for Prussia the implications were clear. If successful, and an Austro-Russian triumph was believed to be inevitable, the campaign would result in Austrian territorial gains without equivalent Prussian compensations; this would have decisively shifted the balance of power in Austria's favour. Hence the new Prussian monarch, Frederick William II, embarked on a campaign to bring Joseph to heel before he defeated the Ottomans. This involved alliances with Britain (1788) and

Poland (1790), as well as covert aid to Habsburg dissidents in Hungary, Galicia and elsewhere. At the same time, the Prussians were demonstratively mobilizing in order to threaten Austria with a two-front war. Some sort of armed conflict in Europe certainly seemed inevitable in 1789–90, but most observers expected it to revolve around the old Austro-Prussian struggle for mastery in Germany. The last thing anybody expected was a prolonged conflagration pitting the young French republic against the Europe of the *ancien régime*. Indeed, both German great powers welcomed France's slow decline into revolution and disorder. 'The present internal confusions in France,' Joseph observed in December 1787, 'are at the moment the best guarantee that that power will not seriously attempt to obstruct our operations against the Porte [Turkish Court].'[3] The Prussian foreign ministry, on the other hand, hoped that the French turbulence of July 1789 – which had its origin at least partly in popular Austrophobia directed against Queen Marie Antoinette – might serve to 'weaken her [France's] liaison with the court of Vienna'.[4]

There was certainly no ideologically inspired desire to intervene on behalf of the old order in France. Despite the firmly anti-revolutionary views of Frederick William II, Prussia was, if anything, keen to foment rebellions abroad, not to stamp them out. Even as France sank into revolutionary bedlam, Prussian agents were stirring up trouble in Hungary, the Austrian Netherlands and Galicia, anywhere, in fact, where they could inflict maximum damage on Joseph. A similarly non-ideological stance was taken by Austria. To quote the incisive words of Kaunitz in September 1791:

The new constitution renders France far less dangerous than she was under the old régime. If it is a bad one, she will be the only sufferer. The alleged danger of the possible effects of the evil example of the French on the other peoples is nothing but a nightmare. Nothing is more insubstantial than the alleged interest of all the powers in co-operating for the more or less wholesale destruction of the new French constitution. The enterprise would be unjust, the success doubtful, the risks and costs incalculable . . . The restoration of the *ancien régime* is an illusion.[5]

This view was echoed in the Third Germany. As one adviser to Karl

Friedrich of Baden wrote: 'We have no right and no need to intervene in France. Do not annoy her; do not support the émigrés; accept the proffered compensation for our rights in Alsace.'[6] Even the ecclesiastical princes, who were far and away the most strident opponents of the revolution and who sheltered many French émigrés, sought only to protect their own interests, not to carry the fight to France.

Similarly, throughout the 'revolutionary' period, developments within the *Reich* remained subject to the primacy of foreign policy, not of ideology. The most striking example of this was the imperial intervention (*Reichsexekution*) against Liège in 1789. Here the prince bishop had been expelled by his estates, the only successful revolutionary endeavour on the territory of the *Reich*. At once the *Reichskammergericht* at Wetzlar instructed the directors of the Westphalian Circle, Frederick William II and the Elector of Cologne, to crush the rebels and to reinstate the bishop. This *Reichsexekution* differed only in scale and not in principle from numerous counter-insurgency exercises in the south and west conducted by the anterior circles in 1789 and throughout the 1790s. Superficially, the *Reichsexekution* might have resembled an exercise in princely solidarity in the face of revolutionary violence. However, unlike those smaller skirmishes, the operation against Liège required Austrian troops; local Westphalian levies would not be enough and the Prussians refused to cooperate. At this point the primacy of foreign policy intervened. The Prussians feared that Austria would use the opportunity to install a pliant coadjutor, an assistant and successor, to the bishop at Liège. Perhaps even more important, the operation endangered Prussian plans for a Belgian insurrection to embarrass Joseph. A vigorous *Reichsexekution* would frighten off the prospective conspirators. In the end, the Prussians pre-empted an Austrian intervention by conducting the operation themselves, but not before conceding all the main demands of the rebels, thus making a mockery of the whole exercise.[7]

It was at this point that the *real* revolution in German politics took place, for in July 1790 Austria and Prussia pulled back from the brink and concluded the Convention of Reichenbach. Prussia pledged support for the candidature of Joseph's successor Leopold for the imperial crown; she also committed herself to ending support for Habsburg rebels. For her part, embattled Austria agreed to break off her costly and only belatedly successful war with Turkey without territorial gains. The terms of the agreement seemed innocuous enough; the very existence of such an agreement was revolutionary. Apart from the brief consensus on the partition of Poland, Prussia and Austria had been in permanent confrontation since 1740; the Third Germany did not find the Polish precedent encouraging. Hence, it was the German revolution which was about to make an impact on France, rather than the other way around. France was the one area of potential Austro-Prussian cooperation not yet paralysed by mutual suspicion: there was no consensus for gains in the *Reich*; expansion in Poland was temporarily precluded by the Prusso-Polish alliance; and the dismemberment of Turkey was not only unattractive to Prussia but specifically ruled out by the Convention of Reichenbach. This left only France, a promising and, as they thought, hapless target. However, although a joint anti-French stand was logical and implicit in the convention, the persistence of dualist suspicions at first made the necessary cooperation improbable. Moreover, like Joseph, Leopold was indifferent, if not sympathetic, towards the Revolution.[8]

In the meantime, a dispute between the new French Republic and the old *Reich* had arisen. At issue was the abolition of feudal rights in France (4 August 1789) and the Civil Constitution of the Clergy (12 July 1790). Both measures profoundly affected the *Reich*: they abolished the feudal privileges of imperial nobles and the diocesan rights of German bishops in Alsace; in essence this was the same problem on which Joseph II had impaled himself. Indeed, the conflict was highly symbolic: on the one hand the strident self-confident rationality of Revolutionary France, on the other the force of imperial tradition and compromise. The matter was brought to the *Reichstag*. It admitted effectively of only two answers: either Alsace must be reclaimed for the *Reich*, or the *ancien régime* must be restored in France; accepting financial compensation was not an option. Not surprisingly, neither the emperor nor the larger territories showed any initial interest in such an extensive undertaking. Indeed, at first the Prussians predictably tried to sabotage the few Austrian efforts on behalf of the endangered western principalities. The *Reich*'s quarrel with France was thus of little significance by itself, but was later to provide a convenient fig-leaf for joint Austro-Prussian action.

What finally created the momentum towards actual intervention was not any sense of monarchic solidarity, nor primarily any sense of obligation towards the endangered western principalities, but rather a combination of four factors. First of all, there was the emergence of concrete Prussian plans for aggrandizement in the west; these envisaged the Prussian annexation of Jülich and Berg, and the compensation of their owners with French territory in Alsace. Secondly, there was the sudden death of Leopold II in March 1792 and the accession of his brother Francis, who was less firmly opposed to intervention against Revolutionary France and more interested in territorial gain at her expense.[9] Thirdly, there were the appeals for assistance emanating from France, especially from the queen, Marie Antoinette, an Austrian princess. Fourth and finally, there was the rush to war in France itself, partly attributable to fear of the monarchic powers, but largely driven by an internal revolutionary dynamic.[10]

Even so, intervention only got under way in fits and starts. The Convention of Pillnitz in August 1791, often seen as a joint Austro-Prussian programme of anti-revolutionary action, committed none of the signatories to immediate action. As for the smaller German princes, the Elector of Saxony, from whose castle the declaration was issued, was so unhappy that he refused at first to have anything to do with it; he was not among the initial intervening powers in the following year. But by February 1792, when Austria and Prussia warned France that a violation of imperial rights and territory would be punished by war, a crisis point was reached. The move had the effect of both stoking French paranoia and concentrating Austro-Prussian minds on the possibility of gains in the west. In the end, the actual declaration of war came from France, which for domestic and ideological reasons welcomed conflict with the powers of the *ancien régime*. For Austria and Prussia, however, the war was not one of ideology, nor, except in the most technical sense, was it a defensive war. It was simply a war of conquest with a subsidiary counter-insurrectionary dimension, a restorationist police action which Louis XVI was expected to reward with territory.[11]

To the casual observer, the Prussian army which lumbered into northern France in September 1792 may have appeared like the avenging vanguard of a European *ancien régime;* in fact, this was far from being the case. Not even the smaller principalities in whose name the whole exercise was ostensibly being conducted, regarded what was obviously a predatory Austro-Prussian venture with any degree of sympathy. Indeed, both great powers had at first tried to block *Reich* participation in the war so that prospective gains would not have to be shared. After the first deceptively easy victories, the commander of the invading army issued a fire-breathing manifesto demanding the release of the French king and aimed at cowing the revolutionaries into submission. But here, too, nothing was as it seemed. In fact, the Duke of

Brunswick had published his declaration most unwillingly; he was not only a prominent reformer and Francophile, but so highly regarded in France that some revolutionaries had intended to offer him the command of the *French* army.[12] A strange ideological war (*Weltanschauungskrieg*) this!

After some early successes, the intervention ground to a halt. Within months the Prussians had been checked at Valmy and then pushed back towards the frontier. By the end of the year French troops were on German soil, where they were to remain for the next two decades. Mainz fell and became the centre of a short-lived experiment in German Jacobinism. In July 1793 it was recaptured by the Prussians. But despite such successes and some deft Austrian campaigning in Flanders, the war now began to go badly. Britain acceded to the Austro-Prussian coalition but was powerless to block the French advance in the west. After the crushing defeat at Fleurus in June 1794, the Austrian Netherlands – Belgium – were lost. By the new year Holland had been occupied. In the summer of 1795 the Prussians concluded a separate peace with France at Basle; only a massive injection of British cash enabled the Austrians to fight on alone. By 1796 the French had overrun most of south Germany. A whole string of smaller states – Baden, Württemberg and Bavaria – were forced out of the war. An Austrian counter-attack in the same year managed to push the French back over the Rhine. But the damage had been done: the political basis on which the erstwhile coalition of Austria, Prussia and *Reich* had been constructed, had been irretrievably shattered.

What had happened? Clearly, the main factor was the overwhelming strength of Revolutionary France, whose armies swept all before them. But that is merely to rephrase the question. For it was not only the impact of the French invasion itself but also the forces it released among the component parts of the *Reich* which decisively determined the course of the next two decades. These forces were not primarily ideological, socio-economic, or even socio-political, but *political* in the purest sense.

First of all, there was the emergence of a Third Germany of smaller territorial states determined to emancipate themselves from Austro-Prussian tutelage. Here French diplomacy, not French ideas, was decisive. For after a brief flirtation with the idea of a war of liberation on behalf of the oppressed peoples of Europe, Revolutionary France pursued a cool *Realpolitik* in Germany. This policy was a lethal synthesis of *ancien régime* tradition and revolutionary ambition. On the one hand,

there was the doctrine of 'natural limits'. 'The borders of France,'
Danton proclaimed in January 1793, 'are determined by nature. We
will achieve them in four directions: the ocean, on the banks of the
Rhine, on the Alps, on the Pyrenees.'[13] This was not so much an extension of the German policy of the French *ancien régime*, which had been
a much more moderate affair aimed at a divided but balanced *Reich*, as
a resumption and radicalization of the expansionist policy of Louis
XIV some hundred years before;[14] the famous renunciation of territorial gains, made in May 1790, was soon forgotten. On the other hand,
there was the entirely traditional policy of cooperation with the larger
territorial states in Germany. As the French envoy Barthélemy, himself
a pupil of Vergennes, warned in 1797, France should take care to preserve the 'second-rank powers' in Germany, which had so far been her
best allies.[15] The events of the 1790s showed that these two approaches
could be reconciled: the natural limits were attained through the simple
annexation of the left bank of the Rhine; the old strategy of supporting the larger states against the emperor was revived through generous
territorial rewards for Baden, Bavaria and Württemberg;[16] and the
resulting despoliation of the ecclesiastical principalities even gave the
whole enterprise a patina of ideological fervour.

The response of the larger German territorial states to the French
invasion was determined by a combination of greed and fear. Now was
the chance to fulfil their long-standing aim of casting off the shackles
of the *Reich* and Austro-Prussian dualism so as to establish themselves
as powers in their own right; to this end, they were prepared to sacrifice both princely solidarity and collective security.[17] They could only
benefit from the geopolitical changes wrought by France: in return for
scattered and vulnerable lands west of the Rhine, Baden, Bavaria and
Württemberg in particular sought substantial accretions of their core
territories. At the same time, the Third Germany risked being caught
in the crossfire of coalitions. Duke Frederick spoke for many when he
expressed his determination not to let Württemberg become a 'play-
ground' (*Spielwerk*; literally, a toy) of the great powers.[18] Yet this resentment was tempered by resignation. As the Bavarian envoy to Vienna
remarked in 1795, 'It depends entirely on Russia, England and France,
what the fate of the *Reich* [and Bavaria] will be.'[19] Moreover, after
1793–4, the smaller states felt they had as much to fear from an Austro-
Prussian *rapprochement* as from French expansionism. As Hans von
Gagern, chief minister in Nassau, put it in 1797, 'The German princes
have so far found themselves in the double misfortune of wishing a *rap-*

*prochement* between Prussia and Austria, and of fearing one when they thought of the example of Poland.'[20] Or, to quote elector Max Franz of Cologne, 'All of Germany is in an uproar, one fears the French less than these two powers [Austria and Prussia] and one generally finds the cure worse than the malady.'

In short, the rewards for collaboration with France were potentially limitless; the penalty for resistance was certain extinction. The result was a precipitate scramble for French favour which began in the mid-1790s and reached its apotheosis in 1805–6. Ironically, although German princes feared the polonization of Germany in general, and of their own lands in particular, in order to avoid the latter they were to facilitate the former.

Secondly, Austrian and Prussian policy was scarcely less destructive. In Prussia, the old *Fürstenbund* policy in defence of the *Reich* as a whole was abandoned in favour of a more narrowly north German focus. By May 1795 the Prussians had withdrawn from the first coalition against France and retreated behind a north German neutrality zone which they undertook to defend against all comers. This certainly destroyed the essential unity of the *Reich* by abandoning the south to Austria and continued war. On the other hand, it is also true that the Prussian neutrality zone enjoyed considerable support in the *Reich* both among the smaller *Reichsstände* covered by it and in the pamphlet literature which constituted 'public opinion' in the old *Reich*.[21] Indeed, the continuation of the war by Austria was seen as more harmful to the interests of the smaller German states caught in the firing line than the supposed 'betrayal' of the *Reich* by Prussia. 'Germany,' the Austrian diplomat Trauttmansdorf (*sic*) noted in 1797, 'where the king of Prussia has already taken on the role of emperor, is entirely lost to us.'[22] This was certainly true of northern and central Germany. But if the neutrality zone itself was not necessarily a mortal blow to the *Reich*, broader Prussian aims certainly were. For, after a brief and opportunistic dalliance with plans for western expansion, Prussia returned to her strategy of disengagement in the west in favour of gains in the north and east.

The result was the final two Polish partitions (1793 and 1795), the completion of which required the withdrawal of substantial Prussian forces from the western theatre of operations. In so doing, Prussia killed three birds with one stone. First of all, she rid herself of the expensive and unsuccessful campaign against France. Secondly, Prussia made much greater territorial gains than she could have expected in the west, albeit – with the exception of Danzig – of questionable economic value. Thirdly, she pre-empted the transformation of Poland from a ramshackle aristocratic republic, which was ideologically abhorrent but politically acceptable, into an efficient enlightened despotism under Stanislaus August, which was ideologically congenial but politically dangerous. In particular, Prussia thereby forestalled her encirclement by a renewed Saxon-Polish personal union under Russian tutelage whose first aim would have been the 'recovery' of Silesia; the territorial pretensions of the Polish rebels in 1794, which were a variant on the *Grande Nation* and the natural limits, showed these fears to have been well-founded.[23]

Meanwhile, in Austria the eclipse of Kaunitz and the rise of Baron Thugut as chief minister heralded a new Austrian policy with a cavalier, almost Josephine, disregard for the *Reich*.[24] This shift was evident in the behaviour of Austrian forces in southern Germany. Through aggressive recruiting and requisitioning they appeared to conduct themselves, and were regarded as, an occupying army rather than saviours of the *Reich*. The new Austrian geopolitical orientation was also uncannily Josephine. Rather than pursue increasingly remote gains on the Rhine, Thugut, much to Wittelsbach alarm, revived the old idea of exchanging the Austrian Netherlands for Bavaria; he also, to Russian alarm, aimed at Habsburg hegemony in Italy. At the same time Thugut resumed the traditional cold war with Prussia – yet another parallel with Joseph – while maintaining a fundamentally anti-revolutionary stance against France;[25] whether he sacrificed the latter to promote the former is still hotly disputed.[26]

French pressure became more acute with the rapid rise of Napoleon Bonaparte after 1795. In late October of 1797 he forced Austria formally to surrender the Austrian Netherlands in return for Venetia and Salzburg; the geopolitical reorientation of Austria away from the west, unsuccessfully attempted by Joseph, had begun. In March 1798 the Congress of Rastatt approved the loss of the left bank of the Rhine and began to discuss the 'secularization' – that is, the annexation and expropriation – of the ecclesiastical states in order to 'compensate' those princes who had lost territory on the left bank of the Rhine. Austria, once the protector of the ecclesiastical states, had already accepted this principle by annexing Salzburg. Rastatt became a feeding frenzy not merely for the two larger German powers, but also, and especially, for the middling states. The imperial Diet at Regensburg, the Prussian envoy Baron Görtz observed, 'now resembled a fair at which lands and souls were traded'.[27] All thought of the integrity of the *Reich* and its institutions disappeared beneath an avalanche of claims and counter-claims. As the young Austrian diplomat Clemens von Metternich remarked in disgust: 'I do not wish to be quoted, but according to my way of seeing things, everything is gone to the devil and the time is come when everyone must save from the wreck what he can.'[28]

For the Third Germany this created a climate of great danger but also of great opportunity. They knew that when the diplomatic quadrilles at Rastatt stopped many of them would find their seats occupied by someone else. For those middling states which had acquired the critical mass to make them viable in a remodelled *Reich* and attractive to the French as allies, the message was clear: only sufficiently large compensations at Rastatt could save them from irrelevance and possibly extinction. But for the smaller and smallest estates, the picture was one of bleak despair. The general mood of bitterness and betrayal was captured by one pamphleteer as follows:

And it happened, as Bonaparte had requested. The high priests, scribes and pharisees assembled in a city called Rastatt and held council about how they would by means of subterfuge capture the *Reich* and kill it. And the *Reich* saw that its hour had come and spake: 'My soul is sad unto death.' And the ecclesiastical council of princes was very concerned and said to the Congress: 'Truly, truly I say unto you, one of you will betray me.' And behold! The Prussian court whispered into Napoleon's ear: 'What will you give me if I betray him?' Bonaparte spoke his judgment over the *Reich*: 'We have a law and according to this law it must die.' Bavaria and Hesse-Darmstadt answer: 'What crime has it committed? I can find no fault with it.' The emperor however said: 'It is better that one should die rather than allow a whole people to go under,' and ordered it to be bound and handed it over so that it should be crucified.[29]

But the *Reich* was not so much crucified as hung, drawn and quartered between France, Austria, Prussia and the Third Germany. The final distribution of territory was agreed at the Imperial Recess (*Reichsdeputationshauptschluss*) in 1803. All ecclesiastical electorates were abolished. The sole exception was Mainz, whose incumbent Dalberg moved to Regensburg. Of the imperial cities, only Hamburg, Bremen, Lübeck, Nuremberg, Augsburg and Frankfurt survived, briefly. The imperial counts and knights escaped to fight another day, but lost the basis of their economic and political strength through the secularization of their strongholds in the ecclesiastical principalities. The beneficiaries were the larger territorial states, Austria, Prussia, Bavaria, Baden and Württemberg, all of which had been compensated to a far greater extent than losses on the left bank of the Rhine would have warranted. Politically, the *Reichsdeputationshauptschluss* had far-reaching repercussions. First of all, it was an object lesson in the benefits of cooperation with France. Secondly, because of the need to integrate disparate new lands, it created an automatic impulse for reform in the middling states. Thirdly, by swallowing up the ecclesiastical territories, it overturned the confessional balance in the *Reich*; there were now Protestant majorities, or at least confessional parity, in the Council of Princes and Council of Electors. At the same time the *Reichskirche*, its diocesan boundaries shattered, went into terminal decline: secularization not only abolished the ecclesiastical principalities, but also involved the expropriation of episcopal and monastic lands. The 'catholicity' of the *Reich* was no more. Fourthly and relatedly, with old Catholic majorities nullified, the *Reichsdeputationshauptschluss* fatally weakened the hold of the Habsburgs on the imperial crown; there was even talk of a Protestant imperial crown.[30] Fifthly and finally, it ratified the geopolitical reorientation of Austria and Prussia away from their western obligations towards the north and east.

The storm on the *Reich* now entered its final phase. In May 1803 the French occupied Hannover, thus violating the Prussian neutrality zone and bringing the war to north Germany for the first time. Throughout 1804 violations of the *Reich* mounted. First, a prominent member of the French royal family, the Duc d'Enghien was abducted from German soil and executed. Then towards the end of the year, the British envoy to Hamburg, Sir George Rumbold, was kidnapped and threatened by French troops. Despite these provocations Prussia refused for the moment to be drawn into conflict with France. Austria on the other hand made yet another ill-fated attempt at coalition warfare in conjunction with Russia and Great Britain. After shattering defeats at Ulm and Austerlitz, she was forced to cede Tyrol, recently acquired Venice, her Swabian lands and Dalmatia at the Treaty of Pressburg (1805). The institutions of the *Reich* now began to unravel. A year earlier, Austria had already announced its own separate Austrian imperial title, a flagrant breach of the imperial constitution. In July 1806, the Confederation of the Rhine, the *Rheinbund*, was set up under

French tutelage. It included almost all of Germany outside Austria and Prussia. The last act followed in August when Napoleon demanded that the Austrians surrender the imperial title, which they did, simultaneously, and illegally, announcing the dissolution of the *Reich;* a new 'Austrian' empire was proclaimed. These months also marked the end of the imperial knights, counts and the remaining imperial cities: they had lost the empire without finding a role. Soon afterwards Prussia was crushingly defeated at the battles of Auerstedt and Jena in October 1806.[31]

The destruction of the Holy Roman Empire was a direct result of the diplomatic revolution unleashed by Revolutionary France after 1792;[32] French power, not French ideas, changed Germany. Of course, the outcome was not inevitable; opinion in Paris on the future geopolitical configuration of Germany was deeply divided. Even as late as March 1806, the French foreign minister Count Talleyrand, by now fighting a losing battle, was arguing prophetically that 'The greatness and power of a state is not absolute. The weakness of Germany is a consequence of its division into so many individual states and it is not in France's interest to reverse this division in those areas near her borders.'[33] It was only after 1797, and increasingly after 1803, that Napoleon resolved this debate in favour of a radical hegemonic solution, which replaced the old medley of small states (*Kleinstaaterei*) with a much smaller number of territorial states under French tutelage. 'The real interest of France,' Napoleon maintained, 'is that the German empire can only be reorganized with the aid of a strong and mighty leadership . . . to sum up: it is in the nature of things that these smaller princes must all be destroyed.'[34]

Napoleonic advances after 1800 accelerated the realignment of the Third Germany with France. These states had little choice. 'The wave of expropriations, mediatizations and roundings-off,' the Nassau minister Hans Christoph von Gagern observed in 1805, 'are getting so out of hand, that there is hardly a third or middle way left between despoiling or being despoiled.'[35] 'If the German emperor cannot help us,' Duke Friedrich of Württemberg argued in September 1805, on the eve of his treaty with France, 'if Prussia suggests simple surrender, then one must join that party which guarantees one's own existence.'[36] Even the smallest states banded together and formed the 'Frankfurt Union' in order to defend their interests. Prussian opposition was shrugged aside by Count Solms Laubach with the words 'Berlin is irritated that we are huckstering too and that we are not allowing ourselves to be led quietly like lambs to the slaughter.'[37] In short, everything spoke for co-operation with France: the French were powerful and close, Britain and Russia were remote; Prussia was neutral and indifferent; and Austria was unsympathetic and expansionist. By 1806, Bavaria, Baden, Württemberg, Saxony, Hesse-Nassau and many other German states were bound to France by ties of formal alliance, interest and complicity.

The rise of French power accelerated the geopolitical reorientation of Prussian and Austrian policy which predated the Revolution by some years. After a brief, and entirely opportunistic, flirtation with western gains in 1792–3, both Prussia and Austria sought aggrandizement further east or south. Prussia looked to Poland and northern Germany; the possibilities for expansion in southern Germany opened up by the acquisition of Ansbach and Bayreuth in 1791 were never explored. Austria looked to Italy, Bavaria and Poland. The French-generated territorial upheaval was thus an opportunity as well as a danger. Indeed, until 1805–6 Prussia and Austria were net beneficiaries of developments since 1792: they were both larger and more concentrated than before.[38] Hence neither power desired a return to the *status quo ante*. They did not even want a Bourbon restoration – in fact, they welcomed Napoleon's decision to crown himself emperor in 1804 – but rather a re-creation of the European balance without relinquishing their gains.[39] Instead, both powers toyed with the idea of a French alliance at the expense of the other.[40] Perhaps surprisingly, no such alliance came about, but the persistence of dualism effectively paralysed any prospect of concerted action against France. The upshot was that, for Prussia at least, the French threat only came into focus very slowly, and much too late.

At the same time, Germany was profoundly affected by the geopolitical transformation of Eastern Europe. In the space of three years in the mid-1790s, Russia had advanced hundreds of kilometres westwards. Instead of a comfortable buffer between Russia and the Hohenzollern state, there was now an extensive and indefensible common border.[41] If the first partition of Poland had increased Prussian security, the final partition drastically reduced it. Austria was equally concerned about the explosion of Russian power. After all, one of the prime motivations behind Leopold's alliance with Prussia in the early 1790s had been to halt Russian advances in the east, especially Poland.[42] He would have been horrified by the partitions of 1793–5; and Austrian diplomats, Metternich among them, almost immediately recognized their mistake in bringing Russia further west.[43]

Moreover, around 1800 Russia began to intervene more actively in central and southern European politics. The major beneficiaries of this were the middling states, especially Württemberg, with which the Tsar enjoyed strong dynastic ties.[44] For the Third Germany, Russia was to prove a useful advocate in the negotiations leading up to the Imperial Recess of 1803; and when Russia and France were of one mind, as in the agreement of October 1801, which set out the broad contours of the new Germany, there could be no appeal.\ The big loser, on the other hand, was Austria, whose coalition with Russia broke apart on the question of Italy, where her annexationist aims ran counter to Russian support for the kingdom of Sardinia.[45] There were also long-standing differences in the Balkans which came to the boil again with the Serbian rising of 1804.[46] Besides, if Russia was a dangerous adversary, she could also be a fickle ally, as Austria and Prussia knew to their cost. In 1800–1 and again in 1805–6, she showed herself apt to withdraw from the German scene, leaving her erstwhile allies to the tender mercies of France.[47]

What had taken place before 1806 was the much-feared (self-)'polonization' of Germany. Throughout the late eighteenth century the same balance of power which had facilitated the partition of Poland had maintained the integrity of the *Reich*. After 1792, the collapse of the European balance inevitably brought the collapse of the delicate German balance in its train: the same great-power interventionism, dualist tensions and small-state pretensions which had once sustained the *Reich* now served to tear it apart.

### Why was there no Revolution in Germany?

It has become a historiographical commonplace to note that there was no revolution in Germany.[48] But there is a tenacious belief in the existence of a sense of crisis before 1789. G. P. Gooch saw the old *Reich* as a country in ferment; Rudolf Vierhaus has pointed to the high level of discontent and subversive opinion among the intelligentsia;[49] and Hans-Ulrich Wehler posits a 'socio-economic and a latent political polarization'. The link between intellectual and political developments is readily assumed. 'Once the realm of the imagination has been revolutionized,' Hegel writes, 'reality cannot hold out for long.' In fact, the opposite is true: Germany in 1789 shows the resistance of political reality to changes in the realm of the imagination.

Most German princes were not only indifferent to the revolution in France, as we have seen, but also largely unworried about the prospects for revolution at home. Indeed, many German governments saw the French Revolution as a vindication rather than a threat. In a famous address to the Academy of Sciences in Berlin, the Prussian foreign minister, Hertzberg, argued that whereas the Revolution in France was justified by the abuses of the *ancien régime*, it was not necessary in enlightened Prussia. Similarly, Joseph II regarded the initial reforms of the new French government as essentially an imitation of his own; and this sympathetic view of events in France was shared by Karl Friedrich of Baden and Karl Wilhelm Ferdinand of Brunswick. They saw no reason to deviate from the well-trodden path of enlightened reform absolutism: for them this was the 'German form of the revolution'.[50] As one Prussian minister famously put it around the turn of the century, 'The beneficial revolution which you have conducted from the bottom up, will be achieved gradually in Prussia from the top down.'[51]

This princely self-confidence proved well-founded. The brief spate of unrest sparked by the outbreak of the French Revolution was dispersed and uncoordinated. Trouble flared in Jülich, Cologne, Speyer and Trier, as well as Saxony, Silesia and Mecklenburg. There was also turbulence in Zweibrücken and parts of Baden. However, these rebels were of the traditional variety: disaffected peasants, journeymen artisans protesting against non-guilded labour, and even high-spirited academic youths.[52] These disturbances were non-ideological, based on local grievances, and directed towards the reclamation of a notional old order, rather than the creation of a new society. They were either crushed or appeased long before the French Revolutionary armies arrived on the scene. Similarly, the brief Jacobin experiment in Mainz showed itself to be primarily an opportunistic reaction to the French invasion, rather than the release of powerful socio-political forces.[53] Subsequent plans for a South German republic came to nothing. Other middle-class conspiracies were easily broken up by the authorities, sometimes with rather more fanfare than they warranted.[54]

To a certain extent, contingent factors militated against a German revolution. The extreme fragmentation of the *Reich* served to disperse subversive potential. There was no revolutionized capital, no single focus of attention, as in Paris, from which the message could be spread throughout the provinces.[55] Moreover, the lack of coordination between rural and urban protest helped to reduce the revolutionary impetus.[56] Conversely, the local levies deployed through the *Reich* military constitution showed themselves quite capable of effective counter-insurgency.[57]

Far more important, however, was the lack of a revolutionary class. The German 'common people' proved themselves extraordinarily resistant to radical propaganda.[58] Unlike France, where they had spearheaded the rural revolution during the *grande peur* of 1789, the German peasantry remained largely quiescent. For a start, in the south and west they enjoyed vibrant imperial institutions which either defused agrarian unrest or, once it had broken out, helped to bring about a negotiated solution; Hohenzollern-Hechingen in 1798 was a classic example of this.[59] The German peasantry were also substantially better off: in West Elbia peasants held some 80–90 per cent, in East Elbia 60 per cent of the land; in France the figure was 35 per cent. Moreover, the number of rural poor in receipt of assistance in Germany amounted only to about 10 per cent; in France the figure was five times higher.[60] Not even the poorest third of society comprising small peasants, day-labourers, apprentices, servants – a veritable 'proto-proletariat' – generated any serious revolutionary unrest;[61] for the most part, they remained beholden to the traditional mechanisms of conflict regulation found in the guild or *Ganzes Haus*. In short, for all its institutionalized inequalities, the German *ancien régime* was a 'stakeholder' society in which a clear majority felt they had more to lose than to gain through violent upheaval.

Moreover, the long-standing tradition of state interventionism to keep the price of grain down helped to defuse popular discontent. In this way, the price crises of 1789, 1794–5, 1797–8 were mastered at minimal political cost.[62] But material factors alone were not decisive. The socio-economic interpretation does not explain why there were revolts both in Mecklenburg, where rural conditions were severe, and in the more advanced areas in western Germany. Geographical proximity to France was certainly a factor in some cases, but not invariably: the exposed western regions were one flashpoint, but so were Saxony in the centre and Silesia in the east. Moreover, whole areas, such as Hannover in the north and Bavaria in the south, remained relatively or entirely quiescent.

Nor did the German bourgeoisie – an amorphous group of bureaucrats, merchants, teachers, entrepreneurs and prosperous craftsmen –

function as a revolutionary class.[63] For the most part, the bourgeoisie was too close to the state and too beholden to the tradition of gradual reform to entertain radical change. In Prussia, for example, the merchant class was hopelessly incohesive: some were protectionist, others free traders, and only a tiny minority could be called politically aware; Marxist historians speak of an 'immature' bourgeoisie.[64] In any case, with very few exceptions, the German middle class did not possess the crucial representative structures which made the French Third Estate such a formidable force in the late 1780s.

This picture was reflected in the remarkable 'immunity' (Epstein) of Germany to French ideas. Despite considerable sympathy with the ideas of 1789, the general intellectual response was characterized by an emphasis on evolution and reform over revolution;[65] later the Terror was to reinforce this attitude.[66] Indeed, the considerable German 'public sphere' proved not only incapable but unwilling to generate a serious political challenge to the authorities. In part, this was in recognition of its common ground with the state. As August Ludwig Schlözer, a professor at the University of Göttingen, remarked in 1791, 'As in France, the [German] Enlightenment rises up from below, but it also finds enlightenment at the head of the state: for where are there more cultivated rulers than in Germany?'[67] Similarly, enlightened writers and polemicists were much more inclined to press their own professional knowledge on the monarch than demand popular political participation.[68] Even the numerous secret societies, such as the Freemasons, tended to shrink from political radicalism: after all, their elitist and hierarchic character was not suited to Jacobin ideas of popular sovereignty and revolutionary violence.[69]

*Ancien régime* Germany was, quite simply, a politically deferential society, passive and respectful in the face of authority: the idea of revolution was deeply alien. In the absolutist states which made up most of the *Reich*, political culture had not advanced much beyond Christian Wolff's quietist injunction that while a ruler must not neglect his duties, he could not be removed even if he did.[70] To quote one pamphlet, suggestively entitled 'A word of encouragement dedicated to the rulers and princes of Germany': 'In these lands no revolt is to be feared, even with complete liberty of the press and opinion. If one broke out, the prince would have no need of soldiers, but would quell a whole crowd of peasants with a word and a stick.'[71] One is reminded of Lenin's famous comment that if a German crowd wanted to storm a railway station they would first buy themselves a platform ticket.

Finally, there was no fiscal-political crisis in Germany.[72] It was the progressive collapse of confidence in *ancien régime* finance and foreign policy – the two were inextricably linked – which had generated the revolutionary situation in France. In Germany, on the other hand, only Austria found herself confronted by an aristocratic revolt in 1789 and the crisis had passed by 1790, well before the local Jacobin challenge, such as it was; the successful revolt in Belgium is more properly interpreted as a traditional anti-absolutist affair, rather than as a 'revolutionary' phenomenon in the modern sense. Prussia and Baden, of course, had no representative assemblies, and their relative financial health excused them from calling any.[73] Even in the many middling territories where such assemblies retained substantial powers, comparatively low levels of state indebtedness meant that the estates never developed into a vehicle for revolutionary change.

This did not mean that relations between princes and estates throughout the 1790s were harmonious, far from it. The Revolution had made the estates both restless and confident, especially in Bavaria and the Hessian states.[74] But the most spectacular example of the cold war between prince and estates after 1790 was Württemberg. If a bourgeois revolution was going to happen anywhere in Germany it was here: almost uniquely, the estates were made up of urban and rural notables, not the nobility. Here the estates were able relentlessly to exploit the rights secured through the *Erbvergleich* (1771): taxes were fixed and could only be increased in an 'emergency'.[75] Just how and by whom this would be defined was left open; truly, as the German lawyer Carl Schmitt says, whoever controls the state of emergency is sovereign. Moreover, the prince was obliged to consult the estates on alliances and wars.[76]

The potential revolutionary situation in Württemberg was created not by the ideological impact of the French Revolution or the impact of French invasion, but by the financial burdens of the war of intervention. Traditionally, the estates had kept the prince on a tight financial leash, even in peacetime. On the eve of the intervention against France, Württemberg could muster only 3000 men, substantially fewer than Brunswick and Hesse-Cassel and only one-tenth of the Bavarian army. The estates now used the fiscal and military demands of war to extract concessions and encroach on the executive.[77] As they explained brutally to the French in 1794, the estates 'grant or refuse the Duke extraordinary monies; the Duke must obtain their consent before either embarking on a war, concluding alliances, levying recruits or summoning the territorial militia'.[78] The prince, on the other hand, claimed that foreign-political necessity justified an increase in his powers: in the case of an emergency, his propagandists argued, 'all assemblies must remain silent'.[79]

It was not long before the estates began actively to interfere in ducal diplomacy. They were instrumental in bringing about the armistice of 1795 between France and Württemberg. By the turn of the century they were sending their own delegates to the conference at Rastatt. Württemberg thus had effectively two foreign policies; this became painfully obvious when the estates opposed the new Duke Friedrich's much-desired elevation to electoral status. In general, the estates opposed territorial gains, not because of any ethical inhibitions, but because they feared that they might serve to make the prince financially independent.[80] For this reason the estates forced the prince to accept the 'incorporation' of new territories: these lands were to be granted corporate representation on the same lines as old Württemberg;[81] this prevented them from being taxed without their consent.

The conflict in Württemberg was power-political and largely free of broader ideological overtones. Unusually for Germany, both sides followed a primacy of domestic policy in which external allies were deployed in the contest for internal supremacy. Duke Friedrich was a passionate admirer of Edmund Burke and critic of the Revolution, but had no hesitation in allying himself with Napoleonic France after the failure of his Austrian alliance.[82] Similarly, the estates were as ready to combine with revolutionary France as with absolutist Prussia, one of the guarantor powers of the *Erbvergleich* and a long-standing, if increasingly ineffectual ally until the end.[83] As one delegate, Georgii, commented in 1798, the estates should follow the French example by 'abstracting from the revolution and acting in purely political terms'.[84]

In the end there was no corporate take-over in Württemberg. Unlike France, the estates never managed to seize exclusive control of the executive. Their power was essentially negative: they could hobble princely authority, but not supplant it. Yet Friedrich's victory was no inevitable, if belated, victory of princely absolutism over corporate privilege. For although the protagonists carried on their struggle under the primacy of domestic politics, its outcome was decided by the primacy of foreign policy. The changing balance of power after 1792 put the estates in double jeopardy. First of all, there was the decline of the guarantor powers, Prussia, Denmark and Hannover. Secondly, there was the corresponding explosion of French power. Even so, the result was no foregone conclusion. Friedrich's Austrian-backed *coup* against the estates in 1799 nearly ended in disaster after the revival of French fortunes a year later.[85] Until 1804 a French intervention on behalf of the estates, as urged by General Moreau, could not be ruled out. And when Napoleon finally decided in favour of the Duke in 1805, he did so simply because the elimination of the estates would better enable Friedrich to fulfil his military obligations towards France.

In fact, the primacy of foreign policy determined not merely the fate of corporate liberties in Württemberg, but that of the revolutionary movement in Germany as a whole. Contrary to their policy in Italy, the French did not encourage the creation of Jacobin republics in Germany, once the experiment in Mainz had petered out. If in November 1792 the National Assembly had announced its intention to back revolutionary endeavours in all parts of Europe, this declaration was quickly repealed in the following spring. Already as early as August 1796, the Directory instructed the advancing armies 'not to change the established authorities of the land' in Württemberg,[86] and to keep local Jacobins at arm's length.[87] This was partly because of justified doubts about their organizational capacities, but mainly because more profitable alliances could be made with the south German princes; west of the Rhine, French interests were best served by outright annexation. When Jacobin emissaries approached French generals in 1800 with plans for a south German republic, they were advised to support governmental reforms at home rather than pursue a forlorn hope.[88] Princely satellites would do as well or better than democratic ones.

The destruction of the *Reich* marked the end of one thousand years of German political commonwealth, yet its demise was in the words of G. P. Gooch, 'unwept, unhonoured and unsung'.[89] The nineteenth-century Protestant nationalist, Heinrich von Treitschke, called it a 'hateful lie', a kind of Habsburg and Roman Catholic racket designed to shackle the German people; James Bryce likened it to a 'corpse . . . ready to crumble at the touch'; and Voltaire famously remarked of the *Reich* that it was 'neither holy, nor Roman, nor an empire'. More recently, Hans-Ulrich Wehler has argued that the *Reich* was dissolved 'under unworthy circumstances, but in accordance with the historical constellation of forces'.[90]

But was the *Reich* really as unmourned as these authors seem to suggest? The death of the *Reich* had been a protracted affair, and very few of its main supporters had survived to lament its passing.[91] The few survivors, such as Dalberg, continued to search for an acceptable common political framework for the rump areas of the *Reich* right until the very end. Nor did the *Reichsidee* die in 1806. Indeed, the general if unfounded expectation that Napoleon would remodel the *Reich*, rather than dismantle it altogether, belies the idea that its demise was greeted with relief; some Germans hoped that he would confer the imperial crown on himself. But even the *Rheinbund* can be seen as a kind of ersatz or replacement *Reich*. Its new prince primate, *Fürstprimas*, Dalberg, was clearly intended to be a kind of surrogate *Reichserzkanzler*. Later on, the debates of 1813–15 were shot through with the wish for the reconstitution of some form of political commonwealth; and the resulting German *Bund* was nothing if not a partial concession to the persistence of imperial loyalties in Germany.

The *Reich* had failed the double challenge of the primacy of foreign policy and modernization. It was unable to ward off the external French threat; and it proved incapable either of modernizing itself or of accommodating modernizing tendencies among its constituent parts. Indeed, the whole ethos of the *Reich* was so profoundly traditional and anti-modern that modernization was not merely problematic, but fundamentally antithetical to its continued existence. On the other hand, the *Reich* was never intended to be a great power or *Machtstaat*; it was always more of a value system than a power structure. Hegel's comment that the German *Reich* was not a state, as it was unable to defend its inhabitants, was thus not so much a criticism as an observation of fact.

Nevertheless, the *Reich* did not implode from within or collapse under the weight of its own supposed internal inadequacies and contradictions. It proved quite capable of dealing with the internal challenges posed by the new era. It was only the combined onslaught of the Revolutionary French armies and the German princes which proved irresistible. Even then the performance of the *Reich*, though ultimately insufficient, was more impressive than on any earlier occasion; never before had the anterior circles of the *Reich* raised so many troops or so much finance.[92] In any case, there was not a single European *ancien régime*, apart from geographically remote Russia and Great Britain, that was not ultimately submerged by the revolutionary and Napoleonic deluge. As Tim Blanning writes, the French Revolutionary attack was 'a chainsaw, which felled an ancient, gnarled, but still flourishing oak'.[93]

## The Reform Era: 'Offensive' Modernization

The radical transformation of the political geography of Germany after 1800 prompted far-reaching domestic changes in Prussia, as indeed in most German states. These developments were not *primarily* a 'revolution from above', powered by a self-confident aggressive bureaucracy, determined both to usurp monarchic authority and keep participatory political demands from society at arm's length. The Prussian reforms were no 'anti-Revolution', a period of accelerated adaptation to modernity resulting from contact with the French Revolution; they were not in the first instance a programme of 'defensive modernization' designed to conserve the social, economic and political *status quo* at home. Rather, the main aim of the reforms, in Prussia and elsewhere, was not so much societal convergence with France as the internal cohesion necessitated by the French-inspired revolution in the European balance of power.[94] It was not Revolutionary or Napoleonic ideas which modernized Germany – however imperfectly – but the impact of French hegemony.

By the Treaty of Tilsit in June 1807, which followed her disastrous defeats at Auerstedt and Jena, Prussia was relegated to the rank of a third-class power. Indeed, she had only been saved from complete extinction by the intervention of Tsar Alexander I. Prussia was deprived of huge tracts of territory and saddled with an enormous debt, a war indemnity and a French occupation; in 1808, the Convention of Paris limited her army to 40 000 men. The main purpose of the reforms, therefore, was to prepare Prussia for the final reckoning with France or at the very least to secure her a substantial role within the new Europe. Only by a thoroughgoing reform of the state, especially the armed forces and the executive, could Prussia ever hope to break out of her client status, regain her rightful place within the pentarchy and help to restore the European balance of power. As the military reformer Gneisenau remarked, 'The Revolution has set into motion . . . the entire French people . . . on an equal social and fiscal basis, thereby . . . abolishing the former . . . balance of power. If the other states wish to re-establish this balance, they must use the same resources.' Though this meant borrowing from the 'arsenal of the Revolution',[95] the intent was not flattering but deadly hostile; the reformers meant to challenge France not to imitate her.

The Prussian reform movement was thus a programme of 'offensive modernization' under the primacy of foreign policy. To a small band of reformers centred on Barons von Stein and von Hardenberg, the military defeat had been too devastating, the shameful surrender of fortresses too hasty, the near universal collapse of morale too evident and the widespread popular apathy to their monarch's misfortune too unnerving, to allow anything but a most radical reappraisal of Prussia's social and governmental system. What was required, Hardenberg argued in his famous Riga Memorandum of 1807, was a 'Revolution in the good sense' in which Prussia followed the French model by awakening 'dormant strengths' and destroying 'obsolete prejudices', Indeed, he continued, the strength of these revolutionary principles was so great that the state had only the choice between adoption and extinction. Similar rhetoric was adopted by Stein's famous Nassau Memorandum, which was to become another classic reforming manifesto.

Despite this rhetoric, the changes after 1806 were firmly within a long-standing Prussian tradition of enlightened reform absolutism. Most of the military, economic, social and administrative reforms had been prepared as far back as the 1790s.[96] In Franconia, the newly Prussian lands of Ansbach and Bayreuth served as a kind of laboratory for Hardenberg and his reformist followers. As minister for trade and excise, Baron von Stein was able to abolish most internal tariffs. And by 1804, agrarian reformers had done away with hereditary bondage on royal domains. But the traditional governing compromise between crown and aristocracy precluded them from liberating the much greater number of peasants on noble estates. This reticence was pragmatically, not ideologically motivated. First of all, the immediate concern around 1800 was not domestic reform but the reorganization of the executive. Secondly, the growing sense of external crisis after 1793 was a disincentive to reform. Even Carl von Clausewitz, the great military reformer, observed retrospectively that 'it would have been very risky to have provoked a great discontent through far-reaching changes, which might not be allayed in time, and which could be dangerous in a time when one needed the support of all estates and classes of the people'.[97] What was lacking before 1806 was not the will but the conscious necessity for radical domestic reform.

Socio-legal privilege had always been functionally justified: the system of inequalities enshrined in the *Allgemeines Landrecht* of 1794 was conceived in terms of positive, not natural law; and the subversive implication was that these inequalities could be overturned by another set of positive laws.[98] This thinking was summed up by the thoughts of the governor of Silesia, Baron Hoym, on peasant emancipation. 'The principles,' he argued on the eve of reform,

> which might have applied sixty years ago are no longer applicable today, and one must not sacrifice the welfare of the most numerous section of the people upon whom the true strength of the state rests (the rural dwellers) to the particular interest of an individual estate (the nobility) or even of just a small number from that estate.[99]

Hence, the programme of attempted radical domestic reform after 1806 was not a breach with Prussian state tradition, but its apotheosis.

The shock of Auerstedt and Jena showed that the traditional military-agrarian complex had failed to ensure the security of the state; new social, economic and military structures were now required. In the search for these new structures, Prussia drew heavily not only on her own rich reforming tradition, but also borrowed extensively, though selectively, from French and British models. The aim was to awaken the immense hidden strengths of the nation and harness them to a project of external liberation and internal renewal. 'Unshackling' (*Entfesselung*), 'ennoblement' (*Veredelung*), 'participation' (*Teilhabe*), 'autonomy' (*Autonomie*) and 'responsibility' (*Verantwortung*) – all terms lifted from the newly fashionable idealistic philosophy – were the key concepts. 'What limitless strengths lie undeveloped and unused in the breast of a nation,' the military reformer Neithardt von Gneisenau argued. If the French were to be beaten and repetition of the disaster of 1806 avoided, then spirit (*Geist*) and state, nation and royal house would have to be reconciled. The individual citizen, in the words of Johann Gottlieb Fichte, should be 'permeated' by the state (*Die Durchdringung des Bürgers durch den Staat*): he should be involved in the state, not a mere passive and indifferent spectator of the ebb and flow of great power politics.

In October 1807, a royal edict promised the emancipation of the peasantry within three years. This measure was a synthesis of idealism, British principles of political economy and long-standing Prussian reform absolutist plans. All restrictions on landownership were to be lifted, thus creating a free market in land. All restrictions on occupations were abolished; aristocrats were now permitted to engage in commerce and the bourgeoisie were legally entitled to own estates. Most important of all, the hereditary bondage of the peasantry was abolished; this created a free market in labour. At the same time, logically enough, the edict terminated state protection of the peasantry (*Bauernschutz*). These measures struck at the heart of the old military-agrarian complex. By abolishing all restrictions on peasant movement and the absorption of peasant holdings, the state potentially lost its regular source of recruits to migration or aristocratic encroachments. At the same time, the old governing compromise, by which the nobility exchanged military and administrative service for socio-legal dominion over the peasantry was radically and unilaterally redefined.

Unsurprisingly, therefore, agrarian reform was matched by military reform. Once again the reformers were guided by a blend of idealism, pre-existing plans and foreign models, especially the French concept of a *levée en masse*. 'One will only be victorious,' Scharnhorst argued in 1798, 'when one has learned to stimulate the common spirit like the Jacobins have.'[100] All inhabitants of the state, Scharnhorst claimed nine years later 'are its born defenders': what better way of permeating the individual with the state, as demanded by Fichte, than by mobilizing him in its defence? That was the moral argument. Pragmatically, agrarian reform and geopolitical exposure made French-style conscription imperative. It was only, to use Scharnhorst's own words 'by arming the whole mass of the people, that a small nation could achieve any kind of parity with a larger nation waging a war of conquest'.[101] Moreover, the abolition of exemptions through the introduction of universal service was the logical corollary to peasant emancipation.

The *Landwehr* law of 1814, which introduced a moderated system of conscription, was the crowning achievement of the Prussian military reform. It was preceded by a series of other measures designed to prepare Prussia for the final reckoning. A radical purge of the officer corps was carried out in the immediate aftermath of defeat; of 183 generals in service in 1806 only eight remained in 1812; this purge accelerated the rise of Scharnhorst, Gneisenau and other military reformers. In 1808 the noble monopoly on officer careers was abolished, at least theoretically. The old aristocratic cadet schools were replaced by a military academy focused on examinations. In the military sphere, no less than in the reform movement as a whole, the aim was to awaken dormant strengths among the population. Everybody, as the saying went, potentially had a field marshal's baton in his knapsack. Corporal punishment – flogging – was abolished: Gneisenau proclaimed the 'freedom of the backs'. Henceforth the soldier was to be a free citizen and a willing shield of the state; this was reflected in the new flexible skirmishing tactics which would have been unthinkable in the desertion-prone armies of the Prussian *ancien régime*. The army, in one felicitous phrase, was to become 'the school of the nation'.

Hardenberg's financial and tax reform of October 1810 was intended both to maximize the short-term income of the state and foster long-term economic growth. He abolished the old guild restrictions and monopolies. Henceforth everybody would be free to practise a trade without the laborious proof of competence required by the guilds; state involvement was limited to a uniform trade tax. Guilds themselves were not actually proscribed, but merely converted into voluntary associations. The financial edict also challenged the noble monopoly of brewing, milling and distilling in the countryside. The theory behind these measures was classic economic liberalism: the state should intervene only to ensure fair competition and the free play of market forces.

The financial edict was not merely generally but also proximately the consequence of the primacy of foreign policy. 'The most pressing concern,' Hardenberg prefaced his edict, 'is the complete fulfilment of our obligations to France.' For in 1810, Prussia had fallen behind with her payments of indemnity; in the event of default, France threatened to annex Silesia. Somewhat optimistically, Hardenberg believed that by removing all restrictions on economic growth, the state could generate enough revenue to keep France at arm's length. In this he was to be disappointed. But the reform of the tax system yielded quicker results: levels of taxation were harmonized right across the monarchy; the distinctions between town and country were abolished, much to conservative fury. Even if the Junkers succeeded in clawing back much of the lost ground between 1812 and 1820, the principle of direct personal liability to taxation was never totally abandoned and represented a considerable modernizing advance on the practices of the *ancien régime*.

At the highest level of government, the personal and structural changes after 1806 were momentous. The disastrous diplomatic and military reverses of 1797–1806 led to a radical reorganization of the executive. Out went the old coterie of advisers, in came responsible ministries. A general reform of the civil administration followed not long after: the division between territorial and subject departments, which had so complicated government, was abolished; the old collegial system of joint deliberation and responsibility was replaced by monocratic ministries. Decision, not discussion, was to be the hallmark of the reformed executive.

At the same time, plans for broader political participation were mooted. Here the thinking was a blend of idealist principles, local corporatist residue and foreign example, both French and British. If political reform before 1806 was socially gradualist and narrowly focused on the executive, the reforms proposed after 1807 were far more radical. Hardenberg called for 'democratic principles in a monarchic government' and Stein advocated a national representation, elected on a property franchise, which would help to mobilize all the strengths of the nation against France.[102] Neither man intended a challenge to royal authority, either before or after 1806. As Mathew Levinger has written, 'Prussian leaders proposed representation and political participation as calculated responses to an external threat. By establishing participatory political institutions . . . [they] hoped not to challenge monarchical authority but to *enhance* it.'[103] For the first, but not for the last time, the primacy of foreign policy was to reconcile royal sovereignty and popular political participation.

Stein's ordinance on urban self-government (1808) was intended as a first step in this direction. It was an anti-bureaucratic measure to curb a remote and interfering officaldom: the ordinance gave communes the power to set their own taxes and direct their own expenditure; franchise rights were linked to a property qualification. As Stein had argued in his Nassau Memorandum (1807),

> If the property owner is excluded from all participation in the provincial administration, then the bond that binds him to the fatherland remains unutilized . . . If the property owner is prevented from participating in the administration, the civic spirit and the spirit of the monarchy are killed; exclusion nourishes opposition to the government, complicates the task of the bureaucracy and increases the cost of administration . . . One must accustom the nation to conduct its affairs on its own and to leave its childish condition behind it.

In short, Stein was hoping to harness the patriotic spirit of the educated and moneyed bourgeoisie for the benefit of state and society; he was reconstructing the very immediate powers which absolutist Prussia had once been so determined to destroy.

But the participatory principles of the City Ordinance were not translated into a more general political reform. The national representation floated in the financial edict of 1810 was stillborn, and the constitution ceremoniously promised in 1815 had still not been granted thirty years later. Some provincial assemblies were revived, chiefly to raise money and secure the consent of the nobility to the sale of crown lands. Here the reformers could build on the burgeoning 'corporate renaissance' which had developed in the Baltic provinces by the late eighteenth century.[104] Indeed, around 1800, many East Prussian nobles were demanding that bourgeois estate owners be granted corporate rights. Political modernization was not just generated by bureaucrats or industrial societies. But the great hour of these rural Prussian liberal aristocrats was to come much later, in the period leading up to the revolutions of 1848.

Symbolically, one of the most important reforms was the Emancipation Edict of 1812, which abolished many of the disabilities suffered by Prussia's Jews. Indeed, with the exception of Revolutionary France itself, Prussia was the first European state to emancipate, as opposed merely to tolerate, its Jews. They were now permitted to own property, marry and travel at will; the question of state employment was left open for future decision. In return Jews were expected to cast off their kaftans and beards, adopt surnames and use the German language. The aim of the reformers was to harness Jewish energies to the state, preferably through full integration. They were impatient with any autonomous Jewish identity, just as the Prussian bureaucrats and liberals were later to oppose Roman Catholicism: the intent was assimilation, rather than toleration *per se*. On the other hand, the relative generosity of the 1812 legislation enabled Jews to choose 'significant' surnames which expressed their Jewish identity; ironically, this later made them easy targets for anti-Semites.[105]

Taken together, the Prussian reform movement constituted a fundamental and essentially unilateral redefinition rather than a 'renewal'[106] of the governing compromise between the nobility and the Prussian state. One prominent conservative, Friedrich von der Marwitz, argued that the Prussian king was not an 'absolute' but a 'limited' monarch, who had no right to abrogate the governing compromise without the consent of the aristocracy.[107] Contrary to the *Allgemeines Landrecht*, these conservatives justified privilege not functionally but in terms of natural law. As Yorck von Wartenburg asked Frederick William III in 1807, 'if your Royal Highness deprives me and my children of our right, what is the basis of yours?'[108] 'Better three more lost battles of Auerstedt than one October Edict' was the mentality attributed to the discontented aristocracy by one jaundiced bureaucrat. It is true: aristocratic resistance to the reform movement put narrow class interests over the foreign-political welfare of the state. But outspoken and principled neo-feudal opposition was the exception rather than the rule among the nobility: when von der Marwitz dared invoke a right of resistance against the king he was thrown into prison.

The nobility were unable to overturn the reforms, but they did modify them considerably. Patrimonial justice, a crucial instrument of aristocratic power in the countryside, was revoked by an edict in 1812, but restored in 1814 after bitter noble protests. Similarly, the lucrative brewing rights were soon restored. The culmination of noble claw-back was the *Regulierungsedikt* of 1816, which laid down the actual terms under which peasant emancipation would take place. Only the better-off peasants who could afford draft horses (*Spannfähig*) were freed, and those who could prove tenure of their land for a fixed period that varied from province to province. The original clause permitting poorer peasants to buy back their land and pay off their labour services was withdrawn. Moreover, the Junkers were able to use the revived local assemblies, which they dominated, to slow down agrarian and financial reform. Thus did the cunning of unreason conspire to make incipient political modernization serve socio-economic reaction.

Besides, there was a significant minority of aristocrats who welcomed the reforms.[109] For the reforms emancipated not merely the peasantry but also, and more powerfully, the landowners. With the full financial force of their credit institutes behind them, they were now able to evict or buy out the unprotected peasants and rationalize their estates. Many nobles had long realized that serf labour was inefficient and unsuited to supplying the growing supra-regional market in grain. Moreover, sharp price fluctuations culled weaker noble producers, created a rapid turnover of estates and attracted bourgeois investors, many of whom were ardent modernizers.[110] Hence, the socio-economic changes in East Elbia after 1800 were to a considerable extent the product of external market-driven modernization beyond state control.

The impact of French power also generated reform within the Habsburg monarchy, or empire, as it became after 1804. Following the defeats of the Second Coalition, Austrian statesmen were forced to reassess their domestic arrangements in the light of external concerns.[111] The parlous state of Austrian finance and credit had been aggravated by the costs of war between 1793 and 1801, ostensibly waged on behalf of the *Reich*, but largely at Habsburg expense after 1795;[112] the loss of traditional capital markets in the Low Countries and northern Italy did not help. Moreover, not merely military weakness but the chaotic organization of the Austrian executive had, so the reformers believed, sapped the monarchy's ability to confront Napoleon. The result was a broadly conceived programme of reforms: the creation of a State Council (*Staatsrat*) of ministers in 1801, which preceded the equivalent Prussian measure by some years; the graded income tax (*Klassensteuer*) of 1800, which preceded Hardenberg's finance reform by a decade; and in 1809, admittedly somewhat later than in Prussia, educational requirements were introduced for bureaucrats.

The core of the Austrian reform movement was the reorganization of the military under Archduke Charles. In the early 1790s, the Austrians had toyed with the idea of a *Volksbewaffnung*, a *levée en masse* to counter the Revolutionary armies. Nothing came of it, partly because the Prussians were opposed, partly because the imperial constitution was too unwieldy, partly because of obvious ideological objections, but also not least because the Austrians feared that a *levée en masse* might emancipate the smaller German states from military dependence on Vienna.[113] After 1800, however, military reform began in earnest. As in Prussia, suspect officers were weeded out, training was improved and equipment updated; and in 1808, six years before the Prussians, a national militia (*Landwehr*), based on a moderated principle of universal service, was created.

These changes were initiated with misgivings that were not primarily ideological but practical in origin. Many Austrians feared that reforms were more likely to precipitate internal collapse and external humiliation than pre-empt it; the trauma of Josephinism ran deep. Moreover, no amount of improvement in the German and Slav provinces alone would suffice to confront Napoleon; Hungary, too, would have to pull its weight. And here the difficulties began. The uncharacteristically deferential Hungarian Diet of 1796 gave way to the Diet of 1802, which was determined, in traditional fashion, to use Habsburg necessity as a lever to extract further concessions from Vienna. The result was a stand-off: the Hungarians voted Francis much less than he had asked for and they got virtually nothing in return. The Austrian chief privy councillor, Count Colloredo, fumed that the Hungarian Diet was 'making His Majesty a slave of this nation . . . he should not have to purchase concessions with sacrifices that could set dangerous precedents and that diminish the very power he is trying to conserve and to increase'.[114] Yet throughout the struggle for mastery in

Germany, this is exactly what the Austrians were repeatedly forced to do.

The Hungarian problem came to a head after 1805. First of all, there was the growing confidence and militancy of the Diet itself, which was aggravated by French agitation. Secondly, the loss of old recruiting grounds in the *Reich* led to a shortage of manpower. The result was an acrimonious Diet at Pressburg in 1807–8: no substantial new funds or recruits were forthcoming. To make matters worse, the *Landwehr* system was confined to the Slav and German provinces, mainly because its extension into Hungary would have enabled the Diet to demand a separate Magyar army; they did not get this until 1867.[115] And in 1811, the Hungarians even refused to pay increased land taxes to cover the indemnity incurred during the war with France in 1809.

Unlike Austria and Prussia, reform in the rest of Germany was not against France, but with it. In the directly annexed areas west of the Rhine, far-reaching changes were instituted by the French themselves: all feudal dues were abolished, French law codes replaced the old society of orders with a more egalitarian bourgeois society, Jews were emancipated and chambers of commerce were created. But in the much more extensive territories controlled by the *Rheinbund* the reforms were carried out by the German princes themselves; they were the direct domestic consequence of foreign-political alignment with France.[116] After the great territorial gains of 1803–6, the main aim of the middling states was internal consolidation with a view to making up in efficiency for what they still lacked in territorial weight. Centralized bureaucratic states, the chief minister in Nassau, Baron du Thil, observed, provided 'better protection against external threats'.[117] More specifically, their client status obliged them to provide Napoleon with funds and recruits well beyond the capacity of the old fiscal-political system.

Like the Prussian reform movement, the *Rheinbund* reforms drew on a blend of local tradition and foreign models. Already in 1796, the Bavarian minister, Count Montgelas, had drawn up a comprehensive programme of reforms involving equality before the law, equality of taxation and conscription, the admission of commoners to high office, religious toleration, the abolition of guild restrictions, agrarian reform, the abolition of mendicant religious orders, the abolition of internal customs dues and the creation of monocratic ministries at the head of the civil administration.[118] Within a decade this programme, part

Josephine, part French-inspired was to become paradigmatic for most *Rheinbund* states. Unlike the Prussian case, however, the initial aim was not so much to refine or even transcend absolutism but to achieve it.

In most *Rheinbund* states, the reformers in the first instance simply picked up where they had left off in the late eighteenth century, especially in Württemberg, where the *Erbvergleich* of 1771 had cut short the absolutist ambitions of Carl Eugen, and in Hesse-Darmstadt, where Moser's reform programme had come to grief a decade later. The first priority, therefore, was the elimination of all political resistance and intermediary powers. In Württemberg, for example, French backing enabled Duke Friedrich to escape 'incorporating' the lands granted in 1802–3 (*Neuwürttemberg*);[119] this doubled his economic and military clout. Soon after, having secured Napoleon's support in the treaty of October 1805, the Elector Friedrich, as he had since become, was able to disband the estates (January 1806). At the same time, throughout southern Germany, the imperial knights were absorbed into the larger territorial states.

The *Rheinbund* reforms addressed administrative, fiscal and military questions.[120] As in Austria and Prussia, high priority was given to the reorganization of the supreme executive, in particular, and the bureaucracy in general. Bavaria led the way in 1799, with the creation of monocratic ministries on the French model; by 1805 Baden, Württemberg, and Hesse-Darmstadt had followed suit.[121] A series of laws (*Hauptlandespragmatik*) defined the bureaucracy as a separate entity in society, with special privileges, including exemption from military service; in this sense, the reforms merely refashioned rather than abolished the old society of orders. At the same time, between 1799 and 1808, Bavaria abolished all internal tariffs in order to encourage economic development and generate more revenue in the long run. Perhaps most important of all was the introduction of conscription on the French model, not for ideological reasons, but out of *raison d'état*; there was no other way of satisfying their obligations to France.[122]

In most *Rheinbund* states, there was also a programme of societal reform. The nobility was made liable to taxation and their exclusive hold on senior administrative posts was broken; however, the years after 1815 were to show that the nobility had by no means lost its old predominance. French law was only introduced in the self-styled 'model states' of Berg and Westphalia. The south German states, on the other hand, managed to keep the *Code Civil* of 1804 at arm's length, partly for reasons of prestige, partly because of aristocratic resistance but mainly because a sudden abolition of feudalism would have bank-rupted the state, which as a major landowner was dependent on feudal dues after 1803.[123] In any case, the egalitarian phase in the 'model states' was short-lived. Very soon Napoleon had 'refeudalized' them by creating a local military nobility, endowed with hereditary titles, estates and feudal dues. This was a crass violation of the principles not merely of the Revolution but also of the Code Napoleon: a more medieval conception of privilege and landholding would be difficult to imagine. Some authors even speak of a 'betrayal of the Revolution'.[124] Yet it was a logical consequence of the primacy of foreign policy. Napoleon simply refashioned the internal structure of Germany to meet his military needs by exchanging one functionally based system of inequalities, the old society of orders, for another. Given time, the new aristocrats would have developed into a Prussian-style Junker class. After all, what is a traditional nobility but a routinized functional elite?

Jewish hopes of emancipation were also to be disappointed. In the French-occupied west bank of the Rhine they were initially freed of all disabilities and granted full citizen rights. However, in 1808 Napoleon introduced repressive anti-Jewish legislation, the notorious 'shameful decree', which not only limited their involvement in commerce but also compelled them to participate in a kind of 'workfare' programme aimed at their moral improvement. In the *Rheinbund* states the picture was equally mixed. The Emancipation Edict of 1809 in Baden explained that 'this legal equality can become fully operative only when you in general exert yourselves to match it in your political and moral formation'; it was the duty of the state to ensure that 'legal equality did not redound to the disadvantage of the other citizens'. In Bavaria, the proposed emancipation legislation of 1813 gave rise to sustained anti-Semitic outbursts; and in Württemberg, emancipation came as late as 1828.

In many ways, agrarian reform was the least spectacular of all the *Rheinbund* measures, largely because in western and southern Germany the gradual abolition of the last remains of feudal servitude, but not feudal dues, had already taken place between 1780 and the turn of the century. *Grundherrschaft* had long replaced *Gutsherrschaft*.[125] Of course, the huge wave of secularization enabled the Bavarian state to strengthen the vital class of prosperous independent peasant propri-etors; it was generally less successful, however, in persuading the nobil-ity to follow suit. In Württemberg, on the other hand, the state actively promoted agrarian reform so as to hobble the newly absorbed nobility after 1803, the *Standesherren*.[126] They, in turn, traded their former political rights for cash compensation, a new governing compromise whose purpose was not to share power with aristocrats but to divest them of it. Real noble participatory political rights in the old mould were now confined to anomalous states like Saxony and Mecklenburg.

In short, the aim of the early *Rheinbund* reformers was to create a dynamic and prosperous society – a 'modern' society if you like – within a centralized, bureaucratized, rational, homogeneous, absolute monarchy. It is thus no contradiction to speak, as Erwin Hölzle does, of Duke Friedrich turning Württemberg into a 'modern absolute state'.[127] For him, political modernity was the kind of late Frederician Prussian absolutism which could provide the funds and the manpower necessary to satisfy both Napoleonic demands and his own diplomatic ambitions. Some influential figures such as Montgelas may have entertained thoughts of broader political participation from the beginning. On the whole, however, the *Rheinbund* princes intended to conserve their newly won power, not to surrender it.

But the momentous political and territorial changes after 1803 generated their own momentum. With the elimination of the estates, the princes had solved their political problems but were left with a financial one: who would now guarantee public credit?[128] Quite apart from the massive military spending since 1792, there were the huge costs of occupying and integrating the new lands, many of which came with large debts of their own attached.[129] The expected bonanza from secularization did not materialize, partly because the glutted market reduced land prices and partly because the expropriated monks had to be pensioned off; they were not simply put on the street. Public confidence in princely credit collapsed. In the long term, the only solution was to resurrect representative assemblies, based on property rather than corporate qualifications, as guarantors of government debts.[130] Of the major states, only Bavaria was to enact a constitution (1808), and a very limited one at that, before 1815; smaller Nassau followed suit in 1814. But by the end of the decade spiralling budgets had forced all of southern Germany to adopt both constitutions and parliaments. In short, the middling German princes were able to effect the breakthrough to a *Machtstaat* only by literally mortgaging themselves politically to their creditors in the political nation; this was to provide a lever for further change in the decades after 1815. Hence, if the Prussian reform movement had begun radically and ended modestly, the *Rheinbund* reforms started modestly as a programme of belated and accelerated absolutism, but ended as the vanguard of political modernity in Germany.

Domestic reform between 1792 and 1815 was not, in the first instance, generated by a social movement or a rising class.[131] Nor was it a response to revolution from below. Rather, reform in Prussia, Austria and the Third Germany throughout the French Wars was powered by the primacy of foreign policy. The result was a period of sustained state-sponsored socio-economic modernization which was, on its own terms, resoundingly successful.[132] Admittedly, in Prussia, the planned free peasantry did not come about, nor did the projected national assembly. Nevertheless, the old governing compromise was unilaterally redefined by the state in the face of extreme external peril: the peasants were emancipated, however imperfectly; Hardenberg pushed through the financial edict rather than surrender Silesia; and the noble stranglehold on the officer corps was broken, at least formally. Similarly, the *Rheinbund* states experienced a huge modernizing surge: the reforms created some of the preconditions for a capitalist, legally equal, religiously tolerant and rationally governed bourgeois society.

Of course, considerable modernizing deficits remained. Patrimonial justice survived not merely in Prussia, but also in Bavaria and other middling states until 1848. The direct universal income tax of 1808 in Prussia was replaced by an old-style taxation system which differentiated between town and countryside. Austria was saddled with a system of inefficient internal tariffs long after 1815. The guilds were far from broken. Educational reform was more spectacular at university than at the local level: many schools remained mired at the level of single-class teaching (*Einklassenniveau*); and often demands for child labour prevailed over school attendance.[133] Political participation, in so far as it existed, was very restricted. This list of desiderata is by no means comprehensive. Finally, with the exception of Theodor von Hippel's famous tract of 1792 on 'The civil advancement of women', none of the reformers even attempted to address the emancipation of women.

Which of the reforms was the more 'modern'? Clearly, the Prussian reform was only 'partial'. Socio-economic change was not matched by commensurate political change in accordance with the Anglo-French paradigm; this has been viewed as a milestone in the German *Sonderweg*, yet another moment when German history failed to turn. Moreover, even socio-legal reform was incomplete in Prussia: in the decade after 1814, the nobility were able to claw back many lost privileges and thus maintain their dominance well into the nineteenth century. The southern German states, by contrast, have been viewed as progressive forces: here the socio-legal break with the past was more radical; here the potential for political change was most advanced. But these criticisms miss the point: thanks to their differing foreign-political contexts, the pace and direction of reform in Prussia and the *Rheinbund* differed out of necessity rather than out of choice.

Paradoxically, in the field of city government, the Prussian reformers were pioneers at the very moment when their *Rheinbund* counterparts were eliminating the last vestiges of urban autonomy within their own jurisdiction. These last bastions of quasi-republican rule, the city-states of Nuremberg and Augsburg, were thrown to the princes by Napoleon. Moreover, it was not too little but too much political participation which was to damage the Prussian reform movement. For the creation of provincial assemblies provided the nobility with a forum from which they could oppose socio-economic change; and the municipal assemblies enabled reactionary artisans to attack legislation against the guilds. This was another paradox: at the very moment when the *Rheinbund* governments were dismantling their traditional estates and other representative bodies, Prussia was resurrecting them.

If modernization was always functional, conditional and ambiguous, this was because the reforms were not merely generated but distorted by the primacy of foreign policy. This was most evident in the *Rheinbund* states.[134] In Württemberg, for example, King Friedrich feared that Napoleon would hobble him by supporting the political rights of the new mediatized nobility, but not enough to issue a pre-emptive constitution.[135] In Bavaria, on the other hand, fears of French intervention motivated Bavaria to issue her limited constitution of 1808 pre-emptively. At the same time, however, external crisis could block constitutionalization. Montgelas himself justified his failure to summon the promised national representation before 1815 with reference to the exigencies of war and diplomacy. The King of Württemberg argued no differently when he defended the lack of constitution in terms of the 'need for dictatorial power during the tempestuous Napoleonic times'.[136]

The progress of the reforms in Prussia and Austria was also related to the broader international picture, be it the presence of a large French garrison in Berlin, or the Austro-Prussian policy of appeasement towards France after 1807/9, or the attempt to use France against Russia. Indeed, the initial reforming zeal in Prussia was dented,

:ast forced underground, as much by direct Napoleonic manipu-
_____ as by conservative opposition. It was French intervention which
led to Hardenberg's second retirement in 1807 and a botched anti-
French conspiracy, rather than conservative intrigues, which brought
down Stein in 1808. Similarly, it was only the shattering defeat of the
*Grande Armée* in Russia that opened the way for Prussian participation in
the final struggles of 1813–14. By the same token, Austrian reform, as
the Archduke Charles argued, was dependent on at least a ten-year
period of peace and consolidation. Instead, Austrian reform was short-
circuited not merely once but twice: during the Third Coalition of
1805 and again in an isolated forlorn hope in 1809. Reform alone, as
the Austrians discovered to their cost was not enough: the international
situation had to be right.

But if reform was motivated by the primacy of foreign policy, this
does not mean that domestic change decided the struggle against
France. Particularly in the military and economic spheres expectations
far exceeded results; moreover, the reforms needed decades to take
effect: they were not a 'quick fix'. Reform alone did not eject Napoleon
from Germany. The uniquely favourable diplomatic conditions after
the retreat from Moscow were much more important. In the end
Napoleon was beaten by the armies of the old régime: they were
merely better led, more motivated, more numerous and less divided
than before. Likewise, most *Rheinbund* states survived the war with their
gains intact, not because they were more modern than some of their
less fortunate neighbours but because they played their diplomatic
cards astutely and turned against France before it was too late. Finally,
Austria emerged victorious from the war in spite of her failure to
reform.

### Nationalism and Liberation

After 1806, Napoleonic hegemony in Germany was incontrovertible. It
was his will which underlay the decrees of the Continental System,
which excluded British commerce from the European mainland. He
alone had smashed the old *Reich* and erected the new *Rheinbund* of bid-
dable German princes in its place. Even the internal transformation of
the new territories was to a greater or lesser degree undertaken in his

shadow. If in some states Napoleon encouraged the process of modernization by threatening the imposition of the *Code Napoléon*, in others he retarded it by stepping in to safeguard the rights of the nobility. Under the protection of the *Grand Empire* the German princes carved out their own niches, concerned only to keep out the encroaching federal apparatus of the *Rheinbund*, especially taxation and conscription. The man whom many now hastened to acclaim as 'the man of the century' had it in his power to redraw the territorial boundaries of Germany almost at will. This had been clearly demonstrated on the occasion of the Final Recess (1803) and then during the great windfalls following the Austro-Prussian defeats of 1805–6. 'The Lord be blessed,' Friedrich of Württemberg exclaimed at the news of Jena, 'nothing can rival the good fortune of Napoleon.'[137] Napoleon gave and Napoleon took away: blessed be the name of Napoleon. The middling German princes, freshly emancipated from Austrian or Prussian tutelage, were happy to play this game, and who could blame them.

But there was a small and increasing band of Germans who were not prepared to play this game. They hated the *Rheinbund* as an alien intrusion. They saw in the new France, the *nation une et indivisible*, both an adversary and a model. Into the emotional and political void left by the collapse of the *Reich* there now stepped, tentatively at first, but then with ever greater insistence, the concept of the nation.

This was a major new departure. Of course, eighteenth-century Germany had known 'national subjects' in literature; Frederick the Great had inspired proto-nationalist patriotic sentiments;[138] and there had been a very keen sense of political commonwealth centred on the *Reich*. Certainly, some German intellectuals affected a strong Anglophilia in order to challenge French cultural hegemony. It is also possible to identify the development of a new national consciousness after 1763.[139] Johann Gottfried Herder's concept of the *Volk*, of a people united by language, custom and history, had gained wide currency at least in intellectual circles. Indeed, by the late eighteenth century a distinct German national culture had emerged, centred on reading and patriotic associations, and coffee-houses, and the Enlightenment undoubtedly existed. However, these 'patriotic' associations were not nationalist in any modern sense: they aimed simply at the improvement of the common weal, in areas such as industry and hygiene.[140] Before 1800 the idea of a *politically* united and *unitary* Germany, which was to become the key demand of the national movement, was practically unknown.

German cultural nationalism was not a creation of the French Revolution and Napoleon, but German political nationalism certainly was, for the explosion of French power had put Germany in a kind of double jeopardy. First of all, French annexation and partition had destroyed the age-old political commonwealth of the *Reich*. The response was a German geopolitics which developed as a kind of 'anti-politics' against foreign domination and arbitrary power. As the geographer August Zeune remarked in 1808, the German is 'like an animal, exchanged, given away, ceded, [and] trampled down . . . like a ball . . . passed from one hand to another'.[141] The new nationalism was determined to put an end to this: there should be, to quote one pamphleteer around 1800, a 'national union [*Nationalvereinigung*], where at last German people would rule over German territory and German forces [*Kräfte*]; and be no more the daily booty of internal tyrants and the constant victim of external policies'.[142]

Secondly, German identity was under threat from the assimilatory programme of French nationalism, partly in the French-occupied Rhineland, but especially in Alsace. 'Who,' the Revolutionary Barrère asked in the early 1790s, 'in the Departments of Haut-Rhin and Bas-Rhin has joined with the traitors to call the Prussian and Austrian on our invaded frontiers? It is the inhabitant of the (Alsatian) countryside, who speaks the same language as our enemies.'[143] The result was a veritable 'linguistic terror' in Alsace in 1793–4.[144] In May 1794 the Abbé Grégoire called upon the Convention to 'annihilate the dialects [*patois*] and to make the use of the French language universal'; and the mayor of Strasbourg, Jean-François Monet, even called for the deportation of the German-speaking majority to the French interior and their replacement by Francophone colonists.[145] By 1800, this approach had given way to a more gradual policy of assimilation. Thus was Alsace-Lorraine, already politically French for a century, finally severed from its German roots.

If the aim of the national movement was the preservation of German cultural and political identity, the motor was inevitably hatred of France.[146] In many cases, such as those of Fichte and Arndt, this had less to do with ethnic prejudices or stereotypes than with disappointed expectations. The enlightened liberators turned out to be more despotic than the wildest excesses of Louis XIV. 'I hate all Frenchmen without exception,' Ernst Moritz Arndt announced. 'In the name of God and my people, I teach my son this hatred. I will work all my life towards ensuring that hatred and contempt for this people finds deep roots in German hearts.' Before long, the nationalist movement could claim its first martyr. The Nuremberg bookseller Palm, author of the inflammatory pamphlet, 'Germany in her deepest humiliation' (*Deutschland in seiner tiefsten Erniedrigung*), was shot on Napoleon's orders in 1806. As Robespierre had predicted, the peoples of Europe did not welcome the armed missionaries of the *Grande Nation*. Partly, this was due to the overt contempt which the French expressed for their customs and beliefs. By 1807, whatever liberating intent the French presence had once possessed had been obscured by punitive taxation and widespread conscription.[147]

It was this anti-French focus which provided the link between German nationalists and the Prussian reformers. The military reforms, in particular, depended on some degree of patriotism. After all, they argued that each citizen of the state was its born defender. 'It is both just and good policy,' Gneisenau observed, 'to give the peoples a fatherland if they are to defend a Fatherland with any conviction.'[148] In 1808 the Spanish rising provided German patriots and Prussian resisters with the model of a popular national insurrection. 'I cannot see,' said Marshal Blücher in 1808 'why we should not emulate the Spaniards.' As Mathew Levinger has written, 'the call to nationhood was a call for political mobilization . . . to forge a unified, active popular spirit that would avenge the depredations of the French'.[149] And while a renewed Prussian patriotism would suffice within the Hohenzollern territories, only a broader German consciousness would enable Prussia to harness nationalist energies to her foreign-political aims.

For this reason, German nationalists criticized the persistence of regional consciousness – Saxon, Bavarian, Prussian and other patriotisms – which impeded the development of a truly national feeling. 'I have but one fatherland and that is Germany, and just as in accordance with the ancient constitution I belong to Germany alone and to no particular part of Germany, so do I give my heart to Germany alone and to no part of Germany,' the Prussian reformer Baron Stein announced famously. 'I am completely indifferent,' he continued, 'in this historic moment to the fate of the dynasties . . . So far as I am concerned you may do with Prussia what you like, you may dismember it altogether.'

The growth of nationalism spawned the growth of political associations; this was a major modernizing shift. In 1810 Jahn founded the *Deutscher Bund* in Königsberg, a subversive organization dedicated to the overthrow of French rule in Germany. At around about the same time the *Fechtbodengesellschaft* and the *Tugendbund* sprang up in Berlin, with similar aims. All of these groups operated covertly; assessing their real size is therefore problematic. Yet it seems clear that the numbers involved were small. The *Tugendbund* had only half a dozen or so members in Berlin, though there were more in East Prussia: its main achievement was facilitating the passage of Prussian officers to fight in the Russian service. The *Turngesellschaft* of 1811, also founded by Jahn in Berlin, was a completely different affair. Targeting specifically the young, especially academic youth, the association, a 'Gymnastics' or 'Keep Fit' society, aimed to instil national values through physical exercise. The *Turngesellschaft* was thus politically formative for a large number of young Germans between 1807 and 1813; many members later became militarily active in the Wars of Liberation.[150] By 1818 there were 150 *Turnvereine* with 12 000 members, two-thirds of them in Prussia and the bulk of the remainder in North Germany. A related phenomenon was the patriotic student fraternities or *Burschenschaften*. Although these only really took off after 1815 and played a minimal role in the liberation struggle, they were significant in that they were directed against the particularism of the traditional *Landsmannschaften*, those regional fraternities in which Germans had previously coalesced when at university.

To most of official Germany, the rise of nationalism was not a welcome phenomenon, nor did it go uncontested. There was the invincible scepticism of the Junker class. Their somewhat contingent loyalty was not to the nation, the 'nationalities swindle' as they called it, but to the monarch and ultimately to their own interests. Indeed, personal loyalty to Frederick William III of Prussia was the most potent alternative to nationalism, not just for the East Elbian landed gentry but for the bulk of the king's subjects and civil servants. Then there were those who were broadly pro-French and anti-Austrian in sympathy. They saw collaboration with France as not merely inescapable but potentially profitable; no sympathy for nationalist ideals was to be expected from them. Indeed, the hardened cynic Leopold von Köckritz, military adjutant and confidant to Frederick William III, once said that the very idea of a *Tugendbund* made him want to found a *Lasterbund*, a league of vice. Finally, there were those who favoured a united Europe under French tutelage, such as the Prussian pamphleteer Friedrich Buchholz, and those such as Dalberg, the former Imperial Arch-Chancellor and Elector of Mainz, who looked to Napoleon, even at this late stage, to resurrect the *Reichsidee* in some form or another.

Established elites were also frightened by the potentially revolutionary character of the nationalist movement. Some of its most prominent propagandists, such as Arndt and Jahn, were outspoken opponents of hereditary bondage and enthusiasts for reform. Both wanted greater popular participation in politics through some form of national representative body. Socially, too, the nationalists were suspect. The gymnasts were apt to sing songs with verses like '*An Rang und Stand sind alle gleich*' – we are all equal regardlesss of rank. Underlying this subversive streak was the primacy of the national interest. In 1808, for example, the military reformer Gneisenau called for a general insurrection in North Germany; uncooperative princes should be threatened with deposition and the traitorous nobility with the confiscation of their estates. Boyen and Grolman argued similarly: 'we must win all of Germany and sweep it along with us. If the princes do not want to follow, the people will.' Perhaps the most striking instance of the unease felt by the established order at the sight of patriotic turbulence were the words of the Austrian Queen in 1809. 'Our current behaviour,' she observed, 'gives our enemies the opportunity to portray the Austrians as the inciters of foreign peoples and as true democrats.'

The strongest opposition to nationalist demands came, however, from the German cabinets. Back in 1795, Prussia had already demonstrated its utter indifference to wider German concerns by ceding the left bank of the Rhine. Later, at the Treaty of Bartenstein with Britain and Russia in 1807, she had specifically denied that the restoration of the *Reich* was one of her war aims. At the very latest after the humiliation of Tilsit, German concerns had slipped entirely from the Prussian agenda, which was one of resuscitation and reform. To the statesmen pusuing Prussia's policy of fulfilment and accommodation with France, nationalism was not an opportunity but an embarrassment. For them, Russia was the key. It had been the tsar who had rescued Prussia from total extinction at Tilsit, and it was on his continued goodwill that the future of the monarchy depended. Without his support there could be no successful challenge to French hegemony. The Franco-Russian *rapprochement* at Erfurt in 1808 thus ruled out any prospect of change or resistance in Germany. This prompted the patriot Scharnhorst to remark that Frederick William put more faith in Russia than in his own people. Never was a truer word spoken! The primacy of foreign policy ensured that Russian support was worth infinitely more than patriotic enthusiasm. It was in disgust at the conciliatory policies of the Prussian government and in despair at the chances of liberation, that many Prussian officers quitted the king's service and went to fight for the tsar.

Surprisingly, it was not in Prussia, where one might have expected it, but in Austria that the new political nationalism struck its first blows. Here the political leadership was divided. In one camp there were statesmen like Sinzendorff and the Archduke Charles, who wanted to emulate the Prussian policy of accommodation in order to provide the framework for internal reform, leaving open the possibility of a later challenge to the Napoleonic domination of Germany. In the other camp were the men of the 'war party,' such as Stadion and Count Metternich, who called for confrontation with France. Among both groups, however, the basis of their thought was not national feeling but an assessment of the foreign-political situation. The peace party believed that the strength of France and the divisions among potential allies ruled out any policy other than that of appeasement, while the war party saw no future for the Habsburg monarchy in a Napoleonic Europe. 'Peace does not exist with a revolutionary system,' Metternich had written in 1808, 'and whether Robespierre declares eternal war against the châteaux, or Napoleon makes it against the powers, the tyranny is the same and the danger is only more general.'[151]

The decision to go to war was thus taken not as a national imperative but as a calculated foreign-political risk. Unlike the classic *Kabinettskrieg* or cabinet war of yesteryear, this effort was to be a *Volkskrieg*, a war of the people. By appealing to patriotic sentiment, the Austrian government hoped to make up in popular enthusiasm for what it lacked in military muscle. Nationalism thus formed only part of a broader programme of internal measures designed to strengthen Austria against Napoleon. By 1809 all the preparations for a blow at Napoleonic hegemony in Germany were in place. The aim: the expulsion of French troops from Central Europe and the reconstitution of an independent European centre. The means: setting Germany ablaze with a popular nationalist rising (*Volkserhebung*). Within months, however, Austria had been defeated. There were initial successes, even a major victory against Napoleon himself at Aspern-Essling, but most of the expected German insurrections did not materialize. The big exception was the Tyrol, where peasant bands under the legendary Andreas Hofer drove out the French and their Bavarian allies.

The German 'nationalism' of 1809 was a complex phenomenon. Its main ingredients were traditional regional patriotism (*Landespatriotismus*), German imperial patriotism (*Reichspatriotismus*) and cultural patriotism. Stadion and Metternich's intent was to restore the *Reich*, not to create a unitary state; both men were, after all, imperial counts.

Similarly, the Tyrolean rebellion was essentially an autonomist revolt with limited and traditional aims. This was a far cry from the united Germany demanded by Arndt and Jahn. Moreover, the Tyrolean rebels were markedly anti-modernist. The revolt had, after all, been triggered by opposition to the reforming efforts of the new Bavarian administration, especially its anticlericalism. The Tyrolean peasants, by contrast, were fiercely clerical and anti-Semitic. Last and not least, it is difficult to impute coherently nationalist motives to a revolt directed in the first instance, not against the French but against their fellow-Germans, the Bavarians.

On the other hand, the war of 1809 did spawn some undeniably 'nationalist' sentiments, reflected in poetry and song, albeit heavily admixed with traditional dynastic loyalties.[152] Similarly, it is difficult entirely to deny the nationalist dimension to the Tyrolean revolt: the Italian-speaking population in the south seems to have remained largely quiescent throughout, suggesting that German ethnicity may have played some role in the resistance struggle. There were also the indisputably nationalist risings of Dörnberg and Schill in North Germany, which aimed to link up with the Austrians; likewise Frederick William of Brunswick, who fought his way from Bohemia to the north German coast, where he was evacuated by the Royal Navy and whose troops later formed the nucleus of the king's German Legion. Ironically, these efforts were mainly directed against fellow Germans in the kingdoms of Westphalia, Saxony and Württemberg. Their failure was as much due to the mistaken belief of the organizers that Napoleon's German auxiliaries would not fire on their kith and kin as it was to a wholly misplaced confidence in the prospect of triggering a general nationalist insurrection.

The main reason why the Austrian challenge of 1809 failed was not lack of nationalist enthusiasm, but because Metternich and Stadion had misjudged the international situation. First of all, they had overestimated Napoleon's difficulties in Spain. Secondly, they had made no effort to wean the *Rheinbund* states away from Napoleon. Thirdly and most important, Metternich and Stadion had relied on Prussian help and, at the very least, benevolent neutrality on the part of Russia. They got neither. Russia was actually obliged by treaty to come to Napoleon's aid in the event of an Austrian attack; moreover, the tsar was more interested in using the resulting confusion to despoil Sweden. Thus, when war broke out, a Russian army threatened Galicia, while another invaded and annexed Finland. Even if the tsar was only going through the motions of honouring his arrangements with France, this tied down valuable Austrian troops and deflected them from pressing tasks in the west. Predictably, the Prussian attitude was entirely determined by Russia. To the passionate entreaties of his own war party, Frederick William replied simply: 'Without Russia I cannot do it.' Once again the primacy of foreign policy over national feeling was asserted.

After the disaster of 1809, Metternich led Austria into a Prussian-style policy of fulfilment and accommodation. This was a belated acceptance of the reformers' demand for a ten-year truce to permit internal renewal, efforts which had been severely retarded by the recent adventure. But the new policy was also a recognition of new geopolitical realities, for Napoleon had reconstituted not only Germany but the whole of Central and much of Eastern Europe. After 1807, Austria was surrounded not merely by the *Rheinbund* in the west but by the satellite Grand Duchy of Poland in the north-east. 'The Confederation of the Rhine,' Metternich remarked in July of that year, 'embraces us on both sides. Any war with France would begin at the same time on the borders of the Inn and the Wieliczka [in Galicia].'[153] After the defeats of 1805 and 1809, Austria had only narrowly escaped partition at French and Bavarian hands; demands for the abdication of Francis were resisted with difficulty. For the time being, therefore, Metternich aimed to supplant Bavaria as the cornerstone of French policy. Counter-revolutionary activists were expelled; popular demonstrations of anti-French feeling were suppressed; and Austria joined the Continental System. An alliance with France was cemented by the marriage of the emperor's daughter, Marie Louise, with Napoleon. However humiliating this might have been for the Habsburgs, it was seen as a *coup* for Austrian policy at the time, not least because it forestalled a Russian marriage which would have consummated the Franco-Russian hegemony mooted at Tilsit. This was the *Rheinbundis-ation* of Austria: if France could not be resisted, she must be appeased and exploited. After 1809, for every Austrian who wanted a Russian alliance to reopen the German question, there was another who regarded Germany as a lost cause and looked to French-backed expansion in the Balkans.[154]

In early 1812 therefore, the general political climate could not have been more unfavourable to nationalist aspirations. Yet the developments of that year were to set in motion the train of events which were ultimately to lead to liberation. For in the summer of 1812 Napoleon, half-heartedly assisted by Austria and Prussia, invaded Russia. By the end of the year, his battered army was on the retreat and the campaign had been utterly lost. All eyes now turned to watch the reaction of Austria and Prussia. Their position was unenviable. It was unclear whether the tsar would press on into Central Europe or whether, as many of his generals advised, he would stop at the Polish frontier. Nor was it clear that Napoleon was decisively weakened. To be sure, he had lost an important battle, a campaign even, but had he lost the war? Those who remembered his resurrection after the Egyptian disaster, and previous temporary setbacks in Germany, were inclined to tread cautiously. 'Rattle your chains if you will,' Goethe warned. 'The man is too strong for you.'

Moreover, Metternich feared that Germany would simply exchange French for Russian hegemony.[155] Austria had long regarded Russian intentions with suspicion. After 1804, Russia used the Serbian rising to extend her influence in the Balkans; during the Russo-Turkish war of 1806–12, which ended in the annexation of Bessarabia, Austria had been undisguisedly sympathetic towards the Ottomans.[156] But even more alarming were Russian ambitions in Central and Western Europe. By 1811, dynastic and political links between the tsar and the southern German states, especially with Württemberg, represented a kind of *Rheinbundist* insurance policy against the collapse of French power and the renewal of Austro-Prussian tutelage. The Prussia of Frederick William III, deeply indebted to Alexander for his support at Tilsit, was potentially if not actually a Russian satellite, the more amenable for fears of being supplanted in the tsar's affections by Austria. To make matters worse, Alexander toyed with the idea of putting the Swedish King Bernadotte, an erstwhile French marshal but now a Russian ally, on the throne of France. This would have exponentially increased the risk of a new Tilsit by which Russia and France would divide Central Europe between them, possibly at the expense of whichever German power had exposed itself most. 'Today the independence of the German great powers,' Friedrich von Gentz remarked in February 1814, 'is secured or jeopardized exactly in proportion as the probability of a close union between Russia and France diminishes or increases.'[157] In short, the last thing Berlin and Vienna wanted in late 1812 was to be stampeded into premature action.

Lying as she did in the path of the retreating French army, Prussia had to make up her mind first; error meant certain extinction. Many figures, such as Ancillon, called on Frederick William to honour his engagements to Napoleon. Others begged the king to throw in his lot with the Russians. Some even exhibited putschist tendencies, planning to depose the king and replace him with a more decisive member of the royal house. For many months the monarch temporized. Then two events intervened to force his hand. The first was Yorck von Wartenburg's unauthorized neutralization of his corps at the Convention of Tauroggen in December 1812; these troops were notionally allied to Napoleon and had covered the northern flank of the invasion of Russia. In Berlin, news of Yorck's insubordination, which threatened to compromise the delicate Prussian balancing act, was greeted with consternation. Even at this late stage, though, Yorck's move did not set off an automatic chain reaction leading to a Prussian entry into the war. Then in February 1813, the estates of Eastern Prussia assembled without the king's permission and approved the creation of *Landwehr* recruited on the basis of universal service.

Finally, in March 1813, by which time much of his country had already been occupied by the Russians, the king decided to accept the *fait accompli* and break publicly with Napoleon. But before he did so, he hastened to secure his foreign-political aims by a treaty with Russia. The result was the Treaty of Kalisch on 27/28 February and the Proclamation of Kalisch on 25 March. The two are frequently confused, but they were quite distinct. By far the most important for the immediate future was the February treaty, in which the tsar agreed to restore Prussia in its approximate borders of 1806. It also meant that Prussia had secured a Russian alliance which she might use to her advantage in any subsequent territorial settlement. In the more famous, but transient, proclamation of 1813 – the Proclamation of Kalisch – the Prussian monarch and the Russian tsar pledged their support for a united Germany. A Russian-backed Central Administrative Council under Baron Stein was authorized to recruit on a pan-German basis and prepare the reorganization of western and southern Germany. At the same time Frederick William of Prussia's appeal – *An mein Volk* – called upon the population province by province to rise up and expel the French invaders; the text made specific reference to Spain, the Vendée and the Tyrol. Subsequent nationalist mythology spoke of this moment as one when 'the king called and everybody came' (*Der König rief und Alle, Alle kamen*), but in view of Frederick William's procrastination it is hard to fault Eckart Kehr's parody that 'everybody called and the king finally came' (*Als Alle, Alle riefen und der König endlich kam*).

Now Austria could not remain aloof for long. Yet when she finally did commit herself, it was not because of any internal pressure: nationalist excitement in Vienna and the western provinces was successfully contained. Rather, Metternich was guided by cool considerations of *Realpolitik*. He feared that Russia might defeat France unaided and thus draw up the postwar settlement without reference to Austria; at the same time, once the subsidy treaty of Reichenbach between Russia, Prussia and Britain had been agreed, Metternich feared being left behind. After Napoleon rejected all of Metternich's mediation efforts the Austrians, too, broke with France and joined the coalition in August 1813.

Metternich had learned from the mistakes of 1807–9. This time the assault on Napoleon would be in conjunction with the great powers. But Metternich had also reversed his policy towards the *Rheinbund* states. If he eschewed the idea of a nationalist *Volkserhebung* on the lines of 1809, it was out of deference to their decidedly unpatriotic sensibilities. The German princes, in turn, became increasingly responsive to such overtures, if only because they feared Stein's Central Commission. Some of the *Rheinbund* states, such as Saxony, were too deeply committed to Napoleon, too impressed by his temporary victories in 1813 and too conscious of partitionist ambitions in Prussia to make the transition. And Metternich, aware that some spoils had to be left for the victors, did not try too hard. But in southern and western Germany, he was more successful: between October 1812 and November 1813, Bavaria, Baden and Württemberg were detached from France in return for territorial guarantees.

The military balance now swung decisively against Napoleon, though the outcome was far from being a foregone conclusion. Napoleon was still capable of winning victories, as at Dresden, Bautzen and Großbeeren, but this time he was facing much larger and better motivated forces than ever before. Thanks to the military reforms, in particular the creation of the *Landsturm* in April 1813, the Prussians were able to match the new inexperienced French levies drafted in from the west. In places, the war took on the character of a bloodthirsty nationalist crusade. 'This is not a war of crowns,' wrote the poet Theodor Körner, 'this is a crusade, a holy war.' Such sentiments found practical outlets in the *Freikorps* or Free Corps of semi-regular artisans and students set up primarily to harness the patriotic energies of non-Prussian Germans. Some of the great theoreticians of nationalism now became its practitioners: both Jahn and Körner fought in the *Freikorps* Lützow; Körner was killed in action. The significance of the *Freikorps* went far beyond their limited military value. Recruits swore an oath, not to the Prussian king but to the *Fatherland*, the German nation; and their dyed black uniforms, red lapels and gold buttons were later to provide the German national colours. This time it was the Prussians, not Austria, who attempted to harness the subversive power of German nationalism to the struggle against Napoleon. Through Stein's Central Commission, they were well equipped to appeal to transregional nationalist sentiment. Now, ironically, it was France's turn to fear that the Prussians would 'revolutionize the left bank of the Rhine' (*révolutionner la rive gauche du Rhin*).[158]

Yet it would be wrong to assume any direct or necessary link between the rise of nationalism and the end of Napoleonic hegemony in Germany; the two developments were chronologically parallel, but they were quite distinct. Napoleon was defeated not by the *Volk* or the emerging modern society of the Prussian reformers. Rather, Napoleon was beaten by the armies of the *ancien régime*, foremost among them the army of the most backward European state of all, the tsarist empire. Not volunteers but conscripted regulars and long-serving professional soldiers bore the brunt of the fighting.[159] Nor does the myth of the universal nationalist enthusiasm of 1813 bear closer scrutiny. With a combat strength of 30 000, the *Freikorps* were important but hardly decisive. Most were artisans; students were in a clear minority. And why should they have been otherwise, given the fact that one of their greatest traditional privileges had been exemption from military service? Peasants were also under-represented, making the *Freikorps* a distinctly urban phenomenon, and a lower middle-class one at that.

Indeed, on the basis of the popular response alone, the war of liberation could never have been fought. The king had always sensed that patriotic enthusiasm, such as it was, would be insufficient. Hence his famous crack at Gneisenau's plan for a national rising: 'Als Poesie gut,' which may be roughly translated as 'Not bad – as poetry.' Hence also his long resistance to the idea of an appeal for volunteers, which he considered a waste of time. 'Calling volunteers is a very good idea,' he remarked, 'but nobody will come' (*Freiwillige aufrufen, ganz gute Idee, aber keine kommen*). In the light of all this, perhaps we should amend Kehr's parody to the effect that the king feared a situation where: '*Der König Alle rief, und Keiner kam,*' where the king called everybody and no one came.

Even the 'national' character of the war can be disputed. To be sure, there was a surge of nationalist rhetoric. But to whom did Frederick

William address his famous appeal *An mein Volk?* Was it to the German nation at large, or only to his Prussian subjects? Those who actually answered his call represented a very wide spectrum of opinions. Some, such as Boyen and Grolman, were indeed unreserved nationalists. Others, such ferocious opponents of reform as Yorck and Marwitz, were Prussian patriots but not German nationalists. Though in some senses their loyalty to the monarchy was ambiguous and contingent, both men were committed to the expulsion of Napoleon from Germany; beyond this aim they had nothing in common with Jahn or Arndt. Others again, such as Hardenberg, were reformers and progressives with a personal concept of loyalty to the king, but not nationalists in any meaningful sense of the word. Finally, there is some doubt as to whether a war in which so many Germans were involved on both sides can be described as a 'national' war. In August 1813, for example, the French army attacking Berlin was largely made up of Saxons, Bavarians, Westphalians and Franconians. Similarly, the decisive battle of Leipzig, which lost Napoleon Germany, is known rightly by German historians as the *Völkerschlacht*, the 'battle of the nations'. On the allied side there were to be found Prussians, Russians and all the peoples making up the Habsburg Empire. On the French side there were to be found French, Poles, Italians and – Germans.

Not national feeling but foreign policy was paramount in the liberation of Germany. It was only the change in the general political climate in Europe, following Napoleon's defeat in Russia, which enabled the national movement, hitherto suppressed for foreign-political reasons, to come to the fore. The wars of liberation were at least as much wars of cabinets as they were wars 'of the people'. The main diplomatic coups of the statesmen in Berlin, be it the Treaty of Kalisch, in which Prussia secured Russian backing, or even the Treaties of Ried, Fulda and Frankfurt by which Metternich won over the smaller German states,[160] mattered far more than a dozen patriotic poems or a dozen *Freikorps*. But if nationalism contributed comparatively little to the process of liberation, the circumstances of liberation contributed a great deal to the growth of nationalism. A myth, a mission and an opportunity had been born. The myth lay in the supposedly universal patriotic enthusiasm of the hour, which acted as a beacon for subsequent generations. The mission lay in Prussia's alleged task of leading the drive towards national unity. Prussia, it was argued, must be the protector of the nation's heritage, she must, in the words of Wilhelm von Humboldt, act as a magnet, converting the rest of Germany by the force of her moral example; as we have seen, this expectation was based on an erroneous interpretation of Prussian policy in 1813. The opportunity, finally, lay in the immense manipulative potential which the national cause conferred on those who could use it. 'The idea of a common German fatherland,' wrote von der Marwitz, 'has taken deep roots. Whoever seizes on this sentiment will rule Germany.'

# 4

## THE OLD POLITICS AND THE NEW NATION, 1815–39

### The Revolution of 1815 and its Consequences

The Vienna Settlement of 1815 was intended to keep the British in, the Russians out and the French down. The resulting territorial dispensation signalled nothing less than a complete geopolitical revolution in Germany, and indeed Europe as a whole. Prussia, once only represented by tiny enclaves in the west, was awarded the Rhineland and Westphalia. This territorial accretion was quite unsolicited: Prussia had originally laid claim to Saxony, a smaller but much less remote prize. It was Britain which insisted on bringing Prussia to the Rhine so as to perform a barrier function against France. Her foreign minister, Lord Castlereagh, spoke of the need

> to tempt Prussia to put herself forward on the left bank of the Rhine, more in military contact with France. I know there may be objections to this, as placing a Power peculiarly military and consequently somewhat encroaching so extensively in contact with Holland and the Low Countries. But as this is only a secondary danger, we should not sacrifice it to our first object, which is to provide effectually against the systematic views of France to possess herself of the Low Countries and the territories on the left bank of the Rhine.[1]

Consequently, Prussia became the guardian of the gate in the west. This was a radical change from her eighteenth-century geopolitical focus, which had been firmly eastern European. Indeed, Prussia had spent most of the Revolutionary and Napoleonic period trying to jettison her outlying possessions in the west in return for gains in Poland and northern Germany.

There was a further striking geopolitical change in Germany: the reorientation of Habsburg interests away from the west and towards southern and south-eastern Europe. For under the new dispensation, Austria had managed to shed her lands in southern Germany (*Vorderösterreich*) and in Belgium, the former Austrian Netherlands. In the eighteenth century these two millstones had cast Austria in the role of European barrier against France in the west; after 1815, this role devolved to Prussia. Hence, while Austria's overall concern with French power remained unchanged, her specific interest in the security of western Germany was attenuated. This tendency was aggravated by the new role which the Habsburgs assumed in Italy, where the Austrians had regained Lombardy and acquired Venetia. Together with a strengthened Piedmont-Sardinia and the Habsburg collateral branches in Tuscany, Modena and Parma, they were to constitute the barrier to France in the south-west. Henceforth the main focus of Habsburg policy was to be found here. This was reflected in the fact that the bulk of the Habsburg army was stationed in Italy until 1848. The resulting tension between Italian concerns and German obligations helped to erode Austria's position in Germany still further. At the same time, however, Austria remained very much of a Balkan power. Relations with the ailing Ottoman Empire were considerably better than in Joseph II's time, but the acquisition of Dalmatia greatly extended her frontier and made her even more vulnerable to periodic incursions by Serb and Bosnian bandits; this tied down Austrian forces even further.

Fundamental geopolitical changes had also taken place in the east, in particular the disappearance of Poland (1793–5) which had been confirmed at Vienna. Except for the elimination of the Republic of Cracow in 1846, the borders in eastern Europe were to remain unchanged until 1918. Domestically, Poland continued to be unstable; in foreign political terms, the area became a backwater, for now neither German great power needed to fear being excluded from a lucrative territorial carve-up. But this did not diminish fears of Russian expansionism. In 1813–14, after all, Metternich had been as concerned to limit Russian influence as he had been to eject Napoleon from Germany. Moreover, after 1815 the newly autonomous Russian

Kingdom of Poland resembled an arrow pointing at the heart of Austria and Prussia; the prospect of an expanded independent Poland including Galicia, which had been sponsored by Tsar Alexander, was only narrowly averted.

Fear of Russia in Prussia remained as powerful as ever, but it was also strong in Austria. If the French threat had now receded, Archduke Johann pointed out in 1815, 'the European situation had changed'. Russia now represented a 'a much more terrible and threatening power' by virtue of her resources and location: 'Against these Austria lacks all defences. Galicia, Hungary, Transylvania are all open to attack.'[2] More than a decade later, this bleak picture was confirmed by General Radetzky's memorandum of January 1828. 'Our borders with Russia and Poland,' he wrote, 'lack all natural or artifical defences. Flat Galicia can be flooded by the enemy at any time . . . Poland is now merely a Russian province. It will form the vanguard of a great northern colossus, which encircles us along the Galician border as far as Transylvania.'[3] To make matters worse, Austria also had to fear Russian subversion among the large Orthodox Serb and Romanian populations of the empire. Hence the Vienna settlement did as much to aggravate Austria's geopolitical exposure as it did to solve it.

Another feature of the geopolitical revolution of 1815 was that the number of individual states in the Third Germany had shrunk drastically. Instead of the huge variety of independent political forms existing in the old *Reich*, there were now only forty-one sovereign territories. Nevertheless, there were still more individual states within the German Federation than in the whole of the rest of Europe put together. Among the medium-sized states, Saxony had come off worst. As a punishment for her loyal support of Napoleon, she lost her northern districts – almost half the state – to Prussia; indeed, she was fortunate to escape total dismemberment. Most of the other middle-ranking territories, however, had emerged from the French wars with their new acquisitions more or less intact. Napoleonic rule in Germany ended as it had begun, with a great horse-trading in territories. Here, geopolitical expediency, not legitimacy, was decisive. For various reasons the great powers all favoured a strong Third Germany. Britain was primarily interested in blocking France. Austria and Prussia were also concerned to keep Russia, as well as each other, out. Finally, Russia aimed not merely to limit France, but to deploy the southern states, especially Württemberg, with which she had dynastic links, in support of her German policy. As a result, the Bavarian Wittelsbachs were restored to their Palatine territories in order to bolster the barrier against France in the west. This, Britain argued, would give Bavarian policy a 'decided German character'.[4] But much to her chagrin, Bavaria was denied the coveted land bridge between her southern and western territories (Palatinate), so as to pre-empt the encirclement of Baden and Württemberg. Indeed, Baden had not only more than doubled her territory over the past twenty years but was permitted to retain the territory of Sponheim at Bavaria's expense. Finally, Württemberg was left in possession of its large Napoleonic gains, mainly as a barrier against France, but also as a curb on incipient Bavarian hegemony in south Germany.

In short, the reconstitution of Germany in 1815 was undertaken with the needs of the European balance of power in mind. But the primacy of foreign policy was not confined to the resulting territorial dispensation: the internal constitutional arrangements of the new German Confederation, the *Bund*, were designed to enable it to function as a bulwark against France. The preamble of the confederal constitution called for a 'strong and durable union for the independence of Germany and the peace and equilibrium of Europe';[5] this would enable Germany to play a collective role in the 'Congress System' designed to uphold European stability in general and to contain France in particular. The eleventh article of the confederal constitution explicitly bound members to provide mutual assistance in the event of an invasion, not to make a separate peace with the invader and not to conclude agreements which threatened the integrity of the Confederation. As a result, by far the most important confederal institutions were the federal military contingents of the individual constituent states and the border fortresses at Mainz, Landau, Luxemburg, and later Rastatt and Ulm. What the old *Reichskriegsverfassung* had failed to do thirty years earlier was now entrusted to the Confederation. Above all, the common forum at the Frankfurt Diet, under the presidency of Austria, was intended to coordinate the actions of Austria, Prussia and the Third Germany against any potential French revival; in particular it was hoped that France would no longer be able to pursue her traditional policy of subverting the smaller members. Finally, the new entity was to be strong enough to keep the French out, yet too weak to develop any potential hegemonic ambitions of its own.

The geopolitical revolution of 1815 contradicted these arrangements even as they were being made. Certainly, in 1814–15 Metternich had rejected Prussian plans for an Austro-Prussian condominium in

Germany, centred on separate southern and northern zones of influence, in favour of a predominant Habsburg role within the *Bund* as a whole. Certainly, Metternich was well aware of the military potential of the Confederation: in 1818, for example, key mountain passes were transferred from Galicia to Bohemia in order to bring them 'under the protective cover of the German Confederation'.[6] It is also true that Metternich sincerely attempted to wean the Third Germany away from narrowly particularist paths and persuade them of the benefits of conservative federal unity. Robert Billinger has called this Metternich's 'school of German nationalism': 'unity' not unification was his watchword; and he 'sought not dominance over Germany but the prevention of that dominance by any other power'.[7] But there was a tension between the legal fact of the Austrian presidency of the Confederation and strategic reality, which cast Prussia in the role of first line of defence against France. Moreover, there was the fraught question of the role of the *Bund* in the event of a member being involved in a military conflict beyond the territory of the Confederation; this particularly affected Austria, with her heavy commitments in Italy and the Balkans.

Finally, there was an unresolved and unresolvable contradiction between the simultaneous desire for security and for independence among the smaller and middling states of the Third Germany. Obedience to Austrian counter-revolutionary measures brought unwelcome Habsburg meddling in internal affairs, but little security against external threats. On the other hand, cooperation with the various Prussian-inspired schemes for federal defence might have been the only sound guarantee in the face of reviving France, but it did entail intrusive Prussian military 'inspections' and submission to Prussian supreme command. For this reason the policy of the Third Germany – to quote the Württembergian chief minister von Wangenheim in 1818 – was simply to 'achieve the aim [of security] with the minimum of effort'.[8] As one statesman from Hesse-Darmstadt pointed out,[9] to compromise the independence of the smaller states in the interests of security was to subvert the whole purpose of the *Bund*. Yet it was equally clear that any effective federal defence required at least some surrender of sovereignty to a Prussian-dominated military high command. Finally and relatedly, there was the paradox that although the *Bund* had been constructed as a Confederation, its allotted task required it to function as a federal state. This was immediately pointed out by the Prussian statesman, Wilhelm von Humboldt. 'The German Confederation,' he wrote, 'is both in intention and fact, a true confederation of states . . . but which has given itself a unity and cohesion in certain respects, to achieve its internal and external purpose, so that, in these areas, we can speak of a federal state.'[10]

In the first decade after 1815, these fissures were latent rather than obvious. This was partly because Prussia and Austria were temporarily agreed upon a common counter-revolutionary policy within Germany itself. But at least as important to the temporary eclipse of dualism after 1815 was the success of the new 'Congress System' in monitoring French policy for any signs of renewed hegemonic pretensions. Much as Prussian statesmen might resent Metternich's dominance, Berlin still needed Austrian backing against external threats in the west.[11] As one French observer commented: 'The [French] danger [to Prussia] was so great that in order to escape it Prussia had to make the very painful sacrifice of throwing herself into the arms of Austria.'[12] So long as the great powers maintained their vigil on the Rhine; so long as Austria upheld the collective security of Germany in the Congress of Europe; for this long, Prussia was content to follow the Austrian lead not only within Germany, but also on the international scene. Henry Kissinger's judgment that Prussia became the 'diplomatic satellite of Austria' may be too harsh; it is undeniable that she deferred to Austria in those instances, such as the South American and Italian revolutions, in which her own interest was remote. The result was a unique decade if not of Austro-Prussian harmony then at least of mutual cooperation and respect.

The inevitable result of this relationship was to accentuate the tendency of the Third Germany towards an independent stance, known as 'trialism', in contradistinction to Austro-Prussian 'dualism'. Here there were two forces at work. The first was constitutionalism: by 1820 all the south German states had constitutions. The second factor was the hope that outside protection, be it the more restrained France of the Bourbon Restoration or the erratically liberal Russia of Alexander I, would guarantee the Third Germany against Austro-Prussian hegemony. Typical of this new 'trialism' after 1815 were the visions of the Württembergian minister August von Wangenheim and the Badenese statesman Blittersdorf.[13] Wangenheim was bold enough not only to call for a separate overtly constitutionalist confederation under Russian protection within the *Bund*, but also to repudiate the principle of anti-revolutionary intervention agreed by the great powers at the Congress of Troppau (1820); this confederation was to carve out its own niche in the confederal military constitution through the establishment of army corps outside the command of Prussia or Austria. But Wangenheim's plan for a trialist confederation in the early 1820s came unstuck. This was due to four factors. French and Russian support was lukewarm, while Austria and Prussia combined to crush it. Moreover, the Third Germany was itself riven by disputes: there was no greater bone of contention in restored Germany than the disputed territory of Sponheim which poisoned Bavarian–Badenese relations. Finally, as we shall soon see, the trialist project was doomed by the new geopolitics of Germany after 1815.

If the unusual Austro-Prussian harmony in the first decade after 1815 was a function of the Congress of Europe, then the subsequent revival of dualism was directly linked to the gradual disintegration of great-power cohesion. The first step was the withdrawal of the army of occupation from France after the Congress of Aachen in 1818. To the victors of 1815, this was meant to signal the reintegration of France into the European states system. To Prussia it meant the disappearance of the first line of defence against France. If previously Prussia had relied upon the guarantees of the great powers, she now had to look to her own security. As General Gneisenau put it succinctly, 'we Prussians may (now) count on having to repulse the first attack (from France)'. Or, to quote the words of Count Bernstouff, later foreign minister of Prussia, 'As France's neighbour, and as a state in possession of provinces which it wants, Prussia is and will remain for a long time, the only object of its revenge, hate, and plans for conquest.'[14] After an unsuccessful attempt to persuade the powers to maintain a European army in Belgium under the command of Wellington, a kind of 'British Army of the Meuse,' the Prussians sought to use the confederal institutions of the *Bund* to organize the defence of western Germany. Yet Prussian attempts to establish a more cohesive military structure at the second Vienna conference of 1820 came to nothing. For the time being, Austrian objections and the suspicion of the Third Germany seemed insuperable obstacles to Prussian leadership in the west of Germany.

Within less than a decade this began to change. From about 1825 onwards, Prussian policy, under the new foreign minister Bernstorff, became increasingly assertive. Already in 1819, she had begun to absorb smaller adjoining territories into her customs system, primarily for narrowly fiscal reasons. Initial attempts to extend these unions were sabotaged by Metternich.[15] But by 1828 Prussia secured a major breakthrough with the accession of Hesse-Darmstadt to her customs system. The 'Central German Commercial Union', a 'trialist' alternative including Saxony, Hesse-Cassel, Nassau and Brunswick, was founded around the same time, but collapsed a few years later. The other 'trialist' alternative, the 'South German Union' of 1829, was handicapped by the absence of Baden, due to differences with Bavaria over Sponheim. Of course, purely economic motives were important in the emergence of the Prussian-led *Zollverein* of 1833/4. But right from the very beginning Prussia had also seen customs unions as foreign-political instruments; indeed, in the case of Hesse-Darmstadt, she traded a net financial loss for diplomatic gain. Increasingly, the middling states appreciated the political benefits too. For after the collapse of the Congress System in 1823 following the spectacular and unauthorized French intervention in Spain of the same year, it was clear that the existing collective security guarantees against France had been seriously compromised.

This predisposed the smaller German states to look more favourably on Prussian proposals for a system of bilateral links. As David Murphy has pointed out, the aim of the *Zollverein* was 'not necessarily anti-Austrian': after all, the Austrians were not shut out for political reasons, but excluded themselves on economic grounds as they feared the effects of customs union on their own trade. Rather, Murphy argues, the *Zollverein* was 'concerned with creating German unity against potential French aggression'.[16] This was evident from the memorandum drawn up by the Prussian finance minister, Motz, in July 1829 in support of a customs union. The political value of such an agreement lay in the creation of German solidarity in the face of France. 'Only in alliance with Bavaria,' Motz wrote, 'is the flank of Rhenish Prussia from the mouth of the Saar to Bingen to be adequately protected against France.' The chief minister of Hesse-Darmstadt, Freiherr du Thil, was even more forthright about the *Zollverein*. 'I do not hide the fact,' he wrote, 'that once we are bound in a commercial way to a great power, we will also be bound in the political sense.'[17] This prediction proved to be premature: the *Zollverein* was not the same as a political alliance and shared economic interests did not necessarily make for political cooperation. Nevertheless, the fact that the smaller German states were beginning to countenance, even welcome, such a link was a direct result of the revival of France.

If the emergence of a more activist Prussian policy in Germany was a consequence of changes in the European states system, then the initial failure of Austria to come up with an effective response was equally linked to the developments in international relations after 1820. To quote the words of Robert Billinger, 'Whereas the German rulers accepted federal duties under the influence of the Metternich system between 1815 and 1824, they asserted their states' rights because of the changing European balance between 1824 and 1830.'[18] Why should this be so? At first sight the escalating crisis caused by the Greek revolt against the Turks after 1821, which pitted pro-Ottoman Austria against Russia, would appear to be unrelated to events in Germany. In fact, its impact on the German scene was considerable. First of all, and most obviously, the collapse of great-power coordination in the Balkans made enormous demands on Metternich's attention just at the time when the renewal of French power was causing unease in western and southern Germany. Secondly, there was a fraying of Austro-Prussian solidarity resulting from Prussia's determination to maintain a neutral stance between Austria and Russia on Greece. Whenever there was a risk of alienating Russia, Prussia could no longer quietly follow the Austrian lead: this rift was quite unrelated to German issues, but it had repercussions inside Germany. Thirdly, there was a widespread fear among the smaller princes that the *Bund* would be dragged into Austria's quarrel against Russia; this fear was stoked by Russian diplomats in order to put pressure on Metternich.

As a result, Prussia enjoyed a relatively free hand in Germany towards the end of the 1820s. Austria was forced to secure her support, or at least benevolent neutrality, in matters Balkan through tacit acquiescence in Prussian gains in Germany. There can be no better illustration of this development than Metternich's response to the customs treaty between Prussia and Hesse-Darmstadt: 'The point will eventually arrive when we will have to assert ourselves but that time has not come, and I especially do not want our higher political relationships with the court of Prussia to be spoiled by a bit of true political rubbish.'[19] In other words, Prussian diplomatic support, or at least passivity, in the Balkan question was more important to Metternich-than the frustration of apparently minor Prussian initiatives in southern and western Germany. For unlike Prussia, Austria was directly affected by Russian advances in Greece. 'Austria can never allow Russia to annex Greece either wholly or in part,' the Habsburg General Radetzky argued in 1828, 'for otherwise Austria would be totally encircled [*umschlossen*] by the Russians, as is now the case for Prussia.'[20]

By the time the *Zollverein* came into operation in 1834, Austria's position in Germany had already been severely shaken by the events of 1830–2. The July Revolution in France, which brought the 'citizen-king' Louis Philippe to power, was followed by revolutions in Belgium, Italy, Germany and ultimately Poland. But whereas Metternich called for an immediate counter-revolutionary invasion of France, the Prussians generally favoured a more cautious approach. This did not mean that the Prussians were any less pessimistic about the French threat; rather, their caution was a reflection of their exposed geopoliti-cal position.[21] Prussia, the foreign ministry pointed out in a diplomatic circular of August 1830, was France's closest neighbour among the great powers. As a result, the eastern powers were unable to agree more than a joint declaration, the *Chiffon de Carlsbad* (August 1830) in which they undertook not to intervene against France, but to repel any attack across the Rhine; rhetorically and politically, the resemblance to the Declaration of Pillnitz in 1791 is striking. In practice, Austria con-fined herself to putting down the revolutions in Parma and Modena. Prussia, on the other hand, moved to defuse the situation rapidly through the unilateral recognition of Louis Philippe.[22] Furthermore, mindful of the disruptive effect of the royalist émigrés in the 1790s, French refugees were excluded from Prussia's western provinces.

If there was anybody who was as mindful of the lessons of the Revolutionary Wars as Prussia, it was the southern and western German princes. In 1792–3 they had allowed themselves to be rail-roaded into the intervention against France; they were the first to suffer from the counter-attacking Revolutionary armies. In 1830, they had no desire to repeat the experience and they were consequently aghast at Metternich's policy of confrontation.[23] The Third Germany and indeed the Prussians were further unnerved by Austrian operations in Italy. For in moving against the revolutions in Italy, Metternich was relying on Piedmont-Sardinia and the German *Bund* as the first line of defence against a possible French intervention. The result was a French-sponsored plan for a south German neutrality zone indepen-dent of Austria and Prussia. But this scheme was stillborn, for within a very short time the revolution spread first to Belgium and then to Luxemburg. The Belgian revolution was undoubtedly of concern to the great powers, for the deposition of the Dutch king and the election of Louis Philippe's son as king threatened Belgium's role as a barrier to French expansion. The revolution in Luxemburg was of direct concern to all Germans, for the duchy was a member of the *Bund*. To make matters worse the Belgian revolutionaries claimed Luxemburg as their own and when the Dutch king of the United Netherlands appealed to the Confederation for help he had every right to expect a favourable audience. But in this moment of foreign-political crisis the *Bund* ducked its responsibility. Unwilling to risk a protracted conflict with the Belgians and their French backers, the *Bund* took the line that the matter was the personal problem of the Dutch House of Nassau alone.[24] Only under considerable Prussian pressure did the Diet agree to tackle the problem, but no action followed. It was now that the shortcomings of the Austrian presidency were most evident. Preoccupied with Italian issues and crippled by financial problems, Metternich was unable to give Germany his undivided attention; the prospect of Austrian military assistance in the event of war with France or Belgium was remote. But the states of the Third Germany had failed too. Their combat readiness had been sapped by more than a decade of parsimony; annual Bavarian military expenditure, for example, had dropped by over one-third between 1819 and 1830.[25] In short, as a mechanism of collective security the German Confederation had spectacularly collapsed.

The only power to emerge with any credit from the whole period was Prussia: it alone demonstrated anything like military preparedness. Although obliged to provide only 80 000 men for the defence of the Confederation, Prussia was realistically able to promise more than double that number. It was Prussia which had pleaded Luxemburg's case before the craven Diet at Frankfurt; and it was the Prussians who used the débâcle to strengthen their political and military links with the Third Germany. As Bernstorff put it to Frederick William III in October 1831: 'Prussia, as the state that would have to bear the greatest burden in the event of a federal war, is therefore called upon to seize the initiative in all areas where successful leadership will lead to greater preparedness and security.'[26] Two years later he spoke of Prussia's 'mission' as being to cultivate 'the union of all German governments and thereby strengthening the unifying bonds of the entire fatherland against external attack'. A glance at the map shows, of course, that this mission had devolved to Prussia by virtue of her changed geopolitical position after 1815.

These Prussian overtures met with less and less scepticism among the smaller and middling states. Unlike his erstwhile chief minister, Wangenheim, who had prided himself on 'doing the minimum' for confederal defence, King Wilhelm I of Württemberg now freely admitted that 'Germany would have to commit many more millions . . . in order to settle the struggle for the Rhine frontier with France sooner or later.'[27] Baden led the way: by the early 1830s she had begun to gravitate away from Vienna towards Berlin, partly because of Prussian support over Sponheim and partly in recognition of Austria's inability to provide adequate security guarantees in the west.[28] True, the Third Germany continued to resist Prussian demands for intrusive military integration and they remained suspicious of Prussian political motives, but the magnitude of the external threat severely limited their room for manoeuvre. Unsettled by French ambitions towards Belgium and Luxemburg[29] they soon abandoned their neutrality scheme and began to move tentatively in the direction of Prussia. 'I know no north and no south Germany,' wrote King Ludwig of Bavaria in March 1831, 'only Germany. I am convinced that safety is only to be found in a firm connection with Prussia.'[30] If particularist sentiment pulled the states of the Third Germany away from the Prussian embrace, the growing French threat pushed them towards ever greater military integration. These fears were based on a slightly exaggerated but fundamentally realistic assessment of French ambitions; in any case, perception was to be as important as reality.

The events of 1830–1 generated numerous calls for confederal military reform, especially the construction of a fourth confederal fortress. Once again, however, the *Bund* was paralysed by political deadlock. Austria wanted the new fortress in Ulm; this was militarily sound but meant abandoning much of south-west Germany to the French in the event of an invasion. The south German states, for obvious reasons, wanted it much further west, at Rastatt or thereabouts; after initial misgivings, the Prussians, led by Josef Maria von Radowitz, enthusiastically supported them. But this incipient Austro-Prussian struggle for control of the confederal military constitution petered out. The death of Motz and the replacement of Bernstorff by the conservative Ancillon as foreign minister in 1832 soon put an end to this very tentative first experiment with the 'German gambit' in Prussian foreign policy. Instead of being the power-political competitor, Prussia became, once again, for the time being, the ideological ally of Austria.

In summary, the events of 1815–31 show that the new geopolitical configuration of Central Europe after 1815 almost predetermined Prussia's victory in the struggle for mastery in Germany. Increasingly remote from the pressing security threats in the west and permanently distracted by events in Italy and the Balkans, Austria progessively lost the loyalty of the smaller German states. Prussia, on the other hand, found that her narrow state interests increasingly converged not only with the German national movement, but also with the interests of the southern and western states of the Third Germany. Secondly, the events of 1815–31 had shown that the *Bund* had utterly failed to fulfil its task of guaranteeing the collective security of all its members. Thirdly, despite a promising beginning, the period 1815–31 marked the beginning of the end of the Third Germany: it was increasingly obvious that the rigorous preservation of particularism and the maintenance of external security were fundamentally incompatible. Even if the sovereigns of the smaller German states were not yet ready to admit it, the objective need for Prussian leadership was now indisputable; in this respect, the Prussian-led *Zollverein* of 1833/4, which marked the abandonment of 'trialism' on the economic level, was indeed a token of things to come. Fourth and finally, the drive towards German unity at state level was not primarily powered by national sentiment, but by the need for a common defence against France.

## Nationalism, Liberalism and the State: Restricted Modernization under the Primacy of Foreign Policy

Writing after 1815, the Prussian diplomat Varnhagen von Ense penned the following description of the Prussian ship of state as it had emerged from the struggle against Napoleon: 'The anchor has been dropped into the feudal system, but the sails on the high seas are filled with popular representation; it remains to be seen which is stronger, the anchor or the wind.'[31] This neat maritime image lends itself to two interpretations. The first is supplied by modernization theory. According to this view, the new ideas and rhetoric of the reform period, the unkept promise of a constitution and a representative assembly were all just superficial rigging, not intended to alter the course or the speed of the Prussian ship of state. The following thirty years until 1815 can thus be seen as a period in which the anchor began to drag as the sails strained with the winds of social and economic change. On such a reading, Restoration politics in Germany was little more than a futile struggle in which the doomed helmsman on the bridge tacked and jibbed in the heavy seas of a changing and increasingly assertive society, trying on the one hand to avoid shipping too much water through concessions to a restive population, and on the other hand to escape the total capsize of revolution. But the contest was in vain, the gales of modernity too strong and the ship appeared to go down with all hands in 1848; the fact that the ship's officers subsequently managed to salvage much of their values and possessions from the wreckage is another story.

But to strain the maritime image a little further, the German states, and especially Prussia, were not merely, consciously or unconsciously, heading for a destination retrospectively termed 'modernity'; they were also acutely sensitive to their own course and position in relation to other states. Each vessel was not simply conducting a lone struggle with the elements, which the first maritime image of a solitary ship would seem to imply, but a *race* in which the different participants frequently risked collision in their determination to draw ahead; this explains the resulting changes of course in the various German states at least as well as any purely domestic or endogenous model of interpretation. In short, foreign-political circumstances and exigencies are as essential as modernization theory to an understanding of German history after 1815.

'Modernization' is the paradigm by which the absolutist, pre-modern state acquires the distinguishing characteristics of 'modernity'. That is: first, the creation of a single nation-state; the traditional dynastic principle of state organization recedes. Secondly, the development of a self-confident and politically assertive middle class; a recognizably 'modern' class differentiation replaces the traditional society of orders. Thirdly, the achievement of representative government. Fourthly, the guarantee of a broad spectrum of civil rights, including religious toleration, Jewish emancipation and, later on, equal rights for women. It is the contrast between this modernization paradigm and the actual historical development of Germany after 1815 that has led many observers to speak of a *Sonderweg*, a special German path of development. The underlying assumption is that modernizing tasks should be attempted and realized in the 'right' order: that is state formation, followed by national formation, followed by industrialization and democratization; failure to stick to this 'correct' order, it was argued, inevitably led to disruption.

The primacy of foreign policy, on the other hand, does not claim to explain everything that happened in Germany between 1815 and 1848 in terms of an all-embracing interpretation: the flapping of diplomatic wings over some foreign-political crisis did not always lead directly to

an uncontrollable societal tempest. Nevertheless, foreign policy interacted with autochthonous, self-generated forces. It set the parameters
of political action in all German states, especially the smaller ones.
Furthermore, foreign-political considerations were inseparable from
the general question of nationalism and constitutionalism after 1815.
Finally, the internal development and behaviour of all German states
was given decisive impulses by foreign-political factors.

A striking feature of the reconstituted Germany of 1815 was the
absence of a united German nation-state. The hopes of German
nationalists had thus been dashed. Given the fact that the creation of
such a nation-state would have meant an upheaval and an expropriation of existing territorial states paralleling or even exceeding that
undertaken by Napoleon, it is not hard to see why the national project
was stillborn. But for nationalists, the political commonwealth of the
*Bund* was a poor substitute. In some ways, the *Bund*, with its Austrian
presidency and Diet in Frankfurt, reflected the structure of the old
*Reich*, with its Habsburg emperor and the *Reichstag* in Regensburg.
Further echoes of the *Reich* can be found in the practice of amalgamat-
ing the smaller states into blocs for the purpose of voting; no less than
six of the seventeen votes at the federal diet were collectively held. This
ensured that the voice of the smaller German states would be given a
fair hearing. But in other ways, the *Reich* and the *Bund* were fundamentally different: whereas the former was a hierarchy of imperial states,
the latter was a league of sovereign states. The concept of *Reichsunmit-
telbarkeit*, of being 'immediate' to the empire, found no equivalent in
the new *Bund*. Nor were there any confederal courts to compare with
the old *Reichshofrat*, to which subjects could appeal against their lords;
the confederal machinery was, regresssively, weighted towards princely
interests.

Another striking feature about Germany after 1815 was the multiplicity of constitutional forms. Here the greatest changes took place in
the south, where constitutions were in place in Baden, Bavaria and
Württemberg by 1820. There were two chief motivations behind this
voluntary semi-parliamentarization. First of all, there was the imperative to spread the responsibility for the massive state debt among the
representatives of the propertied classes. Secondly, a representative
assembly was seen as an indispensable instrument to integrate the
socially and religiously diverse new populations acquired in the course
of the recent territorial expansion. In Bavaria, a traditionally Catholic
state was transformed by the addition of historically Protestant areas

such as Franconia; in Baden the dynasty was Protestant and the new subjects were Catholics. Of course, the resulting constitutional arrangements did not yet mean the breakthrough of popular sovereignty. Parliament's powers were restricted to approval of the budget and collaboration in the drafting of legislation. These powers stopped well short of control of the executive; ministers continued to be responsible to the prince alone. Besides, the composition of the assemblies was still heavily weighted towards the old landed elites. In Bavaria, for example, the Upper House was comprised of mediatized nobles, royal princes, archbishops and royal nominees. The Lower House was made up of elected landowners, including peasants who satisfied the property qualification, delegates from the towns and Protestant and Roman Catholic clerics. Accompanying these structures was a charter which guaranteed a whole range of basic rights (1818) to the population as a whole, though as we shall see there were some important exceptions. These rights were equality before the law, freedom of the press and freedom of conscience.

At first sight, the south German states had resurrected the very intermediary powers which they had previously attempted to destroy. What had begun as anti-participatory socio-economic modernization was transformed into a political modernization in favour of the old elites. In some cases, the '(be-)late(d) absolutist' period lasted no longer than a few years. Yet it would be wrong to see any necessary link between the old vibrant estates of the Third Germany and the triumph of constitutionalism after 1815.[32] Aristocratic representation in the new assemblies was primarily an attempt under strong Austro-Prussian pressure to compensate annexed 'mediatized' former imperial nobles (*Standesherren*) for their loss of independence; it was not the heir to the old estates. They resembled each other only in so far as they were both politically anti-absolutist and socially conservative. Once it became clear that their influence was going to be limited, most of the *Standesherren* lost interest and became absentees. Besides, the corporate power of the nobility in these assemblies was diluted by a substantial bourgeois, largely bureaucratic presence. Only in Württemberg, where the estates had been entirely non-noble, did constitutionalism with its representation for the *Standesherren* represent, ironically, an increase in aristocratic power. Hence, in southern Germany at least, political modernization *pre-dated* socio-economic modernization, a kind of *Sonderweg* in reverse.

By contrast, Saxony, Hannover, Austria and Prussia remained

absolute monarchies in the decade after 1815. But in the Prussian case, this outcome was in considerable doubt until 1819. For in 1815, during the heady days of liberation from Napoleon, the Prussian king had promised his people a 'national representation' in order to encourage them to join the contest against Napoleon. During the following years the reform party within the bureaucracy, headed by Hardenberg, sought to make good this commitment. Conservatives, on the other hand, furiously rejected the suggestion that the popular contribution to the wars of liberation justified broader political participation. Some, such as the German Edmund Burke, Friedrich von Gentz, and the conservative lawyer, Theodor Anton Schmalz, minimized the role of the *Freikorps* and other nationalist enthusiasts. In the implacable words of Gentz

peoples, youth, and volunteers contributed hardly anything [to the defeat of Napoleon]; the princes, the ministers, and the standing armies did all the great and glorious labour themselves, especially the wondrous unity between the courts which had been secretly prepared well in advance.[33]

The crowds of 1813, Schmalz claimed, had been motivated not by patriotism but curiosity, like people who 'hurry over to watch when a neighbour's home is burning'.[34] 'It is true,' Bülow von Dennewitz wrote in 1815, 'the romantics have provided the King with many a courageous soldier, but we must now rid ourselves of these people.'[35]

In the end, the vehement opposition of conservative elements in the bureaucracy and among the nobility won out. It did not help that the king himself was at best lukewarm about the prospect of sharing his power with a national representation. Moreover, many reformist bureaucrats were ambiguous about restoring possible mechanisms for aristocratic obstruction; the refractory assemblies of the reform period had been a chastening experience.[36] Far better, the argument ran, to effect progress from above. As the Prussian philosopher and statesman, Reinhold Barthold Niebuhr, famously put it in imitation of Alexander Pope: 'freedom rests far more on administration than on constitution'. If integration through representation was the watchword in southern Germany, bureaucratization instead of representation became the slogan in Prussia.

To make matters worse, the Austrian chancellor, Metternich, was determined to prevent the Prussians from setting a bad example to those German states, such as Saxony, Hannover and the duchies of Mecklenburg, which had not yet taken steps towards constitutional government. The fall of the liberal General von Boyen as war minister and a meeting between Frederick William and Metternich at Teplitz in 1819 marked the end of the Prussian reform movement and the defeat of the first attempts at constitutionalization in Prussia. In the following year Metternich persuaded the German Confederation to adopt the 'monarchical principle.' This law dictated that princely rule should be the normative form of government in all German territories; the only constitutions and representative assemblies permitted were the so-called *landständische Verfassungen*, that is to say representative institutions based on the traditional estates of yesteryear. Hence, instead of a unified national representation on the Bavarian model, Prussia was furnished in 1823 with a regionally based system of noble-dominated assemblies (*Provinziallandstände*). They were consultative bodies only, with no fiscal powers, and during the early years they were further marginalized by apathy and low turnouts; on the other hand, some 20 per cent of adult male Westphalians were enfranchised, a figure which compares not unfavourably with the pre-1832 electorate in Britain. However, before capitulating to the rising tide of reaction, Hardenberg and the reforming bureaucracy succeeded in passing a measure which was eventually to subvert the whole political status quo. This was the *Staatsschuldengesetz*, or 'state indebtedness law' of 1820: it prevented the state from raising any new taxes or loans without the approval of a 'national' representative assembly.

Clearly developments in Germany, and especially Prussia, were not unambiguously 'modern'. There was the failure to create a unified nation-state; the new German Confederation was but a poor substitute. Furthermore, the failure to match social and economic reform with political progress in Prussia appears to herald a fatal split between  socio-economic and political-constitutional development; this is the alleged *Sonderweg*. As for smaller and middling German states such as Saxony, Hannover and the duchies of Mecklenburg, where princely absolutism persisted, these were not merely politically but also socially backward; here no agrarian reform on the Prussian model had as yet been attempted. Only southern Germany seemed to be taking the right path towards constitutionalism. Indeed, Hans-Ulrich Wehler speaks of the 'developmental lead of the south German constitutional states'.[37] The new mechanism of mutual coexistence in Germany, the German Confederation, receives equally short shrift from Wehler: in view of its rhetorical commitment to the 'monarchical principle' and against constitutional government, Wehler speaks of a 'system of domestic-political illiberalism'.[38]

However, the original purpose of the German Confederation was not primarily the maintenance of a system of political illiberalism. Rather, as we have seen, the Confederation had been created in accordance with the primacy of foreign policy: to curb French power and to achieve sufficient cohesion among the German states to prevent a repeat of the humiliating dismemberments of 1795, 1797, 1803 and 1805–6. Cooperation in the area of security may never have been as intense as many, including German nationalists, would have liked, but in scope and financial outlay it far exceeded common action against real and imagined domestic enemies within.

But the primacy of foreign policy over political reform was also at work within the individual states. The classic case was Prussia. After all, the plan for a national representation had originated in the context of the need for total mobilization against Napoleon. Its advocates among the reforming bureaucracy saw in such an assembly an essential instrument for harnessing the resources of the nation in its struggle against foreign domination. But as the French threat receded after 1815, so did the impetus for political reform weaken. Moreover, just as the reformers had claimed that necessity of state overrode the particular interests of the nobility and other groups, opponents pointed to the foreign-political liabilities of a national representative assembly. There were many senior Prussian figures, such as Moritz Haubold von Schönberg, who argued that whereas smaller territories such as Baden could afford parliamentarization, a fully-fledged member of the European pentarchy of states, such as Prussia, could not allow her freedom of action to be cramped by a representative assembly. This theme was taken up by the justice minister, Karl Christoph von Kamptz, when he noted that 'Poland would not have gone under if it had had a truly monarchic constitution, or if it had had neighbours with Polish constitutions.'[39] Finally, it was not the least concern for the foreign-political implications that motivated Prince Wittgenstein in his opposition to the *Staatsschuldengesetz*. There was a danger, Wittgenstein argued, that such a body would use its fiscal muscle 'to judge the necessity and usefulness of a planned war, and thus also demand the right to be kept informed of and comment upon the course of diplomatic negotiations'.[40] In short, the *Staatsschuldengesetz* risked giving a future assembly a lever over the royal prerogative of foreign policy. This was not mere rhetoric with a view to the retention of social privilege – though it was that too – but was part of a long-standing debate in Prussian history that was to remain unresolved until 1914 and, some would argue, well beyond. Indeed, it is a tribute to the vibrancy of the primacy of foreign policy as a collective political mentality in Prussia that her politicians remained bitterly divided about whether political liberalization at home was the precondition or the nemesis of a vigorous foreign policy.

Austrian domestic policy, too, was conceived under the primacy of foreign policy and geopolitics. 'From the politico-geographical point of view,' Metternich argued in 1817,

> the Austrian state constitutes an open territory in the middle of Europe. Surrounded on all sides by greater or lesser neighbours . . . it lacks . . . a continuous [natural] border. Therefore the monarchy must seek its own great strength in the common spirit of its peoples, and its political, military and financial administration.[41]

For this reason, he continued, Austria needed to generate more internal strength for her self-preservation than any other European state save – significantly – Prussia. Austria, Metternich argued, could not remain secure 'if Austria, as the great central power [of the continent: *Zentralmacht*], does not provide herself with a constitution and the resources which can guarantee security if necessary'.[42] This view was echoed by General Radetzky some ten years later. '[Natural] borders and the shores of the sea,' he claimed, 'determine the geographic situation of the state' and helped to define the needs of the state.[43]

Yet financial weakness cut across Austria's security concerns. Ever since Joseph II's Turkish campaign she had been operating a chronic deficit, even in peacetime, which was much aggravated by the Revolutionary and Napoleonic wars.[44] This led to Austria declaring bankruptcy in 1811; and two years later she faced further massive expenditure in the final push against Napoleon, above and beyond British subsidies. After 1815 some 30 per cent of revenue went on simply servicing loans. The various anti-Revolutionary interventions and demonstrations in Naples, Piedmont and elsewhere were also ruinously expensive. In 1822, for example, the army asked for 55 million guilders, was granted 44 million and spent 66 million![45] The mobilization of 1831 against France wiped out years of increases in indirect taxation. Yet Austrian resources were never extensive enough either to restore Habsburg prestige in Germany or to deter Russian expansionism.

The solution was a radical fiscal-political restructuring of the empire. For the problem was not so much economic backwardness as the tenacious defence of privilege, particularly in Hungary; this meant that economic growth was not adequately reflected in increased revenue.[46] 'Hungary and its dependent territories,' Metternich lamented, 'enjoy privileges which paralyse the machinery of state.'[47] This had already been demonstrated in 1811–12, when the Hungarians had initially refused to accept either Austrian promissory notes or the new debased coinage; and it became painfully apparent after 1833 when the traditional tariff barriers separating the German and Hungarian halves of the empire contrasted with the common economic area created by the *Zollverein*. Moreover, Hungary and Transylvania were not contributing sufficently to the military defence of the empire. Both provinces, the Archduke Johann pointed out, were prevented from mobilizing powerful resources rapidly because they possessed constitutions which were 'obsolete according to the standards of our time'.[48] As in Joseph's time, Hungary was exempted from conscription on Austrian lines in favour of voluntary recruitment; further troops could be raised only with the consent of the Diet.[49] Consequently, the burden of taxation and military service fell very unequally, in this order, on Vienna, Lombardy-Venetia, the Alpine provinces, Bohemia, then Galicia and Hungary. In the German and Slav lands, Metternich was the beneficiary of Maria Theresa, who had emasculated the power of the estates in the mid-eighteenth century; in Italy, ironically, he was the beneficiary of Napoleon, who had abolished all corporate privileges and installed a reformed administrative and taxation system.[50]

One voice for radical change in Austria was the veteran bureaucrat Baron Kübeck. He had been heavily influenced by Adam Smith's *Wealth of Nations*, and rejected the traditionally cameralist view that economic progress was linked to population growth. Ironically, however, Smithian economics in the Habsburg case involved more not less state intervention. He called for restrictions on the power of the guilds, government sponsorship of railroads, the end to Hungarian separatism in matters of trade and taxation, and peasant emancipation.[51] In political terms, however, Kübeck was a staunch defender of the monarchical principle against the attempts of the Austrian estates to recapture some of the ground lost in the eighteenth century: this made him a late absolutist in the Josephine mould, or, alternatively, a proto 'neo-absolutist'.

Metternich was not necessarily opposed to domestic change, as such: his primary concern, as evidenced by his correspondence, was the defence of Austria's position within the international state system. If this meant encouraging the smaller Italian despotisms to forestall revolution and French intervention through timely reforms, or some internal restructuring within the empire, so be it. Indeed, in the immediate aftermath of 1815 Metternich toyed with various schemes of domestic reform, most of them absolutist and centralizing, but some of them corporate, or even semi-constitutional.[52] Yet the very primacy of foreign policy, which dictated change, also set boundaries to it. As in Prussia, Austrian statesmen and generals, such as Radetzky, feared that constitutionalism and a national militia would compromise their security. First of all, because a representative assembly with fiscal powers might cut military expenditure;[53] secondly, because cheap militias were no substitute for expensive fortresses and standing armies. As Radetzky put it:

A state which is surrounded only by states which seek their security in militias needs no fortresses, because it need fear no wars . . . [But] Austria is by no means in such a reassuring situation. It borders on a huge power [Russia] which . . . will probably not receive a constitution within the next one hundred years, and will therefore not reduce its standing armies.[54]

Hence, there should either be constitutions for everyone or constitutions for none.

Yet the absolutist centralizing alternative advocated by Kübeck was also fraught with dangers. Radical measures might be intended to achieve domestic cohesion and external strength; they would be as likely to precipitate domestic unrest and external weakness on the lines of 1787–90. Consequently, Metternich was a firm opponent of any *coup* against Hungary.[55] The trauma of Josephinism ran deep. Even Kübeck counselled against rash moves which had 'resulted only in a reaction that has furthered the re-emergence of the venomous and obsolete'.[56] Instead of a disruptive *Totalfusion*, Metternich pleaded for 'a powerful well-organized central government which would tolerate the commonsensical and long-standing particularities, based on language, climate, customs and tradition, of the various parts of the monarchy'.[57]

Thus, by its very nature, the Habsburg Empire was as incapable of thoroughgoing modernization as the eighteenth-century *Reich*. The upshot of all this was a policy of expedients and managed decline. Determined efforts were made to keep military expenditure down, even at a time of domestic and, especially, international instability after 1825.[58] The price was a manifest loss of military credibility, especially in 1830–1 and later in 1839–40. Periodically, the financial bureaucracy under Kolowrat, Metternich's great rival, succeeded in balancing the books. But in general Austrian budgets after 1815 remained in permanent deficit. These shortfalls were covered by a huge programme of state borrowing from the Rothschilds and other sources. For the time being international capital saved the *ancien régime*; as yet, nobody could guess that in due course the money markets would help to precipitate its collapse.

Metternich's extremely complex attitude towards constitutionalism and reform was also reflected in his policy towards Germany as a whole. If he could not modernize himself, he would prevent others from doing so.[59] In the Prussian case he even went so far as to argue, with false solicitude, but with an unerring sense for Prussian sensibilities that

A national representation of popularly-elected deputies would mean the dissolution of the Prussian state: because such an innovation cannot be introduced in any large state without a revolution, or without leading to a revolution; because the Prussian state, thanks to its geographical location and composition, is not capable of sustaining a national representation in the pure sense, because it [the Prussian state] needs military strength above all, something which is not compatible with a pure representative system.[60]

Simultaneously, however, Metternich encouraged the Prussians to introduce corporate representations or constitutions (*Lanständische Verfassungen*), that is to resurrect the very estates whose absence had contributed to Prussia's superior domestic cohesion in the eighteenth century. If Joseph had attempted to rationalize Austria to catch up with Prussia, Metternich tried to bring Prussia down to his level. This was the inevitable corollary both to Radetzky's reflections on the militia problem and to the impracticality of neo-Josephinism: if Austria could not reform herself into a modern *Machtstaat* then nobody else should either.

At the same time, Metternich feared that constitutionalism in Prussia and south Germany would act as a disruptive magnet within the rest of Germany, and even within the empire itself. This concern was aggravated by the danger of Prussia using constitutionalism to steal a diplomatic march on Austria *vis-à-vis* the south German states.[61] Similarly, both Austria and Prussia worried that constitutionalism would give the Third Germany an unwelcome ideological coherence at their expense. Finally, both Austria and Prussia, in true eighteenth-century style, sought to hobble, though not totally paralyse, the Third Germany with disruptive corporate assemblies.[62] They wanted the Third Germany to be strong enough to fulfil its confederal obligations, but not strong enough to challenge the Austro-Prussian dualist condominium: the lessons of the 1790s, when the estates had helped to choke the imperial war against France, and of the *Rheinbund*, had been well learnt. Hence simple *Realpolitik*, rather than ideology, underpinned Austro-Prussian commitment to the very corporate constitutions (*Landständische Verfassungen*) which they rejected for themselves. These assemblies sought to kill two birds with one stone: to forestall the emergence of southern and western Germany as a beacon of constitutionalism; and to prevent the Third Germany from maximizing its resources through either neo-absolutism or radical constitutionalism.

Finally, domestic arrangements in the smaller states were, if not determined, then at least powerfully influenced by foreign policy. For them, the constitutional gambit was not merely a fiscal necessity but an opportunity to advertise their newly won sovereignty. Thus Nassau and Bavaria promulgated constitutions in 1814 and 1815 respectively, in the first instance so as to pre-empt great-power partition and in the second instance to forestall interference by the *Bund*. In the Bavarian case, the object was also to underpin the Wittelsbach claim to leadership of the Third Germany; the possible alternative of a corporate constitution in return for Austrian-sponsored territorial gains was rejected.[63] Yet, as we shall see, military dependence on Austria and the *Bund* for protection against France forced some constitutional states, especially Baden, to tread carefully. Indeed, domestically unpopular policies, such as military service and increased military expenditure, were often justified to sceptical assemblies in terms of external compulsions; at the same time these measures helped to stimulate internal integration and state formation in the Third Germany.[64] Last but not least, south German sovereigns retained a firm grip on the executive: foreign policy remained exclusively and explicitly their preserve. But in time it became increasingly clear that the simultaneous stipulation that the prince could not surrender land, enact or alter laws, raise loans or taxes, without the consent of the *Landtag* had unavoidably compromised princely control of foreign policy.

It was not long before the new order established in 1815 came under furious attack from many directions: liberal nationalism, conservatism, aristocratic separatism, social unrest and political catholicism.

Admittedly, the more narrowly political and subversive groupings  remained small and isolated. The grand total of revolutionary nationalists such as those headed by Karl Follen in Gießen, the *Schwarzen* or the *Unbedingten*, cannot have been more than a few hundred, if that. But in the decade after 1815, the numbers mobilized directly or indirectly in support of German nationalism already ran into the tens of thousands. Underpinning this liberal nationalist challenge was a transformation of the public sphere characterized by organization through association. The mixed enlightened societies and Masonic lodges of the eighteenth century, in which the nobility had been prominent or even predominant, were replaced by much more self-consciously middle-class associations (*Vereine*); and the numbers involved, at least after 1830, were considerably larger.[65] Spectacular public manifestations of nationalist exuberance followed, at the *Wartburgfest* in 1817, where boisterous student festivities soon mutated into an inflammatory nationalist rally, and then at the Hambach Festival of 1832, where well over 20 000 Germans turned out to show their liberal and nationalist colours. By 1847, total membership of associations exceeded 200 000. As Berthold Auerbach noted in his *Gevattersmann* of 1846: 'There really are no more great men, but rather many of the middling sort [*Mittelschag*], and that is a good thing. The master and ruler of the present day and our future is the hero: association.'[66]

Official parties in the modern sense were forbidden by law. But in 1832 the 'German patriotic association for the support of the free press' was set up; this early experiment in proto-party-political organization soon boasted more than 5000 members across state boundaries and was instrumental in organizing the Hambach Festival. This was a new departure, for it was the first more or less openly crypto-political organization to achieve what was by the standards of the time a mass following. Two years later, Rotteck and Welcker began to publish their *Staatslexikon* (completed in 1843), which was soon to acquire the status of a liberal bible around which liberal agitation could crystallize. There was also an explosion of the press, especially when censorship restrictions were relaxed around 1840.[67] But perhaps the most decisive transformation of the public sphere was its interaction with the new representative assemblies in the Third Germany and indeed Prussia after 1823; this gave liberal nationalists a political lever which the old enlightened public sphere had lacked.

 The main aim of the liberal nationalist public sphere was the definition, expression and advancement of a German national identity based not on race or ethnicity, or even primarily language and economics, but on a sense of a threatened *political* commonwealth. In its most extreme form, this nationalism was *programmatic*. It demanded the completion of the unfinished business of 1813–14: a unified German nation-state on French lines, a structure liberals believed would best guarantee the implementation of liberal reforms. But in its more moderate and widespread incarnation this nationalism was largely *reactive*, with a clear focus on the territorial integrity of the *Bund*. The events of 1830–1 reinforced both tendencies. First of all, they made the case for greater German unity and ultimately unification in the face of the French threat; secondly, they destroyed confederal and Austrian military credibility.[68] As a result, Prussia began to regain the standing with liberal nationalist opinion which she had forfeited after 1815. In Baden the liberal opposition under K. H. Hoffmann, Münch, Schulz, Dahlmann and others began to move in the direction of Prussia; the long-standing liberal idea of a joint crusade with France against tsarist Russia was already under attack.[69] Some, such as the Palatine democrat and Bavarian citizen, Johann Georg Wirth, even called for a league of German constitutional states led by Prussia.

Liberal nationalists subscribed to the primacy of foreign policy no less than their governmental adversaries. Some of them were even prepared to put domestic change on hold for the sake of external security. Daniel Cotta, a Württembergian publisher and doyen of the liberal public sphere, argued in December 1831, in the immediate aftermath of the French invasion threats, that criticism of poverty and injustice should wait. 'Even if all the complaints of the opposition men are true,' he wrote, 'is it *national*, is it *patriotic*, in a time of pressing danger, and under the threat of powerful enemies . . . to sow mistrust between the rulers and the ruled, to spread unrest and disorder.'[70] But more often liberal nationalists argued that political reform was a prerequisite for external security. In 1815–19, Prussian nationalists had argued that their contribution to the struggle against Napoleon entitled them to greater participatory rights. Now they argued that these rights were needed to repel the renewed French threat. 'Practical politics,' Hansemann argued in his famous book *Preußen und Frankreich*, 'consists of the ability to maintain and increase the power of the state both internally and with respect to its external relations.'[71] Prussia, he continued, was much weaker than France. This could only be compensated by harnessing national feeling and dynastic patriotism in the various parts of the state. 'In a word,' he concluded, 'moral forces must compensate for the lack of material ones,' if Prussia was not to be dominated by France or any other of its powerful neighbours.[72] What Hansemann argued for Prussia, Rotteck extended to Germany as a whole: 'Germany [should be] a power infused by a collective national will, an imposing power which deters any potential aggressor.'[73]

Internally, the main liberal political demands were parliamentary restraints on princely absolutism and the granting of a constitution; a property franchise; freedom of the press and of conscience; the abolition of feudal elements in the legal system; and a unified nation-state which would not only articulate national interests within Europe, but also put an end to the old *Kleinstaaterei* and allow freedom of trade and movement. The constitutionalization of southern Germany in 1815–19, and the quasi-representative institutions created in Prussia after 1823, gave liberal forces an arena in which these aims could be pursued. Because the individual state laws did not permit delegates to form political factions in the assemblies, opposition politics were at first somewhat hamstrung. In time, however, liberals were able to exert increasing pressure on state governments by tightening the pursestrings. In the southern states this manifested itself in close scrutiny of the budget; in Prussia this culminated in the refusal of the provincial assemblies to permit new loans or taxation without a genuine representative assembly, as indeed they were entitled to do by the terms of the 'state indebtedness law'. But liberal programmes could also, as we have seen, be pursued through the press and the burgeoning associations. And in the Prussian Rhineland, the structures of municipal self-government left behind by the French helped to furnish liberal elites with what Jeffrey Diefendorf has called 'a practical political education'.[74] A typical political career would lead via the local chamber of commerce and the city council to the regional assembly.

The Rhineland was not merely home to a vocal liberal opposition, it was also the focus for an emerging political Catholicism. Here the sources of friction were twofold. In the first place, the Rhinelanders were attached to the legal legacy of Napoleonic rule, which soon became known as 'Rhenish' rather than French law. Prussian attempts to replace the *Code Napoléon* by the *Allgemeines Landrecht* in 1824 and 1833 met fierce resistance and had to be abandoned. Secondly and relatedly, there was an immense confessional gulf between the Roman Catholic Rhinelanders and the predominantly Protestant Prussian administration. Matters came to a head with a papal decree that children of mixed marriages which had been blessed in church had to become Roman Catholics; the Prussian state took the scarcely more progressive view that the confession of the father should be decisive. The Bishop of Cologne was arrested and thrown into prison; only after the accession of Frederick William IV did the state back down and pursue a more conciliatory policy. But by then the growth of political Catholicism was in full swing. The year 1844 saw mass pilgrimages around Trier, testimony both to the renaissance of popular piety and the growth of Catholic identity. In the Rhenish *Landtag* of 1841 the Catholics had already formed a group of their own, and four years later the first Catholic newspaper was licensed in Protestant Württemberg; for confessional divides had been no less sharp in the liberal south-west.

Yet another challenge to the state in Prussia and elsewhere came from conservative aristocrats. Since the 1790s, conservatives had faced two ways: against the Revolution but also, as throughout the reform absolutist period, against the centralizing state. Whereas reform conservatives in the bureaucracy operated according to the primacy of foreign policy, aristocratic conservatives upheld the primacy of their own corporate interests. In southern and western Germany, the mediatized nobility tried to mobilize the *Bund* in their defence against princely encroachment; after 1815, 'liberty' could mean aristocratic liberty as much as anything else. In Prussia, conservative Junkers agreed with Arndt's observation in 1813 that Frederick William had become 'Germany's first Jacobin, and [that] nearly all German princes have followed his example';[75] but they regarded this as an accusation, not an accolade. Paradoxically, these nobles had suffered *socio-economically* during the reform period, but, thanks to the revival of the estates, had gained power and confidence *politically*. By the 1820s religion became the focus of aristocratic resentment. Pietist nobles put up a furious resistance against Frederick William's union of the Calvinist and Lutheran churches in 1817 and against the abolition of the estates of the *Kurmark* in 1820;[76] their secret prayer conventicles helped to prepare the way for conservative mobilization. Further tension was caused by the *Agendenstreit*, the controversy over the introduction of a unified liturgy in the newly united state church. Western parishes in particular condemned this as unwarranted state interference. At the same time, the primarily Silesian 'Old Lutheran' opponents of the union in the 1830s were part of a broader opposition to the centralizing policies of the state.[77] In short, as in the late eighteenth-century *Reich*, the apparent 'reconfessionalization' of politics after 1815 was subordinate to, rather than constitutive of, broader socio-political alignments.

Many conservatives, of course, were staunch supporters of the state; indeed, as bureaucrats, many of them were *of* the state. They too sought strength through organization. Ernst Wilhelm Hengstenberg founded his *Evangelische Kirchenzeitung* (1827), and the *Berlinisches Politisches Wochenblatt* (1831), founded by the von Gerlach brothers in association with the then Crown Prince of Prussia, later Frederick William IV, helped to create a conservative public sphere. At the same time, there was the emergence of conservative associations to rival those of liberal nationalists, if not numerically then at least conceptually. For example, the *Kriegervereine*, set up with the encouragement of the military establishment, could boast some 50 000 members by 1848 and made a significant contribution to conservative mobilization during the revolutionary period.

The greatest internal challenge facing Austria was traditional aristocratic separatism in Hungary and Poland, aggravated by a growing liberal nationalism. In a series of cantankerous Diets in 1825, 1832–6 and 1839–40, the Magyar nobility succeeded in retaining control of the vital areas of taxation and conscription.[78] They were the beneficiaries of both Austrian preoccupations with Greece and Metternich's fear of another Josephine internal collapse. This old-style anti-absolutist, but not necessarily separatist opposition, which differed little from eighteenth-century Hungarian postures, was led by the liberal magnate Stephen Szechenyi, on whom Metternich increasingly relied to manage Hungary. In return for a minimum of cooperation and goodwill, the Magyar gentry expected state support against their peasantry *in extremis*. But the uneasy consensus of the immediate Restoration period began to collapse after 1830, first of all, because the authorities were slow to react to peasant rebellions in Eastern Slovakia and Romania, both then lands of the Hungarian crown, in 1831. Irate Magyar nobles and townspeople were unimpressed by the Austrian military performance and began to argue for the need to organize their own defence.[79] Secondly, the growth of a more radical form of

Hungarian separatist liberal nationalism under Lajos Kossuth was to gather increasing momentum in the years ahead. Similar problems confronted both Austria and Prussia in Poland. Here the independent oligarchical 'Republic of Cracow', and especially the Russian 'Kingdom of Poland' with its liberal constitution after 1815, acted as a dangerous magnet for the substantial Polish populations in Austrian Galicia and the Prussian east.[80] Metternich reacted to this threat with characteristic repressive vigilance. But the Prussian response was a liberal policy of conciliation: the new governor, Prince Anton Radziwill, was himself a Pole; and the supreme administrator, Zerboni di Sposetti, was not merely an old liberal but a Catholic, in deference to Polish confessional sensibilities. The nobility were co-opted into local government and granted state assistance to weather the agrarian crisis of the 1820s; the peasantry were emancipated.

No good deed goes unpunished. The liberal constitutionalist experiment ended in full-scale rebellion in Russian Poland in 1830/1; thereafter both Prussia and the tsar abandoned their policies of conciliation. The new governor, Flottwell, suppressed the clergy and the nobility, both regarded as carriers of Polish separatism; the peasantry and German, largely Protestant, colonization were encouraged as counterweights; in 1832, German was introduced as the exclusive language of administration; and after 1833, local government was increasingly in the hands of German *Landräte*. Yet in some respects Flottwell was also a liberal, who not merely defended mixed marriages against the Polish clergy, but also greatly improved the lot of the Jews; his successor, Theodor von Schön, was both an avowed liberal and a sponsor of Germanizing policies at Polish expense. The accession of Frederick William IV in 1840 brought the Poles some respite: the rebels of 1830 were amnestied; the Prussian climbdown over mixed marriages eased confessional tensions; and Frederick William's emphasis on corporate Christian conservatism was not, *prima facie*, uncongenial to the Polish nobility. But as the events of 1848/9 were to show, once again a policy of conciliation served to inflame rather than defuse Polish separatist ambitions.

In the German and Slav lands of the Habsburg Empire, liberal nationalism was as yet a much less acute problem. Potentially, of course, German nationalism, with its emphasis on a united *Reich* shorn of its foreign encumbrances, spelt death for the Habsburgs. Such pan-Germanism was already making inroads not merely in the Tyrol and Upper Austria, but also in Bohemia, where the implications were explosive. At the same time, by way of reaction and imitation, the first manifestations of Slav nationalism were to be observed. In Dalmatia and Slovenia, the brief period of French rule had opened a window on the world outside. The most important developments, however, took place among the Slavs of Bohemia and Moravia, where middle-class mainly Protestant Czech intellectuals, such as Franz Palacky, rediscovered the vernacular languages and literature upon which national revivals were based; here the heritage of medieval national heroes, such as the heretic Jan Hus, was to prove important. If in Poland it was the German Protestant oppressor, in Bohemia it was the German Catholic oppressor. Ironically, it was left to the nobility (and the state) to champion the cause of national and confessional coexistence against *petit-bourgeois* chauvinism. Many Bohemian magnates, such as Count Thun, described themselves as neither 'Czech nor German, but simply Bohemian'.[81] But this approach had no future: it could only be either part of a German regional movement or a Czech national movement.

To the Habsburgs, of course, *any* nationalism was suspect. 'Peoples? What is that?' the halfwitted Ferdinand I exclaimed. 'I know nothing of peoples, I only know of subjects.'[82] But Metternich's response to the emergence of the lesser Slav nationalisms was more complex: they were perfect counterweights to German, Magyar and Polish nationalism. In Hungary, where nearly half the population was made up of Slovaks, Romanians and Croats, the Austrians were able to exploit Magyar paranoia. In Galicia, the Habsburgs encouraged the Uniate orthodox-rite church and Ruthenian peasantry against the Roman Catholic Polish nobility and townspeople. And in Bohemia, the Austrian administration even sponsored the growth of a Czech identity through permitting the teaching of Czech in secondary schools (1816), the creation of a national museum in 1818 and other measures, partly out of genuine antiquarian interest and benevolence, but mainly in order to embarrass German nationalists in the province. Austria, Metternich argued, should encourage 'nationality' but not 'nationalism';[83] so long as Slavism 'does not transgress into political daydreaming, then the government should not impede it.'[84] Paradoxically, therefore, the very fractiousness and diversity of the Habsburg Empire was also its potential salvation. 'My peoples are strangers,' Franz I observed, 'of their dislike, order is born; and of their mutual hatred, universal peace.'[85]

Similar strategies were developed to deal with liberal nationalism within Germany itself. In Prussia, the monarchy encouraged a dynastic, narrowly Prussian patriotism. In the southern and western German states there were sustained government efforts to transform traditional particularism into a Bavarian, Württembergian, Badensian, Saxon or Hessian 'nationality'.[86] New points of identification with the state – representational buildings, a cult of the monarchy and so on – were created. It was also hoped that the state representative assemblies (*Landtage*) would increase regional consciousness at the expense of a broader German focus; nationalism and constitutionalism were thus not necessarily coterminous.[87] But the most common response, throughout the *Bund*, was repression. Matters came to a head in 1819 when Karl Ludwig Sand, an emotionally disturbed student radical, murdered the Russian agent and reactionary playwright, August Rost von Kotzebue. Sand was an almost ideal typical German nationalist: as a native of Ansbach, he came from an area which had been forcibly incorporated into Napoleon's Bavarian satellite state in 1806 and which remained Bavarian in 1815; he could consider himself particularly alienated by the compromises of the Vienna Settlement. Sand had fought as a volunteer in the wars of liberation and had studied under tenured radical nationalist professors in Gießen. Metternich, in tandem with the Prussians, now used the assassination of Kotzebue to crush what he saw as liberal nationalist subversion. The upshot was a series of ordinances (the Karlsbad Decrees, 1819). In theory, these furnished the German Confederation with a considerable repressive apparatus: a confederal investigative commission was set up with the purpose of eliminating political radicalism; some crypto-political groups such as the *Tugendbund* had already been banned, the rest were now suppressed; strict censorship was introduced; and individual states were instructed to exclude members of suspect student fraternities or other associations from the bureaucracy.

The main thrust of the Karlsbad Decrees was domestic in origin, but foreign policy also played an important role in their conception and, especially, their execution. For one thing, the great powers knew that the internal stability of Germany was crucial to keep potential predators out; such fears were realized when revolutions in Spain (1823) and Belgium (1830–1) gave France the pretext to intervene, be it in a legitimist or a liberal fraternal guise. Moreover, throughout the 1820s constitutional Baden and Nassau vigorously implemented the Karlsbad Decrees. For unlike Württemberg or Bavaria,[88] Baden was both entirely dependent on Austria and the *Bund* for security against France and lacked another great-power protector. She was also anxious to preserve her favourable territorial settlement of 1815, including Sponheim. Here, as ever, state interest overrode domestic ideological orientation. Conversely, the primacy of foreign policy could serve to mitigate repression. Russia was bitterly opposed to the Karlsbad Decrees, which it regarded as merely a vehicle for Austrian domination.[89] Many southern and western German states, on the other hand, walked a tightrope between genuine fear of revolution, terror of France and an immediate fear of Austro-Prussian tutelage. As a rule, the more remote they were from France, the less assiduous they were in implementing repressive federal legislation. Hence what Metternich did not achieve was as important as what he did achieve: he failed to dismantle existing constitutions in Baden, Bavaria and Württemberg. In this respect, the 'monarchic principle' ordained in 1820 remained a dead letter. This was partly because the states concerned saw representative assemblies as crucial to their own internal consolidation, and partly because the decree was regarded as intolerable outside interference. In the same way, the confederal investigative commission against political radicalism was bitterly resented among the smaller and middling states as a vehicle for Austrian influence. This applied as much to reactionary Saxony before 1830 as it did to progressive Württemberg and Bavaria: to all of them, the threat to their dearly held sovereignty far outweighed the question of ideological principle.

In any case, the wave of Metternichian repression in the 1820s could only delay and not reverse the rise of nationalism as a political force in Germany. By the 1830s and particularly after 1840, organized nationalism was proving impossible to control; half-hearted attempts at conciliation through amnesty were unsuccessful. Despite widespread censorship, chicanery and surveillance, the established order was unable to prevent the revival of the gymnastics associations, the student fraternities and other groups. By the mid-1840s, the successors of Jahn's gymnasts had more than quadrupled their number to about 90 000. Indeed, by this stage well over 200 000 Germans were organized in various student, choral, cultural and gymnastics societies. All over Germany, front organizations of animal- and nature-lovers sprouted; transparently politicized Luther and Schiller clubs flourished; and mass banquets such as the Gutenberg Festival became the focus of public attention.

At first sight, all this would tend to suggest that the German national movement after 1815 was a progressive force, with all the hallmarks of political modernity: a popular base supported by a voluntary associational structure, an emancipatory social programme and a transregional appeal which set it apart from the traditional particularism of the old Germany. Nationalism, in Wehler's definition, 'saw itself as a liberal party of modernization, which believed itself capable of solving the accumulating problems through social and political reforms. In this sense, nationalism continued to be a reaction to the modernization crises and relative backwardness of the German states.'[90] The German Confederation, by contrast, resembles a repressive cartel, determined only to stifle all popular political participation. It had, in Hans-Ulrich Wehler's words, 'revealed itself as a police state, as a system of princely insurance against any kind of political change'.[91]

Yet one of the little-known stipulations of the Karlsbad Decrees was the injunction to maintain standards of public order and common decency towards all citizens equally. This was a direct reference to the rampant anti-Jewish riots which had shaken Germany throughout 1819, especially in liberal Baden, where marauding peasants and artisans accompanied their attacks on the established order with anti-Semitic outrages. But it might just as well also have been a reference to the prejudices of the liberal nationalists who had congregated on the Wartburg in 1817. A brief look at what was ceremoniously burned by the young radicals provides an insight into the ambiguity of modernity. Among the first casualties was the paraphernalia of German militarism, such as a Prussian corporal's baton and a Hessian military pigtail; this would tend to give the whole event a progressive aura. But the burnt offerings to German nationalism also included such alien publications as the modernizing *Code Napoléon*, which offended nationalist proprieties. Perhaps even more problematically, the works of the Jewish author Saul Ascher, who had ventured to criticize the more extreme manifestations of German nationalism, were consigned to the flames, amid noisy anti-Semitic refrains. Hence, uncomfortably for those who see a direct link between political modernization and civil rights, anti-Semitism in early nineteenth-century Germany was also a subversive phenomenon. It was a regular feature of socio-political protest in early nineteenth-century Hamburg, Silesia and elsewhere. The authorities, by contrast, did their best to, in the words of two experts, 'combat rumours and *Pogromstimmung*'.[92] Indeed, German governments were deeply troubled by these outrages against Jewish subjects, not least because they were interpreted, correctly, as a gesture of popular contempt for the established order. Here classic modernization theory breaks down, for it posits anti-Semitism as a manifestation of backwardness, which is later used manipulatively as an integrative ideology by the old elites in their struggle against modernity. In this instance the individual state governments were entirely innocent of manipulatory tactics.

Hence, in terms of civil rights, the repressive apparatus of the German Confederation paradoxically had limited progressive effects; even if it did not grant Jewish emancipation, it curbed xenophobic and anti-Jewish excesses. Moreover, it was in supposedly more politically backward Prussia that the project of emancipation, with all its imperfections, was most advanced; Jewish rights were least well protected in new Prussian acquisitions such as Posen, where the old repressive Polish laws still applied after 1815, and ironically in the Rhineland, where the population clung to Napoleon's discriminatory legislation and resisted the Prussian emancipation edict of 1812; this too was a spirited defence of the French legacy against state intrusion.[93] It was those guardians of ancient liberties, the free cities of Hamburg and Frankfurt, and the supposedly more progressive southern German constitutional states of Württemberg and Bavaria that had blocked Alexander von Humboldt's plan to enshrine the principle of Jewish emancipation in the confederal constitution.[94] When a very limited royal proposal for Jewish emancipation was introduced in Bavaria in 1813, the *Landtag* unburdened itself of its anti-Semitic prejudices in a frank and open debate; this experience was repeated more dramatically in 1849. Indeed, in the southern German states the continued denial of civil rights to the Jews was not in spite of political modernization, but because of it: not for the first or last time, representative assemblies had revealed their anti-emancipatory potential.

Similar ambiguities became evident in the German revolutions of 1830. Many radicals sought political participation in order to reverse socio-economic modernization, especially the decline of the guilds and the growth of the bureaucracy; Hesse-Cassel is a good example.[95] In Saxony, the situation was even more complex. At one level, the revolution, which began *before* the overthrow of the Bourbons in July 1830, simply speeded up political modernization through the extortion of a constitution. On another level, the revolutionary challenge also involved a sectarian assault on Saxony's small and highly unpopular Roman Catholic minority, triggered by royal attempts to moderate the popular Protestant triumphalism of the annual *Confessio Augustana* celebrations.[96]

Moreover, the revolutions of 1830 showed that the German Confederation was no mere transregional reactionary police authority. Contrary to what one might have expected, there was no coordinated confederal action against the revolutionaries. The plea of the Prince of Schwarzburg-Sondershausen for a Prussian intervention was rejected by Bernstorff in October 1830.[97] Similarly, Bavaria opposed the Austrian-sponsored *Bund* decision to move against the Hessian Revolution in September 1830. Indeed, Metternich's plans to crush the disturbances in Saxony were frustrated by Prussia, primarily in order to annoy Austria; there are shades of the sabotaged *Reichsexekution* at Liège here. In the same way, the reactionary government in Hannover backed the anti-absolutist rebels in Brunswick against their duke. It did so not for any ideological reasons, indeed ideological motivations would have inclined the Hannoverians to side with the deposed duke, but because – having failed to mobilize the Confederation on their behalf – it was their last resort in a long-standing disputed succession between the related princely houses. Once again, Metternich's plans for a confederal intervention against the revolutionaries were sabotaged by the Prussians, partly because they wanted to keep the constitutional states onside in the event of a French invasion.[98] Not for the first or last time, the primacy of foreign policy had won out over ideological solidarity.

Furthermore, the primacy of foreign policy also served to subvert the very conservative order which German governments were determined to uphold at home. Autocracies and constitutional states alike were never more vulnerable to liberal or corporate pressures than when they needed resources for foreign interventions. Hence deterrent police actions in Naples and Piedmont during the 1820s were domestically harmful in that they weakened central government against the Hungarian Diet, which it was forced to ask for extraordinary taxes and recruitment. Similarly, liberal oppositions in south Germany after 1830 increasingly used their control over the budget, which included military expenditure to meet confederal obligations, to extract concessions.[99] In 1833 the Württembergian liberals launched a ferocious parliamentary attack on confederal repressive legislation, which they regarded as a diplomatic humiliation of the kingdom and its representative assemblies. One solution for the governments was to capitulate to liberal demands to keep the size of the army down;[100] as we shall see, this was to have embarrassing consequences later. The other option was to embrace the Prussian *Zollverein*: its financial benefits helped embattled governments in the smaller states to keep the liberal opposition at arm's length; this soon resulted in *dependence* on *Zollverein* income with its implied pro-Prussian orientation.

But the most striking example of the link between external events and constitutionalization was Prussia. Here the debate had hardly changed since 1815–19, but it was nearing a temporary resolution. Many, such as Bernstorff, still argued that representative institutions would weaken the Prussian state within the international state system.[101] Others, such as Hermann von Boyen, argued the reverse with undiminished vehemence, and hoped that the military preparations of 1830 would lead to liberalization: no mobilization without loans, he reasoned, and no loans without the long-promised national representative assembly.[102] For the moment, however, the Prussian state temporized by keeping expenditure as low as possible, covering their deficits through secret loans from the Rothschilds and other banks, on the Habsburg model. Only time could show whether foreign political crises would remain an obstacle or become a precipitant for domestic political change.

### A New Society? Social and Economic Development after 1815

If you had walked across Germany in 1815 and taken the same route as in 1780, you would have been struck by some important changes. Starting in Prussia, you would have witnessed a slow transformation of rural society in progress. This had already been in full swing by the late eighteenth century, but it was very much accelerated by the agrarian reforms of Stein and Hardenberg. On the way, you might well have encountered pedantic bureaucrats demarcating the new boundaries between peasant and noble land. This was always a painful process, and you would have been as likely to meet a disconsolate smallholder who had lost the bulk of his land in compensation to the nobles as you would one of the emerging class of viable independent peasant proprietors. You would certainly have come across many more estates managed directly by the nobility, whose share of the land had actually increased. On the other hand, a rising number of those estate-owners, between 10 and 20 per cent, would have been from a bourgeois background; this was the age-old phenomenon of new wealth buying into the privileged elite. In the towns, you would have found that the old guild restrictions were being abolished. So as you moved westwards, you would have noticed that the most backward and static areas of Germany were no longer in the east, but in the north and centre: territories such as Saxony and Mecklenburg still kept the peasantry in hereditary bondage. But if you travelled even further west, you would have found an agrarian society on the threshold of modernity. Here, in the formerly French-occupied Rhineland and Palatinate, feudal dues and practices had been swept aside during the Revolutionary wars; guild restrictions had been abolished; and the introduction of French legal codes had made the decisive leap from a traditional society of orders to a modern civil society. Finally, the total population of Germany had now climbed to just over 20 million and was rising rapidly.

This was certainly a society in flux and it was to change still further by 1848. In modernization theory it was the political pretensions of this restive society which precipitated the political crises of 1830 and 1848. According to Hans-Ulrich Wehler, the decades after 1815 were a period in which 'societal evolution proved to be more powerful than the political defence of the status quo'.[103] Nevertheless, Germany before 1850 was not yet a modern industrializing country and it is therefore misleading to see a direct or necessary link between socioeconomic change and the upheavals of 1848.

German society after 1815 was still overwhelmingly rural, patriarchal and deferential. In Prussia, which included areas as diverse as Brandenburg, Silesia and the Rhineland, some 70 per cent of the population lived in the countryside; this figure had not changed much by 1850. In Austria, the proportion of rural dwellers remained more or less static at around 80 per cent. As in the eighteenth century, the agrarian sector was still the most significant branch of the economy: although the percentage was decreasing, well over half of all German investment went into agriculture long after 1848. Similarly, everyday life in the countryside was characterized by continuity as much as change. It is true that in many areas state-sponsored reforms and market-generated pressures had undermined the traditional household or *Ganzes Haus*. But elsewhere the village community remained resistant to modernization: rather than necessarily leading to 'possessive individualism', or facilitating the move from kinship to contract, the market could lead to the modification and intensification of kinship, such as when the various new functions were carried out within the family.[104] In any case, traditional relationships had always been more pragmatic and cash-oriented than romantic notions of the 'pre-modern' country- side allow. In short, German (rural) society was perhaps less backward at the beginning of the nineteenth century than was once thought, and less modern fifty years later.

Nor had German society become any less patriarchical. 'Modernization' and mental change had not challenged but merely redefined the inferiority of women. On the land, female burdens increased with the intensification of agricultural production:[105] new methods such as the stall-feeding of animals were largely the preserve of women. Hence the horizons of many German women continued to be bounded by the traditional preoccupations and pitfalls of marriage, childbirth and infanticide; some things never change, or change very slowly. In the towns, some women were able to carve out a more active role. The period after 1815 saw the emergence of female philanthropic and charitable associations; this was an emancipation of sorts, even if it only replicated their domestic 'maternal' role.[106] However, politically involved women, such as those attending the Hambach Festival in 1832, were a small minority. Indeed, in many ways 'modernization' had reduced female status and opportunities. The great wave of secu- larization around 1800 meant that women could no longer find fulfil- ment as abbesses. More generally, the rise of rationalism simply replaced the religious definition of female inequality with notions of a 'natural' order between the sexes as dictated by reason. The late eigh- teenth-century concept of the 'division of spheres' attributed beauty, emotion and passivity to women, but power, activity and rationality to men.[107] Unlike the *Ganzes Haus*, where female and child labour was common, the man was now seen as the breadwinner, whereas the care of the family by the woman was defined as a matter of 'character' rather than labour. One form of hierarchical 'harmony' had thus been replaced by another. From the point of view of female status and opportunities, there was little to choose between the gay intimacy of rural poverty and the suffocating prison of bourgeois family life.

The deferential and hierarchical nature of German society was epit- omized by the renaissance of the nobility after 1815. By the end of the eighteenth century, the German nobility had come under fire from both the public sphere, *Adelskritik*, and the reforming absolutist state.[108] Noble values and noble privilege were endangered by the rise of com- petitive examinations; the inflationary creation of new titles by the state; an influx of Polish and French émigré nobles in the 1790s; over-speculation in the artificially buoyant land market of the late eighteenth century; and, of course, the reforms of the Napoleonic period. By the second decade of the nineteenth century, however, the nobility had succeeded not merely in clawing back much of its lost influence, but in adapting its role to changing socio-economic trends.

This was most striking in Prussia east of the Elbe, where the Junkers had simply exchanged their politico-legal for a socio-economic domination of the peasantry; they now became a socio-economic *class*, rather than a privileged legal *order*. They used the emancipation ordinance of 1807 to appropriate large swathes of formerly peasant land through the state-sponsored arbitration schemes. The peasants purchased relief from hereditary bondage through the sale or exchange of land. As one wit put it, emancipation 'liberated the peasants from their land'; many of them ended up as free but landless labourers. The *overt* violence of feudal relationships was replaced by a more subtle form of socio-economic and ideological control.[109] The greatly enlarged Junker estates were now turned into booming capitalist enterprises supplying both the domestic and the growing foreign markets in Britain.[110] In some cases, this eliminated the middling peasant as a labour broker, facilitated the emergence of a class of landless labourers, and thus created paternal relationships which had not previously existed.[111] Moreover, the nobility in East Elbia, Austria and Bavaria managed to hold on to their control of patrimonial justice over the peasantry. Local government in East Elbia continued to be run by the local magistrate (*Landrat*), who was chosen by the king from the representatives of the estate-owners; Hardenberg's *Gendarmerieedikt*, which had replaced noble jurisdiction in the countryside by the state, was withdrawn after fierce Junker protests. Similarly, the Habsburg nobility continued to dominate their peasantry economically and, especially in Hungary and Galicia where serfdom still existed, socio-legally. As late as 1844, for example, peasants in rump Austrian Silesia spent up to one-third of the year working for their lord.[112]

But the resilience of the nobility extended far beyond the sphere of purely agrarian relations: almost every senior post in the army and bureaucracy of almost every German state was in the hands of the nobility. The new Prussian regional governors, *Oberpräsidenten*, were overwhelmingly from an aristocratic background. Even the new constitutional structures erected in southern Germany were weighted heavily towards the nobility. Their control of the upper chambers was complete, while they predominated in the lower houses.[113] Socially, the *Standesherren* of southern and western Germany continued to dominate the countryside: they had been mediatized but not expropriated during the great transformations around 1800. In short, in German society after 1815 land and title were as important as ever.

Another element of continuity was the continued growth of the bureaucracy. The early nineteenth century was widely experienced as a period in which the bureaucracy reached into parts of people's lives they had never reached before. In Baden, the *Beamtenedikt* of 1819 guaranteed administrators security of tenure and independence of action; and in Bavaria bureaucratic power was enshrined in the constitution of 1817.[114] Similarly, the period after 1806 in Prussia has been described as one of 'bureaucratic absolutism' in which a powerful and self-confident bureaucracy pushed the king to one side and tightened its grip on German society as a whole.[115] In the contemporary debate, both conservatives and many liberals were united in their detestation of the bureaucratic plague; to the one they were the agents of state-driven modernization, to the other they were an infuriating brake on individual freedom and initiative. If in the late eighteenth century the question had been how to protect the administration from the arbitrariness of the monarch, then in the early and mid-nineteenth century it was a matter of protecting the population from the arbitrariness and surveillance of the bureaucracy. As Robert von Mohl remarked in 1841 'It almost seems as if one half of the population were constantly preoccupied with the task of controlling the other half.'[116]

But it would be wrong to see Germany simply as a society of snooping and ubiquitous civil servants. It is true that the bureaucracy remained a largely closed and self-recruiting elite throughout the period. It is also true that because of the long unpaid apprenticeships in the bureaucracy, access was effectively denied to all those without private means. However, in Prussia the salaried bureaucracy numbered only about 7000 out of a total population of 17 million; this figure was under constant review as the state tried to limit expenditure. Even if one included the 4000-odd unpaid apprentices there was still less than one bureaucrat per one hundred of population. The figure for south Germany is at least three times higher: over-bureaucratization was more of a liberal-constitutional than a conservative problem. Indeed, it was the relatively *small* size of the Prussian bureaucracy, and its failure to provide an outlet for the waves of educated men leaving the universities, which constituted the main bone of contention between the civil service and society at large; this has been described as an 'excess of educated men'.[117] Besides, it was to the state bureaucracy that the destitute and the poor looked for redress. In short, to adapt Friedrich Dahlmann's famous phrase, the Prussian state was a magic spear that healed as much as it wounded: for every oppressed citizen bemoaning bureaucratic probes, there was another pleading for more state intervention and employment.

One of the main forces of change in this still essentially traditional agrarian society was industrialization. By the 1840s, Prussia had emerged as the powerhouse of German economic development; her only rival, in relative terms, was Saxony. Silesia, the Prussian Rhine province and Berlin-Brandenburg became centres of coal extraction and iron production. Between 1815 and 1850, for example, coal output in Upper Silesia increased almost tenfold.[118] The 1820s saw the first steam engines in Berlin; in 1838 the first Prussian railway linked the capital to Potsdam; and by the late 1840s hundreds of thousands of workers were employed in the construction of railroads.

South Germany, by contrast, was relatively underdeveloped. She had actually taken the lead in 1835 with a line linking Nuremberg and Fürth, but the bulk of the railroads laid down before 1850 were in the north, west and (south-)east. With some exceptions, South German industry before 1850, despite the *Zollverein*, remained far behind developments in Prussia and Saxony, possibly because restrictive practices inhibited entrepreneurial talent. But by far the most backward part of Germany was Austria. In 1828 she had led the way in railway construction, with a line between Linz and Budweis. However, this proved to be a false start, and by mid-century Austria enjoyed no more than a few fragmented lines linking the major cities. And with the significant exception of Bohemia and some pockets in the hereditary provinces, the Habsburg lands were economically entirely pre-modern. As one Austrian observer, Albert Kotelmann, observed just after 1850, Austria compared unfavourably with *Zollverein* Germany in almost every respect. Their products tended to be cheaper and qualitatively superior, wages and purchasing powers were higher, interest rates were lower; their industries were more often manufacturing rather than traditional and craft-based.[119] Metternich, in particular, felt this inferiority keenly. As he remarked to Kübeck in 1841: 'I have just been to Germany in the midst of the industrial developments there; I have observed the forces which are stirring everywhere and the tendencies which they follow, and it has induced in me an acute feeling of inferiority.'[120]

Far more so than her Austrian and South German rivals, the Prussian state made conscious efforts to encourage economic development. It supported foreign travel for the acquisition of foreign expertise; it sought to attract specialists from abroad; it bought machinery; it organized trade fairs; it suppressed the guilds; and, by the tariff law of 1818, it lifted all restrictions on internal and external trade.[121] Above all, the Prussian bureaucracy insisted on free movement within the borders of the monarchy. This human mobility was later to be an important factor in German industrialization.

Paradoxically, however, there is no evidence that state intervention substantially promoted economic growth. It is true that the guild restrictions were lifted, but the greatest growth took place in those branches of manufacture such as textiles, where there had never been any significant restrictions. Besides, guilds were not abolished in thriving Saxony until much later in the century, without this causing obvious damage to her economic development.[122] Nor did government undertake important infrastructural development: until it woke up to their military potential in the 1840s, the state was slow to encourage railways, not least because vast sums had just been invested in roads; here the good was the enemy of the best.

The relationship between economic development and the various Prussian tariff initiatives is equally tenuous. It is certainly debatable whether the law of 1818, which exposed domestic producers to the 'dumping' of cheap mass-produced foreign goods, especially from Britain, helped Prussian manufacturers. Moreover, the *Zollverein* of 1834 was initially of more fiscal than economic significance: the intent had been to maximize tax revenue and release governments from total dependence on representative assemblies or, as in Prussia, to enable them to circumvent the *Staatsschuldengesetz*; the promotion of economic growth, let alone national unity, had been a secondary consideration.[123] Results matched expectations: *economic* growth during the first phase of the *Zollverein's* operation was negligible, but the *fiscal* gains – the reduction of collection costs by a factor of four – were massive.[124] One should not strip the *Zollverein* of nationalist myth only to reinvest it with modernizing pathos. Markets and technology rather than state intervention seem to have been the decisive force behind German industrialization.

In any case, before 1850 Germany was not yet an industrialized or even an industrializing society. In relative terms, most economic growth during this period took place in traditional industries such as textiles, or in agriculture, where productivity was increasing rapidly. There were, of course, significant pockets of industrialization in Saxony, the Rhineland and Silesia; and it is true that important *qualitative* leaps, especially in railways, had been effected during the 1840s.[125] But the real period of 'take-off' in any *quantitative* sense was definitely *after* 1850.[126] All the decisive statistics indicate a surge during the 1850s. For example, if in 1844/6 the transport price per kilometre tonne on railroads had been 13.5 Pfennigs, it was only half that (7.5) by 1854/5; if 27.1 million kilometre tonnes of goods had been moved in 1844/6, it was 643.7 by 1854/6.[127] It was only in the second half of the century that the improvements in transport and communications necessary to power market integration took place. A quick international comparison bears this out. In the period before 1850 the German economy consumed only one-tenth of the British consumption of pig-iron and even less of coal and woollen yarn. Admittedly, these are aggregate figures, which do not take regional factors into account.[128] But then the British figures are also aggregate: they cover Manchester and North Wales, just as the German figures include the Rhineland and rural Bavaria. The significance of the overall figures remains the same: Britain was already an industrialized country and Germany nowhere near one.

Similarly, there was no industrial proletariat yet worth speaking of, though in relative terms a considerable increase took place between 1815 and the 1840s. The absolute number of those employed in traditional 'putting-out' manufactories, or as day-labourers, far exceeded those in recognizably modern factory-style working conditions.[129] In progressive Prussia, for example, there were just over half a million factory workers, whereas there was nearly twice that number of artisans;[130] in other parts of Germany, the disparity was even greater. Nor did the proletariat make up in organization and consciousness for what they lacked in numbers. Admittedly, there were some rudimentary forms of worker self-help: mutual support groups, secret societies and educational associations. But throughout the whole period leading up to 1848, Berlin witnessed only one solitary strike.[131] In short, to adapt Marx's own terminology, the proletariat before 1850 was hardly even a class 'as such', let alone 'class-conscious'.

 In fact, the most dynamic force in German society after 1815 was not socio-economic but demographic. Between 1740 and 1840 the population of Germany almost doubled; and the rate of increase after about 1810 was even greater.[132] If one takes into account regional differentiation, then the picture is even more striking, with areas such as

Saxony and Prussia almost doubling their population in the thirty years after 1815 alone; the southern states enjoyed a much more measured growth. In the long term, this increase was to have significantly beneficial consequences for German economic development. In the short term, however, it led to the phenomenon of rural deprivation known as 'pauperization'. Some stress its localized and temporary nature; others argue that there was merely a greater consciousness of poverty, rather than more of it. Most probably pauperization was the result of relative overpopulation: the existing agrarian economy was as yet unable to accommodate the huge surge in population, especially during periodic bad harvests; it was certainly not a consequence of early industrialization. A new kind of poverty had thus emerged: it was mass, not individual, permanent, not seasonal.[133] But despite considerable population growth, the level of urbanization – a standard index of modernization – throughout Germany remained relatively low; a steady increase was registered in western towns, while those in the east, apart from Berlin, tended to stagnate. There was certainly nothing like the exponential urban expansion that was to take place in the second half of the century.

Pauperization and poverty in general put the authorities under considerable strain. Often, the legacy of French rule and the effect of modernizing reforms proved to the disadvantage of the poor. In Cologne, for example, the French had secularized church assets devoted to poor relief; their Prussian successors had even criminalized begging. In the East Elbian provinces, on the other hand, the traditional welfarist 'grain policy' had been abandoned during the reform period: no longer could the urban lower orders rely on the state to buy up grain in times of plenty for distribution in times of need.[134] A striking illustration of the collapse of the old *Wohlfahrtspolitik* was York von Wartenburg's recommendation 'to let some fifty to sixty thousand starve to death, for no other help is possible here; then the rest will have employment'.[135] German bureaucracies reacted to the wave of pauperized migrants in two ways. In Prussia, the state stuck to the principle of relatively free movement within the monarchy;[136] it even forced cities to pay poor relief to residents of more than three years' standing, regardless of their place of birth. In most other German states, by contrast, bureaucracies and especially city governments frantically sought to stem the flow of migrants, even within their own area of sovereignty. The result was a series of restrictive citizenship laws, which served the twin purpose of regulating immigration and combating pan-German nationalism. Even the Prussian law of 1842 – six years after the *Zollverein* – defined the *Prussian* not the German citizen; this essentially pre-modern and pre-democratic concept implied no associated set of participatory rights or civic attitudes.[137] But it was in the smaller states that the preoccupation with migration, citizenship and sovereignty was greatest.[138] 'Foreigners' – that is, all persons, including Germans, not possessing state citizenship – were subject to various forms of discrimination, such as legal inferiority, higher taxes, and marriage restrictions; even in a minor territory like Hesse-Darmstadt the yearly numbers of deportees in violation of migration laws ran into thousands. The bureaucratic xenophobia which still inhabits German society today has its origins not so much in German nationalism as in small-state particularism.

Restricting immigration was one approach to the problem of pauperization, emigration was another. Sometimes, German states resorted to traditional eighteenth-century practices by dumping paupers on unsuspecting neighbours; this led to demands for confederal regulations against it. But far more important was the relaxation of long-standing restrictions on *emigration*, which had characterized the old *Peuplierungspolitik* of enlightened reform absolutism. Until the 1840s emigration to the New World ran at about 20 000 a year, most of them from southern Germany.[139] Motivations were varied, and included frustrated personal ambition and religious intolerance or political persecution at home, but economic reasons, such as unemployment and inheritance subdivision, were also important. Emigration certainly helped to defuse the problem of pauperization and it was sometimes actively encouraged by government, especially when it facilitated a Cuban-style clear-out of criminals, the destitute and the insane.

At the same time, however, many conservatives and bureaucrats began to address themselves to the growing 'social question' as a problem in its own right. Some figures, such as the Prussian Radowitz, began to demand active state intervention against poverty. 'The state,' he argued, 'will have to face up to its social mission, or be toppled by it.'[140] Indeed, he saw in the rising proletariat a possible ally of the state against the aspirant bourgeoisie: here Radowitz was a proto-Bismarckian. For the time being, however, nothing was to come of this gambit. Rather, as we shall see, Radowitz increasingly came to view the middle classes as an ally in the 'German Question'; as ever, the primacy of foreign policy overrode domestic considerations.

For next to the great demographic surge, the most dynamic force in early nineteenth-century German society was the growth of urban 'bourgeois' society, which was beginning to replace the traditional, largely rural, society of orders. The constitutive force in the development of this bourgeois society in Germany after 1815 was not economic change; this still lay ahead. Rather, the main factor was education, more especially the huge increase in university graduates and the unusually high level of popular literacy: about 80 per cent by mid-century.[141] But what was distinctive about the *Bildungsbürgertum* – the educated bourgeoisie – was not so much education *per se* but the value they placed on educational achievements and qualifications. This set them apart from the nobility and their emphasis on the privilege of birth. Around 1815 they would virtually all have been in some form of state employment as administrators, clergymen and teachers; but by mid-century they were being joined by the 'free' professions, such as lawyers and doctors.[142] Another rising group were the *Wirtschaftsbürger*, the economic middle class engaged in trade or manufacturing. But the numbers involved were still small, probably not more than about a thousand families by 1850. In any case, they were not yet industrial capitalists on the contemporary English model. Rather, the *Wirtschaftsbürger* tended to be bankers or entrepreneurs in traditionally organized industries such as clothing. Both the educational and the economic bourgeoisie were self-consciously middle-class: they cherished specifically bourgeois values such as thrift, domesticity, education and self-improvement. They were thus much less likely to ape the manners of or try to join the ranks of the nobility. Thanks to the wave of government-sponsored (partial) constitutionalization and modernization, these bourgeois liberals enjoyed a wide range of representative fora – state assemblies, city governments, chambers of commerce and so on – to articulate their interests. The classic case here was Baden, where bourgeois delegates comprised about two-fifths of the 1831 *Landtag* and the aristocracy was in retreat throughout the state administration.[143]

Liberalism and the bourgeoisie were not coterminous. Many prominent liberals, such as Hans von Gagern and Theodor von Schön, were noblemen. Indeed, one of the centres of liberalism before 1848 was Junker-dominated eastern Prussia. Nevertheless, the rank and file of the liberal movement came from the mainly Protestant middle classes, especially in the precocious Prussian Rhine province. Here political leadership was increasingly being provided by notables from the world of finance and business such as David Hansemann and Ludolf

Camphausen. Moreover, the anti-governmental animus was fuelled by the pressure-head of resentment building up among unemployed graduates. There were now many more of them competing for a shrinking number of posts in the bureaucracy. This academic proletariat was almost entirely middle-class, not least because noble senior bureaucrats ensured that applicants from the bourgeoisie were the last to be hired and the first to be fired.

The distinction between nobles and bourgeoisie was not always rigid. Many nobles were themselves only recently elevated bourgeois bureaucrats. In Prussia, for example, there was a fivefold increase in ennoblements after the death of Frederick the Great; at least one-third of them were administrators. Conversely, not all aristocrats were *rentiers*: in Bohemia and Silesia they were often at the forefront of industrial development.[144] Many of them were also members of the various bourgeois associations. Moreover, marriages between old status and new money were not uncommon. Nevertheless, there was no real symbiosis between aristocrat and bourgeois: by and large the two groups inhabited separate spheres.[145]

Yet liberalism did not simply reflect the economic interests of the bourgeoisie: it was not the party of modernization *tout court*. Liberals were not necessarily spokesmen for the economically dynamic elements of society. Admittedly, most liberals were determined to dismantle anachronistic guild and other restrictions on individual enterprise. But some liberals, far from being permanently in the vanguard of events, were actually deeply ambiguous about the socio-economic developments taking place around them.[146] In Baden and Württemberg, liberals, fearful for their vulnerable manufactories, were among the bitterest opponents of the *Zollverein*. Even urbanization – that hallmark of modernity – divided liberals. Some, such as Heinrich von Gagern, were all in favour of urbanization; others such as Robert von Mohl, the classic southern German liberal, were implacably opposed. There were even liberals who supported restrictions on movement to prevent their little home-town sanctuaries from being swamped.[147] Indeed, many liberals looked to a strong state to protect them against social disorder.[148] As the Prussian statesman, Josef Maria von Radowitz, famously remarked shortly after the 1830 Revolution: 'The middle class is only interested in the political part of the revolution, [for] the social part of it would militate against them . . . while a common front may be necessary in the struggle against the old order, there is an instant parting of the ways whenever social questions are addressed.'

Nevertheless, liberalism was not just a party of (middle-)class inter-est. At a local level the emphasis was on politics, usually resistance to state-sponsored centralization, rather than socio-economic issues.[149] It could be as inclusive of the lower classes as the old 'home-town' men-tality was exclusive, not least because greater political participation was one of the few strategies which would unite oppositional elements from various socio-economic backgrounds. Indeed, most liberals were not so much concerned to defend class barriers as to transcend them: they sought a classless commercial society of equal citizens rather than an industrial stratified society of classes. The key to this transformation was not the redistribution of wealth, but education: the mass of the people, the *Volk*, would be elevated into bourgeois society through *Bildung*. Of course, these liberals were attached to an abstract ideal of the 'people', not its superstitious, brutal and ignorant reality; they wanted to dissolve the existing *Volk* and educate a new one.

Liberals believed their ultimate victory to be inevitable. As David Hansemann argued with breathtaking self-confidence in 1830, the state could 'delay emancipation awhile through prevarication . . . but in the meantime bourgeois society continues its natural development, its spirit is only suppressed in the external sense, and suddenly it will burst forth again, more strongly than ever.'[150] But this self-confidence could act as a political restraint: rather like pre-1914 German Social Democracy, the doctrine of inevitable victory could induce liberal passivity – *Attentismus* – and a policy of cooperation rather than confrontation with government.

Indeed, the most subversive impulses after 1815 came not from the rising bourgeois classes, but from the declining and frantically insecure artisan class. Overall, artisans made up between about 15 and 20 per cent of the German population during the period 1815–48; this pro-portion was slightly higher in urban areas. The balance of the urban population, about three-quarters to two-thirds, was made up of the propertyless poor. But it was the artisans who were the most activist element: it was they who were most at risk from the macro-economic situation – the decline of trades and the rise of manufactures. It was they who found themselves most threatened by the modernizing ambi-tions of the bureaucracy. In Prussia, where guild restrictions had been lifted in 1810, they sought to turn the clock back; elsewhere in Germany, especially in the south, in Saxony and in Posen, they tena-ciously defended the *status quo*. Further conflict with the authorities – and in this the artisans made common cause with the patriciate –

resulted from the insistence of the Prussian bureaucracy on free movement within the kingdom. This violated all traditions of urban autonomy, permitted the influx of skilled workers at the expense of local
craftsmen and put an intolerable burden on the system of poor relief.
But the greatest rate of increase of artisans was in rural areas, the
result of Prussian deregulation during the reform period: the countryside remained the most dynamic and stable area of society.

It is therefore no surprise to find the artisans in the vanguard of revolutionary movements of the 1830s and 1840s. It was machine-break-
ing and sectarian artisans, rather than bourgeois liberals, who brought
down Saxon absolutism in the revolution of 1830. This did not reverse
the spread of factory-based manufactures which eventually destroyed
their livelihoods, but it did force government into modernizing concessions such as agrarian and constitutional reform. An anti-modern
protest thus had a modernizing outcome – yet another example of the
ambiguity of modernity. Similarly, the hard-pressed Silesian weavers,
underpriced by cheap British imports, abandoned by grain-exporting
Junkers, and unsupported by an ideologically hostile state, broke into
open revolt in 1844; this was but a foretaste of what was to convulse
the whole kingdom, and indeed most of Germany, four years later.[151]

It would be tempting to see Prussian economic success and Austrian
backwardness as the triumph of partial modernization during the
reform period, when the state had ruthlessly pressed ahead with socio-
economic changes, while stalling on the political constitutional front. It
would be equally tempting to believe that the Prussian bureaucracy
thereby created the very capitalist industrialist bourgeoisie and impoverished alienated proletariat whose political aspirations brought down
the state in 1848. *Prima facie* there is a strong case for this. Austria was
much less advanced than Prussia in almost every respect: economically,
in terms of associational culture, a public sphere, and even in the
development of political Catholicism.[152] In fact, the link between state
action and socio-economic change was complex and attenuated. As we
have seen, the creation of an industrial society had begun after 1815,
but it was still very much in its infancy, even in Prussia, in 1850; and it
is doubtful whether state-sponsored modernization was in any sense
decisive, given the high levels of industrial growth in states such as
Saxony where many of the pre-modern socio-economic structures,
such as the guilds, were still place until the 1860s.

Conversely, the link between socio-economic change and political development was far from straightforward. There was certainly no automatic connection between economic and political liberalism. Free-trading Baden rigorously enforced the repressive Karlsbad Decrees while protectionist Bavaria attempted to evade them. With the exception of Saxony, Prussia was socio-economically the most advanced German state, yet political modernization – constitutionalization – had made the greatest strides in southern Germany. However, while the politics of the Prussian state were conservative and in contradiction to the participatory aspirations of the population, the socio-economic policy of the state was liberal, in contradiction to most sections of society, who favoured some sort of socio-economic conservatism, be it the traditional Hohenzollern grain policy, protectionist tariffs, the restoration of the guilds or some other measure. Throughout Germany, indeed, the struggle for greater political participation was often intended to reverse or modify socio-economic modernization. By the late 1840s there were unmistakable signs that widespread material deprivation was on the verge of mutating into political upheaval: mounting artisanal distress; and in 1845–7 a series of bad harvests which produced the last great agrarian subsistence crisis *de type ancien* in Germany. In socio-political terms, the dying convulsions of the old society were to prove as dangerous to the established order as the birth pangs of the new.

To sum up: German society between 1815 and 1848 was still over-whelmingly rural and traditional. Apart from an impressively high rate of literacy, it had yet to acquire most of the distinguishing characteristics of socio-economic modernization: an industrial proletariat, industrialization and urbanization. Major social changes followed rather than predated, or even caused, the political shock of 1848. There was thus no striking disparity between German socio-economic and political development, since the German economy did not 'take off' before 1850. On the other hand, it is indisputable that the period saw the gradual emergence of a distinctive 'bourgeois' society. For the time being, however, its political role was confined to the fiscal gridlock which characterized relations between most German state governments and their representative assemblies in the 1830s and 1840s. Their challenge to the old régime in 1847–8 was to be not socio-political but fiscal and foreign-political.

So if you had taken that same walk from east to west again in 1847, you would have encountered a society which was in most respects similar to that of 1815, a society certainly on the verge of, but not yet undergoing the transformation to a modern class society. You would have seen that the vast majority of the population still lived on the land and that the main sphere of economic activity was still agriculture. You could not but have agreed with Friedrich Engels, who wrote in that same year that 'the countryside dominates the towns, agriculture dominates trade and industry'.[153] You would have lamented that at least every third German you encountered along the way was still subject to the patrimonial justice of his noble lord. You would have been three times more likely to meet a bureaucrat in the west, but you would have found his attentions equally irksome on both sides of the Elbe. To this extent, the new society looked remarkably like the old.

But on your way you would also have noticed unmistakable signs that a period of incubation was taking place, after which, to mix metaphors, the shell of the old society of orders was to be shattered for ever. You would have been struck by the dramatic increase in the numbers of peasants and landless labourers in the fields. At the same time, you would have been aware of the problem of pauperization: the swarm of destitute vagrants on the move in search of bread and employment. But the picture would have been far from one of unrelieved misery: moving west you would have come across healthy medium-sized farms in Saxony; on your last visit in 1815 they would still have been under the total control of their noble lords. You would also have noticed the relatively high level of industrialization. As you continued on your way, you would soon have realized that your progress was much quicker than before, either because you were using one of the many new roads constructed by the Prussian government after 1815 or because you had decided to use one of the few railroads already in operation. And if you were a particularly keen observer, you would already have been able to make out a distinctive portent of the new age: one of the first telegraph poles erected that very year. But you would most probably not have thought that this was an aggressive new society on the eve of bringing its political system into line with its changed socio-economic organization.

# 5

## THE STATE VERSUS THE NATION, 1839–50

### The Breakthrough of the Nation and the Crisis of the State, 1839–46

The revolutionary decade opened with an unexpected drama. In far-off Syria, the ambitions of the French puppet Mehmet Ali prompted Russian, British, Austrian and, nominally, Prussian intervention on behalf of the tottering Ottoman Empire. In order to 'compensate' herself for this humiliation, France then sought to revise the borders of the Vienna settlement at Germany's expense by annexing the left bank of the Rhine.[1] The resulting 'Rhine Crisis' of 1840 was perhaps the most striking instance of the primacy of foreign policy in German history: the flapping of diplomatic wings in the remote Levant caused a storm in Central Europe which was to shake the edifice of the German restoration to its very foundations.

To those who remembered the crisis of 1830–1, there was a certain sense of *déjà vu* about the reaction of official Germany. The comatose *Bund* meekly requested an explanation for French armaments, and professed itself satisfied with the manifestly unsatisfactory reassurances received. Eager both to deter France and forestall great-power tutelage, the South German states amalgamated their forces under the Convention of Karlsruhe, only to fall out almost at once over the question of the supreme command. In any case, not even the Bavarians were optimistic enough to believe that the Third Germany could stop France from crossing the virtually undefended Rhine between Basel and Landau, and very soon they appealed to Prussia for assistance.[2]

They certainly received none from Metternich, whose main concern was to avoid provoking France. His meeting with Frederick William IV took place at historic Pillnitz in Saxony, the same castle where the Austrians and Prussians had published their noisy but meaningless broadside against the French Revolution almost half a century earlier. But unlike Pillnitz (1791), and like Carlsbad ten years before, the Austrians did not subsequently intervene. Instead, they patiently waited for the war fever in Paris to subside. Only Prussia, once again, showed any signs of military preparedness to defend the settlement of 1815 in the west.

What nobody had expected was the popular response: an unprecedented surge of national feeling among Germans, especially in the south and west, who faced being subjected to their second French occupation in a lifetime. In their quest to establish the German identity of the Rhine, patriotic songsters and versifiers went into rhetorical overdrive. The most famous of these new nationalist hymns was Niklas Becker's 'Sie sollen ihn nicht haben, den freien deutschen Rhein'-'They shall not have it, the free German Rhine', which became a bourgeois nationalist anthem, or 'Colognaise'; it was set to music 200 times.[3] So for each predatory rendition of the *Marseillaise* by French revisionist mobs, there was a band of injured German patriots ready to strike up their tunes in response; another of these tunes was Max Schneckenburger's, 'Die Wacht am Rhein.' For the Rhine Crisis was not primarily the result of two mutually escalating and equally culpable nationalisms: such a view does considerable violence both to the contemporary perceptions of patriotic Germans and to the actual sequence of events. In the crisis of 1840 there was an aggressor and a victim. The clear aggressor was an expansionist France bent on reversing the stipulations of the Vienna settlement; the indisputable victims were the threatened Germans of the Rhineland and the Palatinate.

War did not, in the end, break out.[4] But when all the dust had settled, the German political scene had been utterly transformed. For the Rhine Crisis accelerated the emergence of a liberal bourgeois nationalist public sphere in Germany generally, and most significantly in Prussia. The immediate origins of this public sphere lay in a series of programmatic statements by David Hansemann, J. G. Wirth and other liberals during the 1830s, which gained wider currency in the years after 1840. For even more so than the revolutions of 1830, the shock of the Rhine Crisis gave a powerful impulse to geopolitical thinking among liberal nationalists. In 1840, their sense of encirclement was summed up by Hansemann as follows:

> The [German] empire must be mighty and strong if it is to uphold Prussian and German independence; for we have dangerous neighbours in east and west. [In the east] the most consistently expansionist state since Roman times [tsarist Russia], which has already taken up a threatening position in the heart of Prussia [i.e. in Poland] and has naturally staked its claim to the possession of the land between this position and the Baltic [i.e. East Prussia] . . . Here in the west there is a state which is dangerous because of its internal cohesion, the warlike and excitable character of its inhabitants and because of their tenacious and unhappy belief in the need to control the Rhine border sooner or later.[5]

This liberal geopolitics bore a striking resemblance to the sober analyses of German – and especially Prussian – cabinets down the ages. Hansemann's stress on the importance of the missing Polish buffer was a staple of Prussian debates after 1795;[6] and his stress on Germany's vulnerability to France was no different from that of statesmen throughout the Confederation. Indeed, during the Rhine Crisis itself Metternich accused France of regarding Germany as an

> arena . . . for merciful blows and the purse for forced exactions . . . [indeed] it might seem as if Germany regarded itself as a body without a soul or a body, as a field, which belongs to the first person to take possession of it, and which only carries the name of a political body without having its dignity.[7]

All of these sentiments might equally have been expressed by a liberal nationalist.

Where Metternich and the liberal national public sphere differed was not in the diagnosis, but in the cure. Whereas Metternich saw the salvation of Germany in a loose, conservative federation of conservative princes, liberal nationalists were openly scornful of the *Bund*. As far as they were concerned – and the Rhine Crisis seemed to bear them out – diversity meant weakness. For when bibulous German nationalists gathered on picturesque mountain crags overlooking the Rhine to sing 'They shall not have it, the free German Rhine,' there was one crucial verse they left out. This ran: 'But by jingo if they try, we have the men, we have the guns, we have the money too.' Indeed, they *could* not sing this verse, because it would not have been true. For what the French threat of 1840 cruelly exposed was the hopeless inadequacy of the security arrangements on the western border. Between them, the front-line southern German states of Württemberg, Baden and Bavaria could muster only a fraction of the forces needed against France; the Austrians, cursed with a cantankerous Hungarian Diet and crippled with a massive debt, were in no position to act. This paralysis extended to the *Bund* as a whole: for while the Confederation had provided a framework for political coexistence in Germany for the past thirty years, it proved quite unable in 1840 to provide the external protection stipulated by the constitution. In this respect the Confederation faced and failed the same challenge that had brought down the old *Reich* some forty years earlier.

The effect of this was to focus the wrath of the liberal nationalist public sphere yet further on the *Bund* in general and Metternich in particular. High on the list of the historical charge-sheet against the old *Reich* had been its failure to defend ancient German territories, such as Alsace and subsequently the Rhineland, from alienation. During the Revolutionary and Napoleonic period, the nationalist indictment ran, the *Reich* had failed to transcend its universal values to protect specifically German national interests against the pretensions of France. In this respect, Gustav Jahn noted, the French Revolution had preached 'a penitential sermon to the German people'. After 1815 nationalism drew much of its strength from the sincere if erroneous belief that the exertions of the nation, rather than the princes, had freed Germany from Napoleon. Now these same German nationalists were not impressed by the parsimonious dithering of the south German princes, whose concern for the implications of confederal military measures for their own sovereignty seemed far to outweigh fear of French aggression. Nor were they impressed by the feeble Austrian performance, which was the more shameful because of her chairmanship of the Confederation. However, they *were* impressed by the Prussian response. Unlike the rest of the German states, or the Confederation as a whole, Prussia had moved with relative alacrity to put the western fortresses in order and to set the state on a war footing. Within a very short time nearly 200 000 Prussians were under arms and facing westwards.

The long-term effects of the Rhine Crisis were complex and in many ways paradoxical. First of all, it accelerated the decline of Habsburg influence in Germany. Thanks to her changed geopolitical orientation after the Vienna settlement, Austria was no longer perceived as the guardian of the gate in the west. Yet Austria was not merely unwilling, but also *unable* to champion German interests on the Rhine. The complex political economy of the empire was not equal to the task of sustaining the diverse strategic commitments entered into at Vienna. Austria's military budget was not disproportionate in relation to her population; in fact, Prussian expenditure was significantly higher in percentage terms. The problem was that Austrian military expenditure was 'too high' in relation to her fiscal-political structure: the survival of regional and social privileges frustrated both increased taxation and the introduction of military reforms on Prussian lines.[8] This was the same problem which Joseph II had unsuccessfully tried to address. In the 1840s, many Austrian statesmen – among them the finance minister, Kübeck – redoubled their calls for custom reforms and tax reforms to put finances on a sounder footing. Still fearful of a repeat of the Josephine trauma, Metternich refused to challenge the Hungarians: he believed that any fiscal gains on the swings would be lost on the roundabout of the resulting political unrest. The result was a fiscal-political deadlock which forced the Austrian military to resort to a series of expedients leading to the fiasco of 1840: retiring officers on half pay, demobilization and short-term savings on equipment. Not for the first or last time, Hungarian obstruction had decisively influenced the struggle for mastery in Germany.

Secondly, the Rhine Crisis exploded long-standing particularist pieties in southern Germany. The ill-fated Convention of Karlsruhe proved to be the last gasp of the Third Germany, and the long Francophile tradition in Bavarian foreign policy now came to a definitive end.[9] For the second time within a decade, western and southern Germany had been threatened with invasion, and for the second time in a decade only Prussia had proved able to defend the territorial integrity of the Confederation. The writing was thus on the wall: even if the smaller German states still stubbornly refused total military subordination to Prussia,[10] they were now forced to concede that an independent military deterrent against France was unrealistic.[11] This started a process of convergence which was not even complete by 1866, still less 1850. Nevertheless, from now on, for each step back towards a particularist past, the southern German states took two steps forward into the Prussian future.

Above all, the Rhine Crisis subverted the attempts of the Third Germany to construct alternative regional or dynastic national identities. Even if cultural, religious and historic considerations dictated reserve, the emerging liberal nationalist public sphere increasingly recognized, as the princes did, that Prussia alone could guarantee the political integrity of Germany against external threats. As one deputy of the Württembergian *Landtag* conceded, it was only the Prussian military system which had saved the day in 1840.[12] This was a remarkable view for any South German liberal to take, but one which was to gain increasing currency.

Thirdly, the Rhine Crisis restarted the halting process of *rapprochement* between the Prussian state and the German national movement. The first alliance had been during the wars of liberation; that proved to be a false dawn, as indeed the hopes of the 1840s were to be cruelly dashed. The basis for this *rapprochement* was neither naivety nor sentimentality but a geopolitically informed sense of liberal national interests. It was recognized that the revolution of 1815 had turned Prussia into the guardian of the gate in the west. As David Hansemann had already pointed out in his programmatic memorandum of 1830: 'Prussia has not been given large territories to suffer amputations . . . but in order to guard Germany's borders the more safely.'[13] 'But it is Prussia's sublime destiny,' Hansemann continued, 'to be the leader of Germany and secure her power and welfare and to unite Germany with strong ties in a Prussian-led union. Austria, which rules mostly over non-Germanic peoples, has no such destiny.'[14] Indeed, as Hansemann repeated in 1840, a policy of German unity was in Prussia's own geopolitical interest: 'Located as we are between two powers which endanger our security, Prussia's policy seems to us to be dictated by circumstances.'[15] If Prussia could unite Germany, Hansemann claimed, 'then Prussia would no longer be the cockpit [*Tummelplatz*] of all major European wars'.[16] Similar views were expressed by South German liberals.[17] In arguing geopolitically, liberals the length and breadth of Germany joined a venerable German school of thought stretching from Metternich back through Leibniz to the Great Elector of Brandenburg.

This focus on Prussia may have been opportunistic; it was by no means sentimental. Liberals saw clearly that the only way forward was to harness the German national cause to Prussian state interest. 'Hopes for Germany's future,' Heinrich von Gagern observed in 1845, 'depend on Prussian ambition (*daß sich Preußen nicht selbst genügen könne*).'[18] Or, as Karl Biedermann, Professor of Philosophy at Leipzig, put it in 1842, the *Zollverein*, 'mapped out the path for the reconciliation of Prussia's interests with those of the rest of Germany, without involving the sacrifice of either'.[19] Moreover, in the Prussian-dominated *Zollverein* German liberals saw a vehicle not only for the achievement of national unity and security but also for the defence of their economic interests.[20] As one observer put it in 1842, the desire for national unity 'now still expresses itself largely in material relationships; industry and trade serve as its vehicle'.[21]

If the events of 1840 boosted Prussian prestige among German nationalists, they also exponentially increased the liberalizing pressures on the Prussian state. For the hard-headed primacy of foreign policy espoused by the liberal nationalist public sphere tended to subvert rather than reinforce the established order. Prussian foreign policy was now expected to serve the national interest; often this clashed with, rather than bolstered, official views of *raison d'état*. If liberal nationalists and the Prussian state found common ground against France, they were far apart on the question of Russia. Liberals were implacably opposed to the tsar, partly because of a series of acrimonious trade disputes which erupted in the 1840s, but mainly because they perceived Russia to be both ideologically and geopolitically threatening to the national interest.[22] By mid-decade, the Russophobes were firmly in the ascendant over the Francophobes.

One by-product of this was the rift over Poland. In part, liberal enthusiasm for the resurrection of an independent Poland was ideologically and sentimentally based; the rash of pro-Polish and pro-Greek associations across Germany testified to the romantic appeal of these causes. But among prominent liberals considerations of *Realpolitik* were dominant. They believed that an independent Poland was an indispensable buffer between liberal Germany and reactionary aggressive tsarist Russia to the east. As liberal hostility sharpened after 1840, Heinrich von Gagern's astute observations acquired a new urgency:

> Poland's independence is a consequence of Germany's independence; both aims cannot be achieved separately. Prussia's dominance in Germany and a breach with Russia are correlates. A united Germany needs a strong Poland and a strong Sweden between itself and Russia . . . A united Germany can give the Poles the Grand Duchy of Posen and united in the east we will be able to come to an arrangement with France about the 'natural borders' unaided.[23]

Not for the last time in German history, liberal opinion was prepared to trade the welfare of their co-nationals in the east for diplomatic gain.

Official Prussia saw it differently, not primarily because of any sentimental attachment to *Deutschtum* in the east – which was still something of a liberal preserve – but because the Prussian state was traditionally friendly or at least respectful towards Russia. After all, it was Russia which had saved the monarchy from total extinction in 1807; conversely, it was Russia which had nearly snuffed out a stricken Prussia in 1759, and left Frederick the Great with nightmares ever after.

Poland and Russia were serious liberal preoccupations, but they were soon to be overshadowed by the emergence of the Schleswig-Holstein question. Of the two duchies one – Holstein – was a member of the *Bund*, the other – Schleswig – was not; Holstein was overwhelmingly German, whereas Schleswig contained a sizeable Danish population. Both territories were ruled by the childless Christian VIII of Denmark, whose death was expected to trigger a succession dispute. At the same time the Danish government began a policy of late absolutist centralization and Danification in the duchies in 1840. All this provided German patriots with a heaven-sent liberal nationalist platform against an alien neo-absolutist prince. By mid-decade Schleswig-Holstein had replaced the Rhine as the focus of liberal nationalist concern, culminating in the Schleswig-Holstein choral rally (*Sängerfest*) of 1844, a kind of Hambach in the dunes, attended by some 12 000 revellers from all over Germany.

There was another sphere, a related one, in which the aftershock of 1840 was to resonate with considerable effect: that of the political economy of Prussia. For while the Prussian response to the French threat had been by far the most formidable, the enormous financial cost involved cast doubt on the ability of the monarchy to wage a conflict of any length. It was now that the implications of the *Staatsschuldengesetz* of 1820 made themselves felt. By its terms, the monarchy had committed itself not to raise any fresh loans without first securing the approval of a representative assembly. During the period of comparative international security between 1815 and 1829 and 1831 to 1840, the government had coped by keeping military expenditure as low as possible, although it still stood at a staggering 40 per cent of total budget; this was done largely by calling up a fraction of those liable for military service. But in the light of the Rhine Crisis, such stratagems no longer seemed defensible. Yet if the situation was to be improved, the fiscal deadlock would have to be resolved. Indeed, ever since the mid-1820s, the Prussian bureaucracy had been warning that in the event of a foreign-political emergency, the creditworthiness of the monarchy would be essential.[24]

This fiscal-political deadlock was to provide the lever to prise open absolutist government in Prussia and insert a liberal wedge. But in doing so the liberal nationalist public sphere continued to honour the primacy of foreign policy. Of course, liberals demanded domestic changes such as freedom of the press, representative assemblies and equality before the law, not least for their own sake. However, they were also, and most importantly, calling for a revision of the traditional governing compromise between state and society in Prussia. During the reform period, such a partial renegotiation had already taken place in order to confront Napoleonic France; now, liberals demanded the dismantling of the still substantial noble privileges.[25] 'Since 1807 Prussia has understood that the strength of the state can no longer be based on the old system of feudal relations, militarism and absolute government,'[26] Hansemann argued and continued, 'Why did feudal dues have to be lifted and the power of the guilds have to be broken? . . . Because the first principle of states is the need to increase their strength . . . [and] because this principle could no longer be served without abandoning the elements which hindered its fulfilment.'[27]

Underlying this argument was an acute sense of geopolitical exposure. As Hansemann noted in 1840, 'Prussia's provinces are not concentrated but are widely dispersed.' For this reason, he continued in the same breath, 'the patriotism of the Prussian people must be correspondingly vibrant, general and national . . . Only freedom can create such a patriotism in Prussia.'[28] In other words, just as old Prussia had sought to make up in internal cohesion for what she lacked in territorial mass, so did liberal nationalists seek to compensate for their geopolitical vulnerability through a programme of internal reforms. 'If you unify and liberate the nation at home,' Robert Prutz argued, 'you will also make it great and powerful externally.'[29] In particular, liberals called upon the state to harness the power of the middle class: only public opinion, a popular militia and 'homogeneity of principles' could guarantee national security; traditional monarchic power was no longer enough.[30] It was only by tapping into the power of the people through a genuine representative assembly, Hansemann argued, that the Prussian monarchy could hope to mobilize its subjects against the external enemy. The debate, in other words, had turned full circle back to the Reform period. Once again, the subversive potential of the primacy of foreign policy was manifest: remove the functional justification for privilege, and privilege itself would have to be redistributed.

To the Prussian government, liberal nationalist demands were both a threat and an opportunity. Many statesmen, such as the foreign minister von Werther, were opposed to them on diplomatic grounds.[31] They were not about to loosen tried bonds with Russia or embark upon a nationalist crusade against France; moreover, they believed that any such venture would alienate vital Austrian support.[32] Others, such as Prince William of Prussia, saw a representative assembly with a fiscal veto as a threat to the military preparedness of the monarchy.[33] This was an anti-emancipatory interpretation of the primacy of foreign policy and one which – as William I of Prussia – he was subsequently to revise. Finally, there were those who were ideologically implacably opposed to liberal demands. The conservative pietist *Camarilla* around the king and other conservatives were hardly Austrophile, but they were deeply sceptical of what they called the 'nationalities swindle' and its subversive potential at home. Frederick William himself was a more complex case. He was undoubtedly a German patriot, and had been a firm opponent of French pretensions during the Rhine Crisis.[34] On the other hand, Frederick William was in no sense a classic dualist: he was not prepared to use what he termed 'the sacred fire' of German patriotism for exclusively Prussian purposes.[35] His patriotism was archaic, corporate (*ständisch*) and intensely cultural; the considerable liberal expectations of him in the early 1840s were thus to be disappointed. If anything, Frederick William tended to defer to Austria in political terms. 'Oh,' he told a visiting Austrian general in 1841, 'if [Austria] were only so mighty, yes, among us Germans still mightier than it is and was . . . I would certainly be its truest subordinate. You can believe me, I want nothing for myself: I want only Germay's greatness.'[36] In his romantic vision, the *Bund* should be a revived *Reich* under Austrian political leadership with Prussia acting as a trusted military vassal. 'We must force Austria,' he argued, 'to be German.'[37]

But to many Prussian statesmen liberal nationalist demands were also a great opportunity. Ideological sympathies played some role, but the primacy of foreign policy was paramount. Men such as Canitz, Bunsen and Radowitz saw the national issue as a platform through which Prussia could seize the initiative and decide the struggle for mastery in Germany. Unlike Frederick William, they wanted Prussia to be German in order to force Austria out. In particular, they wanted to harness the immense power of bourgeois nationalism to Prussian state interests. Even such a sceptical observer as Bismarck was later forced to concede that nationalist enthusiasm in 1840 had had 'the effect as if we had a few more army corps on the Rhine than was actually the case'.[38] Indeed, the 'German' faction within the Prussian leadership was prepared to indulge liberal demands for internal reforms. As Boyen and Eichhorn put it in 1841, it was necessary that the nobility 'should surrender its privileges for the greater common interest . . . as expressed in the duty to defend the Fatherland and in the whole military organization of the state'.[39]

Easily the most prominent advocate of the 'German' faction in Prussia was Frederick William's confidant, Carl Maria von Radowitz. He knew well the dangers of German division: he had first seen action as a Westphalian soldier against his compatriots in 1813.[40] 'Prussia,' Radowitz argued, 'is a European state, but thanks to its internal character it is primarily a German state, so that Prussia's policy must be a German policy through and through.'[41] This meant that Prussia must aim for an undoubted hegemony in Germany. This hegemony was to be moral and political – Radowitz sought to lead the smaller states, not to annex them – rather than imperial, but it was a hegemony none the less. The result was a twin-track strategy. At *Bund* level, Prussia now began to press ever more insistently for a reform of the ramshackle federal military constitution. In particular, Prussia pressed for the construction of a new federal fortress in southern Germany; her resolute stance contrasted favourably with the bickering between Baden, Württemberg, Bavaria and Austria on its location. Prussia also demanded larger individual contingents to reflect population growth, shortened mobilization times, a fixed proportion of state budgets set aside for military purposes and regular inspections. Naturally, Austria and the Third Germany opposed these initiatives as a vehicle for Prussian hegemony, but they were forced to submit to a military inspection in 1841. When the heavily massaged report was produced in 1843, withering judgments were passed on the military preparedness of the smaller and middling states: training periods were too short, equipment inadequate, exercises few and far between, and the paper strength of many federal contingents proved to be ludicrously exaggerated.[42]

At the same time, the 'German' faction sought to ride the liberal nationalist tiger at home. In the Rhineland, for example, Prussian administrators sought to stimulate a specifically Prusso-German nationalism directed against France. But far more important was the attempt to bolster Prussian prestige through constitutionalization; this would both defuse domestic tension and put Prussia at the head of the national movement. As Heinrich von Gagern pointed out, a truly liberal representative assembly in Prussia could not fail to act as a magnet for the rest of Germany. 'And what will then happen to the legislative activity of the Federal Diet [at Frankfurt]?' he asked. 'And what effect will that have on other states? Who will want to be a Hessian, a Bavarian, or Hanoverian if there exists in Prussia a German parliament in which no important matter is discussed which does not concern the whole of Germany?'[43] But when in 1844 Frederick William finally relented and summoned a United Diet for 1847, not even Gagern could have foreseen its spectacular consequences. For the complex link between taxation, representative institutions and foreign policy exposed a loose thread in the Prussian polity which was progressively to unravel royal authority.

### The Defeat of the Nation and the Triumph of the State, 1846–50

The revolutions of 1848 began in 1846. On 8 August of that year, Christian VIII of Denmark issued his 'open letter' claiming the duchies of Schleswig and Holstein for the Danish monarchy. In so doing, Christian bowed to the demands of the 'Eider-Danish' movement for a unified Danish nation-state. At the same time, he was trying to improve state finances by forcing additional taxation on the estates; resistance to Christian thus came from both 'modern' nationalists and 'traditional' corporate interests. The *Bund* did not react, not least because it had no legal basis to do so, unless the Danes tried to separate the duchies. Metternich, in particular, was determined to resist popular pressure for action. 'The public, both of the speaking and the singing variety,' he wrote, 'has no right to interfere.'[44] Official Germany, in fact, demanded not action against the Danes, but suppression of nationalist protest. All this had the effect of both inflaming and emboldening the liberal nationalist public sphere. In Baden, the radical Friedrich Hecker threatened the dispatch of volunteers to Schleswig-Holstein if the *Bund* proved unwilling to protect German interests; but prominent moderate liberals such as Welcker, Brentano and Bassermann were also outraged.

The liberal nationalist critique of German diplomatic weakness now moved into sharper focus.[45] In Heidelberg, the liberal G. Gervinus taught that foreign policy was 'the really decisive factor' (*eigentlich bestimmende element*) in the state.[46] For him an active foreign policy and the liberalization of the Prussian state were inseparable: 'Prussia must put herself at the head of Germany, but this requires three things: Prussia must promulgate a constitution, it must allow freedom of the press and it must attempt a forceful foreign policy.'[47] In Prussia, the liberal Heinrich Simon called upon Frederick William to pursue a German foreign policy. 'We entreat you,' he wrote, 'to protect the borders of the [Prussian] state against Russia . . . [and] to ensure that Schleswig-Holstein is not alienated from Germany.'[48] This new sense of liberal foreign-political engagement was exemplified by the founding of the *Deutsche Zeitung* in May 1847. Its programme consisted of three main demands: a competitive position for German goods on foreign markets, an end to the diplomatic dependence on Russia and an active 'German' foreign policy in pursuit of political unity; these were to be achieved through an alliance between the Prussian state and the nationalist movement.[49]

What was qualitatively new about this liberal nationalist critique was its pretension to executive power. When Carl von Rotteck's *Staatslexikon* called for 'a voice in the formulation of foreign policy' (*Stimmberechtigung in Sachen der auswärtigen Politik*), he spoke for many liberals.[50] Hitherto, all over Germany, foreign policy had been strictly the preserve of the cabinets; representative assemblies had no right of consultation.[51] But if, before 1847, the liberal nationalist public sphere in Prussia had lacked an institutional mechanism to articulate its views, this was soon to change.

When Frederick William IV summoned the United Diet, he was not primarily indulging his romantic medieval notions of a new age of corporate liberties, nor was he simply giving in to domestic liberal pressure. Rather, Frederick William was guided by the joint dictates of modernization and the primacy of foreign policy. For in 1844–6, the Prussian state was forced to come to terms with the question of railways. In 1840 there had been 185 kilometres of railroads in Prussia; by 1845 this had jumped to 1106 kilometres. But by mid-decade, an impasse had been reached. Private entrepreneurs were unwilling to fund risky large-scale projects to open up the east; the state was reluctant to help out, partly because it had just completed an enormous programme of road construction, partly out of ideological commitment to private enterprise, but largely because of lack of funds. Yet the state had an undoubted interest in further railroads. First of all, a line linking the eastern and western halves of the monarchy – the *Ostbahn* demanded by liberal opinion – would greatly enhance the economic and political integration of Prussia. Secondly, and perhaps even more important, there was the increasing military significance of railways. As the young Helmuth von Moltke observed in 1843, 'Every new development in railways is a military advantage; and for the national defence, a few million on the completion of our railways is far more profitably employed than on our fortresses.'[52] In the autumn of 1845, the French government had begun the construction of a network of strategic railways threatening the western border of the *Bund*;[53] in April 1846, a federal commission stressed the need for a system of German strategic railways; and in January 1847, the same arguments were repeated in a Prussian-authored federal report.[54] Predictably, however, the *Bund* did not respond: petty particularist jealousies intervened, and the southern German states were unable even to agree the gauge of an integrated rail network. If Germany was to have the system of strategic railways she so desperately needed, Prussia would have to act alone; but if Prussia was to act, she would have to submit to a fundamental reform of her political economy. The only way out of this fiscal-political gridlock was to call a United Diet in order to sanction the extraordinary taxation required for railway construction.

The adjutant-general, Ludwig von Thile's keynote address to the Diet in June 1847 made the link between geopolitics, foreign policy and finance clear. 'The main purpose of the state treasure,' Thile argued, 'is the defence of the Prussian monarchy against external threats, to increase its power in the midst of states which are far more formidable in terms of size and population, and always to have the means to hand to arrive first on the scene with armies wherever possible.'[55] 'The Prussian state,' he continued,

lies in the midst of all the European great powers, as Germany lies in the middle of Europe . . . In terms of population and material wealth [however] we are far behind our powerful neighbours. The state is stretched out in a narrow 200-mile strip, from the border of one large empire to the border of another . . . What kind of means do we possess to counter these disadvantages? No other than the old Prussian spirit, speed and decisiveness in execution . . . We have at times been hailed the champion of Germany, and I believe that we can accept this title without immodesty. We are not the most powerful state in Germany, but the more powerful state which borders us is not called by its geographical location to be the champion of Germany as we are. We, however, have this destiny, because our lands everywhere comprise the vanguard of Germany and enemies first have to step over our bodies before they can penetrate further into Germany.[56]

There it is in a nutshell: the German *Mittellage*, the Prussian 'mission,' the irrelevance of Austria, the need for increased military expenditure and (implicitly) an acceptance of resulting domestic concessions. In short, the great liberalizing experiment of 1847 in Prussia was a direct, if delayed, consequence of both Hardenberg's state indebtedness law and the geopolitical revolution of 1815.

On the whole, the Diet was sympathetic to this analysis. As delegate von Saucken put it, the Russian threat made the construction of the *Ostbahn* imperative. 'I now regard us Prussians as on a losing wicket,' he argued, 'when faced with this great giant of the north. If our brothers cannot hurry to our aid, then we shall be . . . flooded by Cossacks, Kalmuks and Kirgizians.'[57] Similarly, David Hansemann considered the *Ostbahn* a 'pressing necessity,' not merely for economic reasons but for strategic reasons: now that Poland had disappeared, eastern Prussia needed every military protection it could get.[58]

Of course, Frederick William called the Diet not because he wanted to hear the opinions of the estates, but because he wanted to persuade them to part with their money; any constitutional changes would have to be wrung from him. None the less, liberal forces were now able to insert a wedge which was progressively to corrode absolute government until its final collapse the following year. For a start, they refused to approve monies for the *Ostbahn* until Frederick William granted them regular *Landtage*. The liberal majority also extended the emancipatory (Jewish) legislation of 1812 to the kingdom as a whole; the lengthy debate showed that this issue had a symbolic significance quite out of proportion to the number of individuals concerned. Finally, liberal critics attacked what they regarded as the government's feeble defence of Prusso-German commercial interests, especially those arising from Russian tariffs and the Austrian occupation of Cracow.[59]

Amidst all this, the old order in Prussia was determined not to concede two things. The first was a constitution; the second was exclusive royal control of foreign policy. As Frederick William pointed out, the two were related. 'Just as in an armed camp, only one man can command, without risking great and foolish danger, so can the affairs of this country only be conducted by one will.'[60] Thus the same primacy of foreign policy which liberals used to challenge monarchic authority was used by the king in its defence. Imagine Frederick William's fury, then, when Foreign Minister Canitz conceded that foreign-political matters did fall within the remit of the Diet; this concession was quickly revoked, but the pass had been sold. Soon after, Hansemann moved to demand Prussian action in support of German interests in Schleswig-Holstein. Wittgenstein's warning some thirty years earlier, that a representative assembly would attempt to encroach on the royal prerogative of foreign policy, had proved prophetic.

In the Third Germany, liberal advances in the years leading up to 1848 were even more spectacular. As in Prussia, increased military expenditure after the Rhine Crisis played into the hands of the opposition. Baden, for example, was obliged to strengthen the garrison at Rastatt in line with new federal commitments. Her military budget, which had stood at 12.9 per cent of the total in 1832 and fallen to 10.4 per cent in 1837 rose to 15.5 per cent in the immediate aftermath of the French war scare; by 1848 it was consuming 24.9 per cent.[61] In theory, liberal oppositions across the Third Germany were not unsympathetic to security concerns.[62] Yet in practice they were committed to low taxation and 'cheap' militias, rather than expensive standing armies: it had always been common for them to exhort the need for national spirit and national defence in one breath, and reject a specific increase in the military budget in the next.[63] Nor were liberals loath to use these concerns as a lever to extract political concessions.

Liberal advances in the Third Germany were facilitated by the fact that representative assemblies had been in place since around 1815. In Bavaria liberal resistance had succeeded in halting the clericalist drift under Abel by mid-decade. The notorious *Kniebeugungserlaß* by which *all* soldiers of the Bavarian army – Protestant and Catholic – were forced to attend Holy Mass, and kneel at the appropriate places, was withdrawn in 1845. By 1847 Abel had been sacked and replaced by a more liberal ministry under Oettingen-Wallerstein. Moreover, the king's relations with conservative Catholics were strained by his public affair with the actress Lola Montez. In Württemberg too, liberal forces were in the ascendant. After a good showing in the elections of 1844, they won the right to scrutinize expenditure on foreign policy, hitherto a strictly royal preserve. But it was in Baden where the liberal movement was to make its most spectacular gains. Throughout the 1840s, the liberals advanced an ambitious reforming agenda which included demands for a militia, a new criminal code and the separation of justice and administration. In 1843 the reactionary ministry of Blittersdorf was toppled through a vote of no-confidence. Significantly, the constitution gave the opposition no such power; they simply arrogated it.

In Austria, the revolutionary period began with a Polish rebellion in 1846. This uprising had strong modern nationalist overtones, but it was also an old-style aristocratic separatist revolt, which was intended both to restore ancient Polish liberties and pre-empt government-sponsored peasant emancipation. It was suppressed quickly and with considerable bloodshed. The forces of law and order were assisted by peasant masses, partly because they had been inflamed by crafty Austrian bureaucrats, but largely because of genuine long-standing socio-legal grievances. A state policy of divide and rule may have exploited peasant discontent, and the tensions between Polish nobles and Ukrainian serfs, but it did not create it. This was the first class war of the revolutionary decade and it cost some 1000 lives; 500 manor houses were burned to the ground. As a result, the last vestige of Polish statehood, the autonomous republic of Cracow, was eliminated.

No sooner had the Polish danger subsided than Metternich found himself facing revolution and liberal triumph in Switzerland. Here the victory of Protestant liberal cantons, led by Berne, over the smaller conservative Catholic cantons of the *Sonderbund* endangered the 'Metternich system' in two ways. First of all, it threatened to act as a magnet for revolutionary tendencies in southern Germany, from where events in Switzerland were being closely watched. Indeed, German liberals launched a massive petition campaign in support of the Swiss liberals; they were particularly impressed by the performance of the liberal militia, which they wished to adopt as a model for themselves.[64] Secondly, according to the Vienna settlement, the great powers were the guarantors of the Swiss Constitution, and thus obliged to intervene on behalf of the *Sonderbund*. Yet despite frantic efforts, Metternich proved unable either to bring about a great-power consensus for action or to find sufficient Austrian troops to mount a unilateral intervention.

In their respective ways, the Polish revolt and the *Sonderbund* crisis both epitomized and aggravated the difficulties facing Austria on the eve of 1848. First of all, the Polish revolt merely reflected increasing nationalist pressure elsewhere in the empire. In Hungary, the Magyar gentry bulldozed Croatian objections aside in 1843 and made Hungarian, rather than the traditional Latin, compulsory in the Diet; Croat opposition was shouted down. Ominously, a new, more radical Hungarian leadership under Lajos Kossuth was beginning to over-shadow moderates such as Szechenyi. 'Hungary,' Metternich observed in 1844, 'is already in the infernal antechamber [*Vorhölle*] of Revolution.'[65] Austria faced similar problems in Italy. After 1840, mounting evidence of liberal nationalist agitation, subversion in the navy and French infiltration put Metternich in a quandary. On the one hand, he wished to minimize expenditure to help balance the books, on the other, he was concerned to avoid false economies in Italy which might encourage unrest, or French invasion, or both, and cause more expense in the long run.[66]

Of course, the root cause of the financial *misère* was structural rather than contingent. Here the problem was not so much Austria's manifest economic backwardness as the traditional political Magyar gentry stranglehold in Hungary which prevented the state from extracting a proportionate share of revenue. Yet Metternich, haunted by the memory of Joseph II, continued to reject neo-absolutist nostrums; domestically, the trauma of Josephinism proved much more enduring than that of the French Revolution. 'That country [Hungary] is not suited to the policy of integration,' he was to remark shortly before his death. 'There can be no question of anything more than a policy of mutual cooperation [*Anlehnen*].'[67] As a result, the Austrian state found itself more and more dependent on international banking houses – especially the Rothschilds – to fund her spiralling military and infra-structural expenditure after 1840: the vast sums required to fund the railway system begun in 1842 and the garrison in Italy had to be found somewhere.[68]

Moreover, the problems facing Austria were not merely individually and cumulatively enormous, they were also mutually reinforcing. If fear of Italian liberal nationalism made Metternich more inclined to intervene on behalf of the *Sonderbund*, he was correspondingly less able to do so, for every soldier stationed in Lombardy-Venetia was unavail-able for operations in Switzerland. If borrowing on the international money markets spared ministers the scrutiny of Magyar or liberal assemblies, it made them all the more dependent on public confidence in Austrian foreign and domestic policy. For when the Vienna syndicate agreed to advance substantial loans to government, it did so on condition that the level of public bonds – *metalliques* – did not fall below par; this was the Austrian equivalent to the *Staatsschuldengesetz* and it meant that foreign-political setbacks or internal unrest had to be avoided at all costs. The empire thus found itself in an impasse: financial restraints prevented anything more than symbolic help to the *Sonderbund* or very limited reinforcements in Lombardy-Venetia; this in turn reduced public confidence and threatened to push the *metalliques* below par, thus precipitating collapse. In short, repression cost money; raising money forcibly invariably provoked resistance, which required expensive repression; raising money consensually involved constitutional concessions such as summoning a representative assembly; and borrowing money put government at the mercy of public confidence, which often amounted to the same thing. In 1847–8, therefore, the Austrian state found itself being slowly and inescapably strangled by a fiscal-political gridlock. Something would have to give.

The showdown came in the winter of 1847–8. First came the defeat of the *Sonderbund*, which both gave an immense filip to Italian liberal nationalism and further depressed public confidence. Then, when Metternich finally authorized more reinforcements for the Austrian commander in Italy, General Radetzky, the finance minister, von Kübeck, dissented, on the grounds that increased expenditure would lead to a crisis of public confidence and the withdrawal of creditors.[69] By a twist of cruel irony Metternich, who had been so determined to learn from Joseph's mistakes, now found himself locked into a vicious circle of foreign-political confrontation, domestic unrest and fiscal deadlock, which resembled nothing so much as the crisis of the Habsburg monarchy in 1787–90. Throughout January and February 1848, the *metalliques* continued to fall until the banks finally pulled the plug in early March.[70] On 12 March, *before* the outbreak of the revolution in Vienna, the Austrian government was now forced to summon an estates-general in order to dig itself out of the financial morass.

The crisis of the *ancien régime* in Germany was thus primarily fiscal-political, rather than socio-economic in nature. By the eve of the revolutions absolute governments in Austria and Prussia had *already* capitulated. This explains, at least in part, the remarkably feeble resistance which greeted the outbreak of revolutionary violence in March 1848. It was rather like the France of 1789, where the strength of the established order had been comprehensively eroded by a searing fiscal and foreign policy critique from the vibrant public sphere, long before revolutionary Paris took to the streets. The poor harvests of 1845–6 and rampant pauperization did not singlehandedly cause the collapse of the *ancien régime* in 1848. Indeed, the monetary credit crisis began in 1847 and exploded in 1848, *after* the start of the political revolution, whereas the agrarian crisis was more or less over *before* the revolution broke.[71] Nor was there any *necessary* link between material deprivation and revolutionary behaviour: eastern Prussia was among the hardest hit areas in 1846–7, but remained quiescent in 1848.

Nevertheless, socio-economic crisis was a powerful contributory factor to the crisis of the *ancien régime*. Business recession, widespread bankruptcies amd subsistence crises reduced taxation yields and aggravated the fiscal-political deadlock. At the same time progressive immiseration inflamed the peasantry and the artisans. The peasants struck the first blows against the rural *ancien régime* in Baden, Württemberg and throughout southern Germany, but also in Saxony and Silesia, during January and February of 1848. But from March onwards it was the artisans who spearheaded the revolution in the capitals: Berlin, Munich, Leipzig and throughout most of Germany. If bourgeois sappers in the representative assemblies had already undermined the *ancien régime* from within, the artisans were the shock-troops of the revolution; they supplied the vast majority of those who died on the barricades in Berlin and elsewhere. In this sense, the revolutions of 1848 were an artisanal event.

The revolutionaries of 1848 have been usefully described as German Jacobins.[72] At first it seemed as if they would re-enact the script of 1789. In almost all German states – Prussia, Bavaria, Saxony, Baden, Württemberg and so on – liberal revolutionaries seized power and freed political prisoners; in the countryside, peasant mobs set about overturning the last vestiges of the agrarian socio-legal *ancien régime*. Kings were bullied into acquiescence; the new ministries pledged themselves to the German national cause, in particular that of Schleswig-Holstein, which had just expelled its Danish garrison. A pan-German parliament was assembled at Frankfurt; a cascade of liberal legislation at both regional and at federal level soon followed. In Austria, there were revolutions in Vienna and Prague. In Hungary, Lajos Kossuth called for 'a responsible ministry, full legal rights, and the abolition of all privilege',[73] except for Magyar privilege, of course. The Transylvanian and Croat Diets were abolished; Croat, Serbian, Romanian and Slovak national demands were brushed aside.[74] Finally,

the Austrian position in Lombardy-Venetia, long starved of reinforcements, came under fierce attack from Italian revolutionaries and
Piedmontese regulars and collapsed.

But whereas the French Revolution radicalized and progressed, the
German Revolutions stagnated and regressed. Already in June 1848,
Austrian troops had cleared Prague; reaction followed revolution in
Berlin (December 1848); nationalist expectations were deflated by the
humiliating armistice of Malmö and the subsequent Danish triumph in
Schleswig-Holstein; and by mid-1849 radical uprisings in Baden and
Saxony had been crushed. Outside the federation, the revolution fared
no better: the Italian revolutionaries and their Piedmontese allies were
defeated by Radetzky; Polish rebels surrendered to Prussian forces in
Posen; and in the autumn of 1849, the Hungarians finally succumbed
to a combined Austrian and Russian onslaught.

One of the reasons for the defeat of the Revolution was the deep
divisions among the revolutionaries themselves. Indeed, the gulf
between moderate Liberals and the more radical Democrats long pre-
dated March 1848.[75] The Liberals wanted a limited, property-based
franchise and a constitutional monarchy as a precaution against social
unrest; the Democrats wanted universal male suffrage and a republic.
Whereas one group desired little more than an arrangement with the
traditional order, the other would be satisfied with nothing less than a
revolutionary new creation. Broadly speaking, these positions also
reflected a social divide between the middle-class Liberals and the
Democrats, many of whom were artisans, or in some other form of
marginal employment; of course, master artisans and journeymen were
themselves split on hierarchic and economic lines. By 1848, this split
between Liberals and Democrats had led to a radical revolt in Baden
under Gustav Struve and Friedrich Hecker.

None of this meant that rioting democratic artisans were the more
genuine champions of modernization; far from it. Freedom of movement, often seen as a classic liberal demand, was only accepted in principle by the Frankfurt parliament after furious resistance from south
German liberal 'home-town' communitarians determined to maintain
their restrictive residence laws (*Heimatrecht*).[76] Similarly, German liberals
– infuriated by foreign tariffs – were protectionist throughout the
1840s; the grain-exporting Junkers, by contrast, were at that time free
traders.[77] On the other hand, the artisans wished to restore the restrictive guild legislation upon which their livelihoods depended. Indeed,
the question of the free exercise of trades (*Gewerbefreiheit*) proved so

fraught at Frankfurt that the delegates agreed to delay a decision until a later date. Hence as far as both freedom of movement and the guilds were concerned, the free-trading Prussian *ancien régime* of 1847 was, and had been for some time, considerably more liberal than some of its revolutionary successors.

But perhaps the best example of the ambiguities of modernization in 1848 was the question of Jewish emancipation. This had been a key, if somewhat ambiguously formulated, liberal demand for some time; it was a staple of liberal programmes in 1847–8; and in December 1848, the national assembly finally delivered itself of an emancipation law. But while liberal grandees made tolerant speeches at Frankfurt, the artisanal and peasant shock-troops of the revolution were reading from another script. In southern Germany, the agrarian unrest of 1847–8 which did so much to topple the princes was accompanied by an unmistakable strain of anti-Semitism. Many of these rebels were guided by a bizarre blend of prejudice, social grievance and utopianism: they demanded the 'destruction' of the nobility, the 'expulsion' of the Jews and all of the princes, the 'murder' of bureaucrats and that 'Germany should become a free state like America.'[78] At Rust near Ettelheim in Baden, the mob called for 'Freedom, equality, and the murder of the Jews.' Well might one Jewess from Baden observe: 'How relieved we were when one day Prussian Uhlans [cavalry] came riding in.'[79] When the restored conservative Bavarian government introduced emancipatory legislation in December 1849, the response was a spontaneous campaign of popular protests characterized by all the trappings of incipient political modernity, including petitions and a press campaign.

The people had spoken, but it was not what any modernizing liberal would want to hear. It is therefore erroneous to assume that Jewish emancipation was positively linked to the process of political emancipation in Germany generally.[80] If anything, the two were negatively linked: political freedom allowed peasants and artisans to vent ancient sentiments, which had hitherto been, mercifully, disenfranchised. Conversely, political repression could be the prerequisite for Jewish rights: in the end it was not the revolutionary governments but the restored autocracies which introduced the necessary legislation, albeit under liberal pressure.[81] For Jews at least, political emancipation also meant the political emancipation of anti-Semites.

Another reason for the triumph of the old order was the policy of partial modernization. Moderate liberal opinion was appeased by constitutional concessions: the imposed constitution of December 1848 in Prussia, for example, granted a parliament elected by a broad middle class, but which excluded those in receipt of poor relief. This was followed in May 1849 by the famous three-class electoral law which gave the better off a disproportionately large representation; it reinforced the political dominance of the propertied bourgeoisie. Thereafter, moderate Prussian liberals stood to lose more from the revolution than from cooperation with the princes. To a greater or lesser extent this pattern was replicated across Germany. Similarly, the old order was able to divert peasant discontent by granting agrarian reforms, be they the abolition of the last feudal residues, as in southern Germany, of patrimonial justice, as in Prussia, or of serfdom itself, as in many parts of the Habsburg Empire. This did not mean that the countryside totally 'withdrew' from the revolution,[82] and it is an oversimplification to say that the peasantry 'turned conservative' to a man, but it is undeniable that agrarian radicalism was decisively reduced. In many areas, especially the Habsburg Empire, the authorities were even able to deploy the peasantry against middle-class liberal nationalists and aristocratic separatists. This had already happened in Galicia in 1846; the pattern was to be repeated in Italy and Transylvania throughout 1848–9.

Finally, partial modernization also involved the political mobilization of conservative opinion; as the reactionary Hermann Wagener observed in September 1848, 'we must learn from our enemies'.[83] The broad contours of a multi-party system began to emerge in 1848–9, with conservatives rallying around the newly founded newspaper, the *Kreuzzeitung*. There was also a proliferation of conservative societies, veterans' associations and patriotic leagues: total membership increased from 20 000 in 1848 to 60 000 in the following year.[84] The natural recruiting ground for these bodies was not only the nobility and many bourgeois, but also the rural population. Monarchic sympathies were deeply ingrained throughout German society,[85] and even many landless labourers were not merely socially conservative but firmly monarchic. One example would be the Westphalian peasantry, afflicted by the collapse of crafts and crop prices. They had wanted state assistance in times of need and were as disappointed by the indifference of the Frankfurt assembly as they were impressed by the interventionism of the Prussian monarchy.[86]

The revolutionaries were also deeply divided on religious lines. The events of 1848 considerably accelerated the growth of German political Catholicism. Of course, there were differences among Catholics: some were liberals, others were old-style corporate conservatives.[87] Nevertheless, region and confession, not class proved to be the strongest bond between the deputies at Frankfurt.[88] Catholics now wanted to use their new rights to reduce state interference in church affairs, and even to demand compensation for the expropriations of the revolutionary era. But perhaps the most striking example of the confessional divide was that the largely Catholic south and west tended to favour Austria, or at least the 'Greater German' model (*Großdeutschland*) including the 'German' Habsburg lands of present-day Austria and Bohemia, whereas the largely Protestant north and east supported a Prussian-led 'Small Germany' (*Kleindeutschland*) excluding all Habsburg lands. This marked a temporary lull in the steady migration of southern and western German opinion towards Prussia, which was resumed with a vengeance in the 1860s.

Yet another political weakness of the Revolution was its failure to seize executive power, in particular military power. At first sight this is surprising, for liberals had thought long and hard about the military question. They were consistent in their demand for a popular militia which would be not merely cheaper than a standing army but more effective and less domestically repressive; the success of the Swiss liberals only reinforced this view.[89] Nor was the Frankfurt Assembly oblivious of questions of security: this was one of its major preoccupations. Indeed, the Frankfurt parliament recognized the need for a larger German army and accepted Radowitz's suggestion that the forces of the *Bund* be doubled to 700 000 men. Much of this increase was to be borne by Austria and Prussia, but the balance was to be provided by a general mobilization (*levée en masse*) of 2 per cent of the population.[90] As far as the Democrats were concerned, these changes were not radical enough: they demanded a unitary German democratic army based on universal, rather than selective, conscription; this made them far more militarist than their princely adversaries. Indeed, the Bill of Basic Rights passed by the Frankfurt parliament in 1849 abolished the traditional exemptions from military service enjoyed by pacifist Christian communities such as the Mennonites;[91] such were the ambiguities of modernity in 1848.

This was the theory. In practice, however, German liberals did not seem to expect ever to have to use violence *themselves*, but merely to sanction or to co-opt the force of others, namely the armies of the *ancien régime*.[92] No serious attempt was made to introduce, rather than merely plan, conscription and increased military budgets. The first moment of truth came in August 1848 with the armistice of Malmö, by which Prussia withdrew her forces from Schleswig-Holstein and left the German nationalists to their fate. The second moment of truth came a month later, when Frederick William resolutely refused to surrender his supreme command over the army; this provoked the resignation of the ministry.[93] To make matters worse, the army not merely refused to act as an executive organ of the Frankfurt parliament, but mutated into an active and semi-autonomous counter-revolutionary force eager to suppress disorder. As General von Roon remarked in 1848 after Frederick William's temporary capitulation to the revolution, 'the army is now our Fatherland'. Liberals now found themselves totally dependent on volunteers and donations; in practice, these were few and far between. There were, to carry the Jacobin comparison further, no revolutionary quartermasters like Carnot, no revolutionary deficit-financing devices like the *assignats*, no terror and no actual *levée en masse*. Moreover, where revolutionary militias did mount serious resistance, as in Berlin, Vienna or Baden, regular goverment forces prevailed;[94] this was an empirical refutation of liberal beliefs in the superiority of a militia over a standing army.

There was another area where liberal beliefs were to be fatally controverted: nationalism and national interests. Many German liberals had been quite unsentimental and pragmatic about the incompatibility of national ambitions in Europe well before 1848. After all, the pre-revolutionary period had been characterized by nationalist antagonism towards the Danish nationalist movement in Schleswig-Holstein. Nevertheless, the majority shared the common expectation of a united European liberal nationalist front against reaction. The swift descent from the brief liberal nationalist fraternity ('springtime of nations') in March into ethnic strife was thus a considerable shock. Of course, Germany was not unique in this regard: the Hungarians, for example, found themselves at odds with Croat, Slovak and Romanian aspirations. Indeed, the ferocity of the Magyar-Romanian conflict in Transylvania far exceeded anything found in Germany. Moreover, the level of anti-Semitic fervour directed by Polish nationalists against German-oriented Jews in 1848 left developments further west in the shade. But nowhere else in Europe were there quite so many areas of tension as in Germany; this was an inevitable consequence of her central location. Some of these disputes caused relatively little friction: a skilful Dutch policy of conciliation and a clear veto from the great powers defused the conflict in Limburg, where local German nationalists unsuccessfully demanded separation from Holland.[95] Similarly, Italian aspirations in the Tyrol – where they made up almost half (44 per cent) of the population – were seen off; here historic, legal and demographic arguments favoured the Germans.

But the most serious conflicts arose in the east and south-east. In Bohemia, the revolution had begun with the customary rhetoric of brotherhood and unity: 'Czechs and Germans are of one body,' so the slogan ran. But very soon a Czech national movement emerged and ceremoniously turned down an invitation to attend the German national assembly at Frankfurt as irrelevant to their needs; instead, a pan-Slavist Congress convened in Prague in June 1848. It was, to quote one historian, 'year One in the political life of the Czechs'; the tide of modernization in Germany had gripped them too: 1848 saw the first Czech constitutions, elections and daily newspapers.[96] This took German liberal nationalists entirely by surprise and produced derision as well as irritation. Friedrich Engels observed that 'the chief champion of the Tschechian [*sic*] nationality, Professor Palacky, is himself but a learned German run mad, who even now cannot speak the Tschechian language correctly and without foreign accent'.[97] The Czechs had indeed successfully (re-)invented themselves; later they suggested that the Habsburg Empire would have to be invented if it did not exist. In many ways Bohemia was a Schleswig-Holstein in reverse: demographically the Czechs were in a clear majority of 2.6 million over 1.7 million Germans. Historically, however, the province was indisputably part of a German political commonwealth, formerly the *Reich* and then the *Bund*. All attempts at compromise failed: the two sides were diametrically opposed with German nationalists calling for inclusion in a united German state and the Czechs demanding either independence or, at least, a more prominent role in a reconstituted Habsburg empire. There were calls in Frankfurt for federal intervention against the Czechs, but no German state, not even Prussia, was prepared to risk such a colossal infringement of Austrian sovereignty.[98]

Similarly, in Posen, which had been Prussian more or less continuously since the 1790s but which was not part of the *Bund*, Polish and German demands were incompatible. The new Prussian liberal ministry, ideologically sympathetic to Polish aspirations for independence, and bent on a joint crusade against Russia, proposed an amicable partition. This was problematic, for Posen was much more of an ethnic patchwork quilt than Schleswig-Holstein, where Germans and Danes were heavily concentrated to the south and north respectively. In the town of Posen itself, Germans and the German-oriented Jews combined were a slender majority, but Poles dominated the surrounding countryside. Overall, the Poles were in a clear two-thirds majority, and they rejected all partition plans as a transparent attempt to manipulate the territorial distribution to their disadvantage; it is certainly true that all the proposed schemes left a disproportionate number of Poles within a united Germany. Unlike the Tyrol, both historic and demographic arguments tended to work against German nationalist aspirations.

On the other hand, broader Polish aims were equally maximal. They demanded no less than the reconstitution of Poland in the borders of 1772; a substantial number even called for the return of Pomerania.[99] This was as unreasonable as a German nationalist demand for the return of Belgium, which had been part of the *Reich* as late as 1790. Moreover, it might have included more Germans, Ukrainians and Lithuanians than Poles; it would certainly have included proportionately far more minorities than an outright annexation of Posen would have included in Germany. The result was not merely a split between German and Polish nationalists, but among German liberals themselves. Some, such as Robert Blum, argued that the Germans should now apply the same principles which they had invoked in Schleswig-Holstein and cede the province to the Poles. German nationalists, on the other hand, argued that the borders should be drawn not on the basis of the pre-partition Polish borders of 1772 but the Vienna settlement of 1815; this was a curious line for any liberal nationalist to take.[100]

Deprived of the familiar historical and demographic arguments, the Posen question forced German liberal nationalists to resort to a lethal Hobbesian cocktail of chauvinism and special pleading. In a highly influential speech, Wilhelm Jordan called for a 'healthy national egoism' (*gesunder Volksegoismus*). 'Our justification,' he added, 'is none other than the right of the mighty, as the right of the strongest.' Indeed, he went on to speak of the 'superiority of the German nature'. Hence, he concluded, there should be 'Freedom for Poland, but Germany above everything' (*Freiheit für Polen aber Deutschland über alles*).[101] Summing up the liberal nationalist point of view, the *Deutsche Zeitung* stated: 'What is German or became German, must stay German.'[102] This was the new inverted nationalist categorical imperative: what is yours is mine, and what is mine is my own. Truly, as Franz

Grillparzer observed in 1849, the new spirit led 'from humanity via nationality to inhumanity (*Bestialität*)'.

The result of all this was not merely the collapse of any liberal pan-nationalist common front against European reaction. It also provided the basis for active collaboration between liberal nationalists and the old order. In Posen, for example, the best guarantor of German interests turned out to be not the suspiciously Polonophile Frankfurt assembly, but the Prussian state which finally suppressed Polish rebels in May 1848. Similarly, many – though by no means all – German nationalists vigorously applauded both the suppression of the Prague Revolution and Radetzky's victories in Italy.[103]

Above all, the outcome of the Revolutions was shaped by the primacy of foreign policy. For the February Revolution in Paris was not just a signal of things to come, but also, and much more importantly, a potential threat to German security. The new French government was widely believed to harbour the same revisionist designs on the Rhineland which had been thwarted less than a decade before. As the liberal Friedrich Daniel Bassermann pointed out, he might welcome the ideological implications of the February Revolution, but he was also painfully aware that Germany might not be able to defend itself against a rejuvenated France.[104] German Liberals wanted not only to imitate the French, but also to oppose them, if necessary. Indeed, in late March 1848 much of Baden and parts of Württemberg were convulsed by a 'false French alarm', an inchoate fear of invasion by a rabble of destitute workers from across the Rhine; armed bands set off to defend the frontier. This paranoia gripped not merely rural areas, but even towns the size of Freiburg.[105]

If the popular and liberal attitude was ambiguous, that of the cabinets was uniformly wary. The *Bund* went into permanent conclave and voted monies for the equipment of the federal fortress at Rastatt; Prussian forces in the west were mobilized at once; and Frederick William's brother, Prince William of Prussia, was sent to take charge as military governor of the Rhineland and Westphalia.[106] But it was among the southern German states that the initial fear was the strongest: as in 1830–1 and 1839–40, they feared a repeat of 1792–3, which made them determined both to prepare for the worst and to avoid any precipitate intervention.[107] Shaken by the transparent inadequacy of their western defences – for the third time in two decades – Baden and Württemberg were temporarily stampeded into seeking Prussian protection and guidance; only Bavaria remained aloof.[108]

In the end, as on the two previous occasions, the invasion did not materialize. It very soon became clear that France would neither launch an annexationist war, nor would it hurry to succour struggling revolutionaries further east. This was to have important repercussions throughout Europe, but particularly in Germany. First of all, it damaged the national cause in southern Germany: as the French threat receded, the princes became less inclined to jump on the Prussian-driven patriotic bandwagon. Secondly, unlike their Jacobin predecessors in Mainz, the German revolutionaries were now on their own; there was no French crusade to help them.

Yet while there was no international revolutionary solidarity, there was certainly no lack of counter-revolutionary solidarity. A good example of this was the Russian intervention in Hungary in May 1849. Another instance would be Prussia's refusal, after initial hesitation, to support dissident movements within the Habsburg Empire; this was in marked contrast to her opportunistic exploitation of Austrian difficulties in 1787–90. But perhaps the most spectacular example of outside intervention was Schleswig-Holstein, where British and Russian pressure forced the armistice of Malmö, by which Prussian troops were ignominiously forced to evacuate the duchies, thus precipitating the collapse of nationalist hopes. Here the motivation was not primarily ideological – in this respect Britain and Russia were polar opposites – but power-political. It was not so much that the great powers fundamentally objected to German political unity; this tenacious historiographical myth has long since been laid to rest.[109] Indeed, Palmerston is said to have remarked in 1849, that 'There can be no objection to the idea of German union except that no one seems able to achieve it.'[110] At one level, Russian and British concerns were not so much about union *per se*, but about its character: in theory, Britain positively welcomed the idea of a liberal ally in Europe, while Russia, again theoretically, was not ill-disposed to the idea of a unitary monarchic and conservative Germany. Yet in the end, these considerations were not decisive. For when both powers intervened so decisively in Schleswig-Holstein, it was not because of any generalized reservations, ideological or otherwise, about the German national cause, though these existed, but out of opposition to the illegal despoliation of Denmark, which threatened the balance of power in the Baltic.[111]

Prussian policy throughout the revolutions of 1848–9 was also guided by the primacy of foreign policy: the national cause, constitutionalization and *raison d'état* were all to become inextricably intertwined. For by late March 1848, the state faced a triple crisis in the shape of the French threat, confrontation in Schleswig-Holstein and, of course, revolution not merely in Berlin but throughout Germany. What followed was the triumph of the 'German' faction in the Prussian leadership. Instead of cooperating with Austria and confronting the revolution, Prussia now decided to confront Austria and co-opt the Revolution.

Just as the great liberalizing experiment of the United Diet had been launched well before the outbreak of revolutionary violence, the nationalist gambit was not simply a desperate response to internal unrest. Indeed, the principles which were to govern Prussia's brief cooperation with the forces of revolution were well-established by March 1848. Nationalism, as Radowitz had argued in late 1847, was 'still the most popular and powerful force moving our people; [and] represents a most dangerous weapon in the hands of the enemies of the legal order'; it should therefore be seized from their grasp and turned to more positive use. 'Prussia,' he continued,

has risen through circumstances into the ranks of the European pentarchy, and will need to defend the position assigned to her. But no matter how militarized and powerful it might be, it cannot be denied that on its own it does not enjoy the same weight in the great affairs of the world as the other four states [of the pentarchy]. Only in the closest connection with Germany can it [Prussia] find the additional strengths it needs. That Germany should be mighty and united is a crucial precondition of Prussia's existence.[112]

The decisive impulse for this analysis came with the French threat in February–March 1848. A crown council in Berlin on 28 February concluded that Prussia could only repel a French attack 'if the German governments ally themselves closely with the spirit of the nation'.[113] That same day Radowitz argued that popular opinion could only be won over if German governments, especially Prussia, could address both the national and foreign-political needs of the hour.[114] With this end in mind, the Prussians – initially in uneasy tandem with Austria – launched a twin-track policy of liberalization and military preparedness at federal level. In early March, Prussia persuaded the Federal Diet to liberalize censorship, at least *de jure*; Austria withdrew its long-standing objections in return for a Prussian guarantee of Austrian possessions in Italy against French attack, yet another victory of foreign policy over ideological principle. At the same time, the Prussian government sought to broaden its base of support domestically through further liberalization. For on the night of 17–18 March – after the French and Austrian revolutions, but *on the eve of* the revolution in Berlin – the Prussian government finally decided to grant a constitution.[115]

For Prussia, therefore, the upheavals of March 1848 were an opportunity as well as a danger. They were a danger because internal unrest threatened to derail her new 'German' policy; a congress of princes scheduled for mid-March had to be postponed. On the other hand, nationalism and liberalism could now be employed as an instrument in the struggle for mastery in Germany.[116] Indeed, the news of the Viennese Revolution was received with dismay by the Prussian foreign ministry, because Canitz feared that Austria might herself take on the 'German mission' and thus steal a march on Prussia.[117] Conversely, the Austrian revolution was potentially beneficial in that the resulting turmoil allowed Prussia to seize the initiative. By the same token, Berlin was initially in no rush to confront outbreaks in southern Germany: not only were nationalist energies to be harnessed rather than suppressed, but they also had the beneficial effect of making the southern princes more amenable to Prussian guidance.

Hence, Frederick William's 'capitulation' to the revolution can equally be seen as a calculated, if brief, dualist bid for mastery in Germany. His Patent of 18 March called for a unified German tax and customs system, a code of weights and measures, a trade law, free movement of individuals, freedom of speech, an all-German military system on the Prussian model, a navy, a constitutional court and a national representation for the whole of Germany; this programme put him at the head of the national movement.[118] On 21 March he proclaimed that 'Prussia shall henceforth be absorbed into Germany.' That same day the new liberal ministry under von Arnim even approached France with the offer of a joint crusade against Russia on behalf of a reconstituted Poland;[119] this was a long-standing liberal demand. Last but not least, Prussia now enthusiastically took up the nationalist cause in Schleswig-Holstein where an attempt by the new Danish king to annex Schleswig had provoked open rebellion in early April.

In the end this policy failed: it resulted neither in a united Germany nor in Prussian hegemony. In part this was due to a lack of nerve. At each crucial moment Prussia flinched. When confronted by Britain and Russia over Schleswig-Holstein, she blinked; when offered the German crown by the Frankfurt parliament in April 1849, Frederick William turned it down; and Prussia was to fold yet again when Austria called her bluff at Olmütz in December 1850. In part, the abandonment of the 'German' policy was due to deep divisions within the Prussian leadership itself. Key figures such as the new foreign minister, Baron Heinrich von Arnim-Suckow, and the former foreign minister, Count Dönhoff, were enthusiastic exponents of the new line and determined to exclude Austria. Frederick William, on the other hand, had only been a very reluctant convert. Back in the autumn of 1847 he had warned, 'The lord should spare me from the prospect of Austria being pushed out of the Confederation and of Prussia taking her place. Germany without Trieste, Tyrol and the glorious arch-duchy [of Austria] would be worse than a face without a nose.'[120] After March 1848 he still tried to work with Austria if possible, and against her only when necessary; his brief dualist lurch was never as wholehearted as that of his ministry. Frederick William's rejection of the German crown was thus consistent rather than craven. Once again, Frederick William IV broke the dualist mould: a Frederick the Great would not have hesitated; nor would Frederick William II have hesitated; and in due course Wilhelm I did not hesitate.

But to a considerable extent Prussian caution was also the product of cool *Realpolitik*. There were sound foreign-political reasons for pulling back from the brink. First of all, the Russian veto over Schleswig-Holstein was decisive; a rejection of Malmö would have meant war not only with Russia and Britain but also with Austria, and possibly France as well. Instead of harnessing the nationalist tiger, Prussian policy had led into a diplomatic cul-de-sac. If Bismarck later succeeded where others had failed, it was with a quiescent Russia. Secondly, the 'German' policy was dependent on the cooperation of the smaller German states; once the French threat had receded, all the old particularist preoccupations with sovereignty resurfaced. Thirdly, the survival of the Habsburg monarchy closed the narrow window of opportunity which had undoubtedly existed between March 1848 and mid-1849.

Indeed, it was the revival of Austrian power which put paid to the last gasp of Prussia's German policy. This was the 'Union' project of 1849–50 by which Prussia assembled Hannover, Saxony, Hesse-Darmstadt, Mecklenburg, Baden, Brunswick and a number of other territories under her leadership; Württemberg and Bavaria remained aloof. The constitutional element of the plan was a Union assembly based on a safe three-class property franchise; otherwise, the general tenor was overwhelmingly monarchic, conservative and confederal. Frederick William now graciously accepted from his princely cousins the same German crown which he had contemptuously rejected from the Frankfurt parliament. The aim was to reconcile conservative federalism, moderate constitutional liberal nationalism and Prussian leadership. This was Prussian hegemony 'on the cheap,' without any of the subversive domestic implications of March 1848; as Metternich pointed out, its predecessor was the League of Princes (*Fürstenbund*) of 1785.

Austrian resistance was correspondingly intense. Fresh from their successes in Vienna, Italy and Hungary, the Austrians rejected a Prussian-dominated *Kleindeutschland*. Instead, the Austrian Chancellor Count Schwarzenberg proposed a federal rather than unitary *Bund* of 'seventy millions' which was to include all of the Habsburg Empire;[121] this was an audacious attempt to turn Austria's liabilities into an asset in the struggle for mastery in Germany. Not least among Austrian motivations was the desire to commit German resources to the defence of Lombardy-Venetia against French and Piedmontese attack, a long-standing aim of Habsburg policy.[122] At the same time Schwarzenberg rallied much of Third Germany against the Union project. Now that liberal nationalist pressure in the smaller states had abated with the suppression of revolutions, Saxony and Hannover were emboldened to join Bavaria and Württemberg in a League of Four Kings (*Vierkönigsbündnis*) under Austrian tutelage in February 1850. The crunch came in late 1850 when Prussian troops attempted to sabotage a federal intervention on behalf of the Elector of Hesse-Cassel, not because of any ideological sympathies with the rebels but in order to embarrass Austria; echoes of Liège 1789 here. Shots were exchanged and war was only averted when Prussia backed down in the face of Schwarzenberg's Russian-backed ultimatum and accepted the 'Punctation of Olmütz'. This was undoubtedly another Prussian humiliation, more painful still than Malmö. Yet even such a Prussian hegemonist as Bismarck argued that the decision had been the right one: war with Austria and Russia over the Union was neither in Prussia's interest nor winnable.[123] In short, Prussia abandoned the German mission for reasons as realpolitical as those which had propelled her to embrace it in the first place.

Similarly, Liberal attitudes throughout 1848–9 were influenced by the primacy of foreign policy. The Offenburg meeting of the south-western Democrats in late 1847, for example, had demanded not merely a constitution, freedom of speech, the abolition of privilege, a militia, and the establishment of public works to alleviate economic hardship, but also a more forceful foreign policy: 'Justice and freedom internally, [and] a firm stance towards the outside world are what behoves us as a nation.'[124] A few months later, the Democrat Struve, speaking at the Frankfurter *Vorparlament*, referred to Germany's 'long period of abject humiliation' (*Lange Zeit tiefster Erniedrigung*) a conscious echo of the executed bookseller Palm's pamphlet in 1806. This humiliation was perceived to be both internal and external. Germany, he continued, 'has more than once been brought to the brink of disaster. It has lost many of its most beautiful provinces [and] others are already under grave threat'; [125] this reference to the loss of Alsace and other former German territories was a staple of liberal and democratic nationalist rhetoric at the time.[126] Similarly, the south-western Liberals, meeting at Heppenheim in late 1847, were even more preoccupied with foreign policy. They had no expectation that the *Bund* would do anything for the 'promotion of national concerns'. 'The federal military constitution,' it was noted, 'has provided neither a general *levée en masse*, nor an integrated federal army.' Nor had it done anything for trade and industry. On the other hand, the Prussian-led *Zollverein* constituted 'the only common Bond of German interests'. Indeed, these Liberals argued that 'The aim of uniting Germany under a German policy and the common defence of national interests will probably be more easily achieved if one wins public opinion for the expansion of the customs union into a German union.'[127]

These south-western Liberal grandees espoused the same proto-Bismarckian alliance between the Prussian state and the liberal nationalist movement which Hansemann and other Prussian liberals had pioneered since about 1830. When Prussia championed the nationalist cause in Schleswig-Holstein, they applauded. 'Germany's enemies,' the steering committee of the Frankfurt parliament proclaimed, 'have been shown that the times when one could interfere in German affairs with impunity . . . are over.'[128] Yet there was a price to be paid for this alliance. First of all, there was the Austrian problem. Should it be reconfigured, dismantled or simply excluded from the new Germany? Almost to a man, German Liberals and Democrats agreed that the hereditary lands (Tyrol, Styria, Upper Austria, etc.) and Bohemia and Moravia were German; they also agreed that it was undesirable to incorporate large numbers of non-Germans. As Heinrich von Gagern observed in Frankfurt, 'Allowing a dozen nationalities to convene here with us is not consistent with the principle of nationality.'[129] Yet very soon strong arguments emerged in favour of excluding Austria and unifying the rump under Prussian leadership; this was known as the *kleindeutsch* solution. Prussia would never accept an Austrian-led union; furthermore and relatedly, Austria excluded herself through the Kremsier Declaration of November 1848, which reaffirmed Austrian sovereignty *vis-à-vis* Frankfurt and rebuffed any suggestion of a break-up of the Habsburg Empire. In short, for a majority of Liberals the *kleindeutsch* option was the necessary consequence of the alliance with Prussia; in the end just enough Catholics – who feared minority status in the new Germany – were persuaded.[130] The second price for Prussian support was electoral: in the crucial vote of March 1849, when the Frankfurt parliament finally opted for a *Kleindeutschland* under Frederick William IV, the Democrats only accepted a Hohenzollern head of state in return for liberal agreement to universal male franchise.[131] Once again, the national imperative had had fundamentally subversive domestic implications.

Liberal foreign policy in early 1848 was not purely defensive, aiming to preserve German interests against external threats. On the contrary, liberal foreign policy was openly aggressive: the new Prussian ministry under von Arnim planned a revolutionary nationalist crusade against the tsarist empire, primarily on behalf of Polish nationalists; and the Frankfurt *Vorparlament* declared the partitions of Poland a 'humiliating injustice'.[132] German liberal nationalist sympathies with Italian, Polish and Hungarian nationalists in 1848 were not just ideological, they were also based on considerations of sound *Realpolitik*. In general, there was a common interest against the reactionary cabinets of Berlin, Vienna and especially St Petersburg; in particular, there was the need for a Polish buffer state in the east, behind which the liberal nationalist transformation of Germany could take place undisturbed.[133] Conversely, German liberals were irritated by the attitude of the smaller peoples of the Habsburg Empire: Czechs, Croats, Serbs and others. This hostility was not just chauvinism or hypocrisy. Liberal nationalists had always believed that nationalities had to achieve a certain critical mass; they could see no justification for the rights of 'unhistoric' 'new' nations.[134] Moreover, Croats, Serbs and especially Czechs were seen not merely as pro-Habsburg but a potential pro-Russian Slavic fifth column.[135]

As a result, 1848–9 saw some strange alliances. A common opposition to the Habsburgs, and to Slav nationalism, caused Viennese radicals to ally themselves with the same Magyar nobles who were suppressing Hungarian radicalism in Budapest. Conversely, all over the Habsburg Empire, the subject races ended up supporting the government against aristoractic and middle-class separatists: Ukrainian versus Pole in Galicia, Croats, Slovaks and Romanians versus Magyar in Hungary, and middle-class Czech versus German in Bohemia. Perhaps the best example of the resulting topsy-turvy alliances was when the middle-class Czechs supported the compensation of landowners after the emancipation of the peasantry in the Habsburg Empire, partly in order to annoy German radicals and partly to support the government, which they still saw as the best guarantor of their interests.[136] This was despite the fact that they were clearly much closer to the middle-class Austrian German radicals on socio-economic matters than they were to the conservative imperial administration; such were the ambiguities of modernization in 1848–9. Similarly, the Czechs were as hostile to an embattled Magyar delegation, under attack from pro-Croat imperial forces, as the Austrian German radicals were sympathetic. Whereas the Czechs saw the Hungarians as oppressors, the German radicals saw the pro-imperial Croat forces under Ban Josip Jellacic as a menace to the revolutionary cause in Germany. Who, the Bohemian German Ludwig Löhner asked, had countersigned the decree allowing Jellacic to invade another state?[137] Again, domestically, Austrian middle-class radicals had more in common with Czech bourgeois than with Magyar aristocrats: this was the primacy of the nation over material interests.

In the short term therefore, the events of 1848–9 had the effect of reforging the bonds between the Habsburg Empire and its Slavic populations; this was an affair of the head, not of the heart. In Bohemia, for example, many Czechs were 'nationally' Czech, but 'politically' Austrian: they regarded the Habsburgs as the best guarantor of their national rights against German dominance. 'Truly,' the Czech leader Franz Palacky famously observed in April 1848, 'if the Austrian Empire did not already exist, we would have to hurry to invent it not merely in the interests of Europe but of humanity.'[138] This sentiment may not have been original – we now know it to have been anticipated by many journalists and bureaucrats well before 1848 – but its echo was massive. Palacky's words were true then, and they were to remain true long after they had been forgotten by his political heirs.

German nationalists were quite right: the smaller Central European peoples threatened revolutionary foreign policy in 1848, which was predicated on a joint pan-nationalist crusade against the old order; on this Liberals and Democrats were agreed.[139] But the aggressive Liberal foreign policy of early 1848 was also motivated by the need to maintain the domestic initiative against the Democrats. The Liberal Gablentz spoke of a 'means of salvation against internal storms' while Heinrich von Gagern invoked a revolutionary war against Russia as a 'salutary means of calming fermenting elements' (*heilsames Mittel der Beruhigung der gährenden Stoffe*).[140] This was a fundamentally new departure in German history: the first manifestation of a primacy of domestic policy, a *Primat der Innenpolitik*. The *Flucht nach vorn*, an external adventure designed to stave off domestic unrest, was first mooted by embattled German Liberals in 1848.

As we know, Liberal plans for a revolutionary crusade blew up in their faces. Those same German nationalists who had once enthusiastically supported Italian nationalism registered Italian demands on the Tyrol with dismay. Similarly, Germans in Posen soon realized that von Arnim's call for the restoration of the old Poland was an explosive charge which could go off in both directions; it was subversive not merely of tsarist Russia but also of German national interests in the east. And in Bohemia the emergence of the Czech national movement not merely embarrassed but baffled German liberals: when Windischgrätz suppressed the Prague revolution, the assembly in Frankfurt could not agree whether this was victory for the German national cause or for reaction! Indeed, the realization of incompatible national aims engendered differing reactions among German liberals. Some opted for a chauvinist confrontation with Germany's neighbours; others favoured a more nuanced and pragmatic approach. As Robert Blum pointed out in 1848, Germany could not 'declare war on the whole world',[141] which was what maximal nationalist demands – however defensible they might be individually – amounted to collectively. To many Liberals and Democrats, especially in the south and west, the logical course was to jettison their German brethren in the east in return for Polish support against Russia.[142] In this way, the primacy of foreign policy allowed particularism to creep in through the back door.

The revolutions were not a watershed in the relationship between German liberals and the Prussian state. Liberal opinion had *already* looked to Prussia well before 1848; after the disappointments of 1848–50 this faith in Prussia was not only unchanged but reinforced.

'Prussia,' the *Deutsche Zeitung* observed in December 1848, three months after the betrayal of Malmö, 'is Germany's natural border-guard in the west, north and south.'[143] Such sentiments had formed part of Liberal rhetoric since 1815, and certainly 1840. After all, it was precisely because Liberals looked to Prussia's 'German mission', that they were so critical of the humiliations of 1848–50. Olmütz, Droysen argued in 1851, was the 'death of 200 years' of Prussian dualism. Yet the consequence of this was merely to make liberal nationalists more rather than less dependent on Prussian *raison d'état*. When confronted with the force of facts, 'spiritual Germany' had failed to overcome Germany of the cabinets. 'Realities,' Droysen noted, 'began to triumph over ideals, [and] interests over abstractions . . . Not from 'freedom', not through national resolutions would the unity of Germany be achieved. What was needed was one [great] power against the other powers.'[144] This was both an empirical observation and a political programme.

But German Liberals drew two further lessons from 1848–9. First of all, they became acutely aware of their dependence on the Prussian state to protect Germans where they were in a minority (Posen); Polish separatists, on the other hand, did not recognize that the same Prussian state was still their best guarantor against extreme German nationalism. Secondly, German liberals became more profoundly conscious of the need for domestic unity in the face of external threats. As the liberal Georg Beseler remarked in May 1849, if Germany was to achieve world status she would do so not by 'chasing after abstract desires for freedom, but by cohering as a nation, and acting in such a way that we are also respected abroad . . . That is what has only just become clear.'[145]

# 6

## CONCLUSION

The decisive force in German history between 1780 and 1848 was the primacy of foreign policy. Thanks to her geographic location, Germany was uniquely sensitive to shifts in the general European balance. Not only were geopolitical factors objectively important, they were also subjectively experienced at the time. Metternich, writing in 1850, described Germany as 'an archipelago of small, medium and large states that lies in the middle of the European continent'.[1] The liberal Carl Nauwerck told the Frankfurt parliament in August 1848 that it was Germany's duty 'to be involved wherever there is a European question to be solved. Because Germany is located in the centre [of Europe], Germany should hold the balance of power in her strong hands.'[2] On this, most Germans, Liberal and Conservative, Austrian and Prussian, thought alike. In the 1780s, Joseph's Bavarian exchange plan was an unsuccessful attempt to cast off onerous obligations in the west in favour of a more secure position in Germany. Some years later, Hertzberg's grand plan aimed to disengage Prussia in the west and concentrate on expansion to the north and east; this remained Prussian policy until 1815. The Vienna settlement, therefore, amounted to a geopolitical revolution in Germany. Prussia replaced Austria as the guardian of the gate in the west; both Prussian statesmen and the emerging liberal nationalist public sphere agreed that this made her the champion of 'German' interests.

With the exception of a brief eclipse in the 1780s, France not merely maintained but enhanced her traditional influence over Germany. From being a joint guarantor of the imperial constitution before 1792, she progressed to being an undisputed hegemon thereafter. After 1815, especially in 1830–1 and 1839–40, fear of French power remained the single greatest concern of German cabinets. But there was also the impact of Russian power, epitomized by Catherine the Great's elevation to the rank of guarantor of the *Reich* in 1779. In 1807, it was the intervention of Russia which saved Prussia from total extinction at Tilsit; it was the failure of Napoleon's gambit in Russia which encouraged German powers to break with Napoleon; and it was fear of replacing French by Russian hegemony that underlay Metternich's hesitation in 1812–13. Throughout our period, Russian power put German cabinets in a geopolitical double-bind. On the one hand, Russia was uncomfortably close to the eastern borders of Austria and Prussia and thus had to be appeased at all costs. On the other hand, Russia was so remote as to be useless in a contest with France; the resulting dilemma was to complicate policies not merely between 1792 and 1815, but thereafter, especially during the crisis of 1830.

The struggle for mastery within Germany between Austria, Prussia and the Third Germany was part of a broader European contest and yet also subordinate to it. Sometimes the force of external events served to unite German powers: this happened briefly in the early 1790s and again between about 1812 and 1825, when dualist tensions receded. More frequently, however, the protagonists sought to enlist outside powers on their side. During the 1780s, for example, the rise of Russia and the decline of France encouraged Joseph to embark on an ambitious programme of expansion and reform. Similarly, during the Revolutionary and Napoleonic period, Prussia courted France in the hope of maximizing her 'compensations' at the *Reichsdeputationshauptschluss*. The Third Germany, in particular, benefited from French and, later, Russian backing. Finally, the general European balance could distract protagonists from the struggle in Germany. Throughout the late 1820s, for example, Austria was too preoccupied with the Eastern Question to address the growth of Prussian power within the *Bund*.

Domestic considerations were usually secondary or instrumental. The 1790s and 1820s showed that ideological cooperation in the face of internal threats was generally spasmodic and half-hearted. No power hesitated to use ideologically suspect forces for short-term diplomatic advantage, as witness the Prussian support for Habsburg dissidents, the débâcle at Liège, the stillborn interventions of 1830 and of course the widespread cooperation with Revolutionary France after

1792–3; interests rather than opinions prevailed. On the other hand, the primacy of foreign policy helped to determine the domestic agenda throughout Germany. First of all, it could serve to stabilize the existing order. In Prussia the socio-legal inequalities of the military-agrarian complex were a function of the external needs of the state; so long as the system 'worked' there was little incentive to reform it. Conversely, precipitate change might encourage internal unrest and thus external weakness; this had been Joseph's experience in the 1780s. In particular, the primacy of foreign policy was frequently deployed to justify restricted political participation, especially after 1815. Secondly, external intervention could decisively shape domestic events. In the old *Reich*, for example, the great powers often intervened to support the estates against the absolutist pretensions of the lesser princes; after 1815, Austria sought to hobble the southern states with traditional corporate constitutions. Conversely, during the Revolutionary and Napoleonic period, France reversed her traditional policy and backed the *forces vives* of modernization and partition; in the long run, this proved to be something of an 'own goal'.

But the primacy of foreign policy could also have profoundly subversive and emancipatory effects. Most German states pursued policies of directed internal modernization aimed at improving their performance in the struggle for mastery. This was often accompanied by a radical redistribution – or abolition – of privilege, particularly after defeat or a period of decline: the toleration edicts, peasant emancipation, economic reforms, universal military service and ultimately representative assemblies were the result. None of these measures was primarily intended to forestall revolution at home: modernization was thus less partial and defensive than directed, selective and offensive. Conversely, a receding foreign-political imperative, as in Prussia after 1815, reduced the modernizing impulse.

Foreign policy was also decisive in the development of German nationalism. The experience of invasion, partition and occupation at the hands of France traumatized a whole generation of Germans. After 1815, and unmistakably after 1840 an emerging liberal nationalist public sphere reacted to and interacted with the international scene. The resulting German identity was primarily defined not ethnically, nor even culturally or linguistically, but *politically*; it was focused on the territorial integrity of the German political commonwealth, the *Bund*. Each new French threat to the Rhine frontier hastened the formation of a hard-headed liberal nationalist *Realpolitik*.

Moreover, the national movement was now linked to representative assemblies and an associational structure.

By 1850, Germany had undergone considerable modernization: huge population growth, peasant emancipation, an increase in religious toleration, a self-confident middle class, the highest level of literacy in Europe, representative assemblies and a burgeoning national movement. The society of orders had begun to give way to a recognizably modern class society; feudal privilege had been abolished. Traditional restrictive practices which had once held back the economy were now in full retreat. 'There is no path back into the happy valleys of medieval contentedness,' one observer remarked of the old craft guilds in 1850. 'Humanity drives us forwards.'[3] Some of this modernizing momentum was self-generated within German society: by the growth of supra-regional markets in grain and textiles, by population increase and by the expanding middle class. Nevertheless, the dynamic modernizing role of the state was crucial to overcome societal resistance to modernization.

But there were also considerable modernization deficits in Germany. German society was still overwhelmingly agrarian; the nobility remained immensely powerful, especially in eastern Germany; working-class consciousness was minimal; women had yet to achieve full socio-legal rights, let alone the franchise; and the 'take-off' into sustained economic growth was yet to come. Moreover, empirical reality often lagged behind modernizing intent: compulsory schooling had existed in Bavaria for some fifty years, yet only half the population could sign their names by 1850.[4] The system of taxation was far more equitable than it had been in 1780, but it was still highly regressive and weighted against the poor; modern progressive taxation was only introduced after 1880.[5] Above all, most German states had yet to experience political modernization and the triumph of liberalism; this set them apart from developments in Britain and France, though not necessarily from the European mainstream.

The causes of this uneven pattern of modernization were twofold. First of all, the primacy of foreign policy encouraged the selective modernization of economy and society rather than politics. Political participation was actively discouraged, not least because it was believed to compromise internal cohesion; only after 1840 did the idea of harnessing the nationalist middle classes gain wider currency. Moreover, the reformist impulse tended to be attenuated with the passing of an external threat. Secondly, conservative resistance by the nobility and artisans was often highly effective. Yet it would be wrong to attribute Germany's uneven modernization entirely to governmental policy or aristocratic obstruction. Many nobles were extremely successful entrepreneurs or capitalist farmers: they did not oppose the emergence of a modern market-oriented society *per se*. Ironically, had Joseph II succeeded in forcing his reforms on the aristocracy, Austria would probably have been less rather than more modern; the same applies to the emancipation of the Prussian peasantry. The future lay in encouraging not the smallholders, but large landowners. Similarly, a revolutionary victory in 1848–9 would not necessarily have modernized Germany. If only, the argument runs, liberal economic policies and a radical franchise had prevailed; if only the emergence of an illiberal expansionist German *Machtstaat* in 1871 had been avoided through a democratic transformation from below. But what if radical artisanal economic policies and liberal foreign policy had triumphed? This perfectly plausible permutation would have produced not the grail of modernity but aggressive war and economic backwardness. Similarly, as the anti-Semitic agitations of 1848–9 showed, free speech and political participation produced not merely weak blossoms of enlightenment and progress, but also luxuriant growths of prejudice and obscurantism. The modernization process was thus highly ambiguous. No conflict in German history was ever a clear contest between modernity and reaction.

It is true: Germany in 1850 was not yet 'modern'. Socially, politically and economically, it was still hidebound and deferential; this contrasts unfavourably with liberal industrial Britain and the new unstuffy American individualism so beloved of modernization theorists. But modern or not, Germany was a much more humane society. As the Russian dissident Alexander Herzen observed on his arrival at Königsberg in 1847, 'The unpleasant feelings of fear [and] the oppressive feelings of suspicion, were all dispelled.'[6] Moreover, if Herzen had traversed the country from east to west, he would not have come across lynched slaves or butchered natives; these were a routine sight in the New World. Though life for the German rural poor was hard, especially in East Elbia, it never approached the grinding poverty of Mediterranean *latifundias*, let alone serfdom further east. And not even the worst excesses of *Pauperismus* in the 1840s resembled the mass famine which had just been visited on the Irish in 'modern' Britain; no German state ever shovelled quite so many paupers into disease-infected emigration ships with lectures on political economy and providentialist homilies ringing in their ears.[7] Finally, the Germans had not lost their universalist streak: in November 1840, at the height of the Rhine crisis, extensive collections were carried out in major German cities on behalf of flood victims in the French city of Lyons.[8]

The struggle for mastery had not yet been decided by 1850. It was far from obvious that Prussia would eject Austria from Germany in less than two decades; if anything, the humiliation of Olmütz had reaffirmed Habsburg dominance. Moreover, in mid-century, a vibrant Third Germany was showing no signs of giving up its hard-won sovereignty and merging into a Prussian-led united Germany. And yet, the ultimate triumph of Prussia was implicit, though far from inevitable, by 1850.

This was not because Prussia was more modern, though she was. The assumption that the struggle for mastery was primarily decided by education, railways, coal and steel is an enduring one. The year 1866 has been described variously as the triumph of coal and iron; of Protestantism over Catholicism; and even as the 'victory of the Prussian schoolmasters'.[9] Indeed, Marx and Engels observed presciently in 1845 that 'One can hardly say of the Austrian people that it belongs to the civilized world, and as consequently it has submitted tamely to paternalist despotism, Prussia is the state that must be regarded as the centre of modern German history.'[10] But the link between socio-economic modernization and political strength was always attenuated and sometimes paradoxical. After all, Prussia was not primarily defeated in 1806 because she was backward, nor did Russia and Saxony survive because they were progressive; geography and diplomacy mattered. Moreover, throughout our period, Prussia was never stronger than during the socio-economically comparatively static later reign of Frederick the Great. Conversely, Prussia was never more abject than immediately after 1815 or in 1849–50, when the modernization gap between her and Austria had never been larger and was widening.

Rather, the reasons for Prussian strength and Austrian weakness were narrowly political, foreign-political and geopolitical. First of all, Austria had to contend with a double dualism: with Prussia inside the *Reich* and later the *Bund*, and with Hungary within her own empire. Whereas in Prussia foreign-political crises tended to strengthen domestic cohesion, in Austria they enabled the Hungarians to extort a series of anti-centralist and anti-modernizing compromises. And after the trauma of Joseph II, Metternich was determined to avoid confrontation in Hungary through a policy of cooperation and appeasement. The size and population of Austria was thus always deceptive; unlike Prussia, a substantial proportion of the empire was not pulling its weight. If one were to identify one domestic reason why Austria lost the struggle for mastery, it would be Hungary.

Secondly, the primacy of foreign policy tended to favour Prussia. The experience of invasion and partition after 1792, and the threat of revanchism after 1815, had shown that Germany needed tighter federal or even unitary rather than loose confederal bonds. The *Reich* had failed. This was not because it had failed to modernize. Admittedly, even the most skilled carpenter could hardly fashion a modern state out of the crooked timber of the old *Reich*. On the other hand, it proved quite capable of containing any self-generated dynamic, modernizing or partitionist; at the same time the *Reich* had ensured a pluralism of views, religions and universities unparalleled in Europe. But it proved unable to protect the German political commonwealth from external predators and ultimately from itself: this marked the temporary end of a trusting German belief in the juridification of political conflicts. After 1815, this pattern was to be repeated with the *Bund*; it too tolerated a multiplicity of political existences. But like the *Reich*, it was not capable of providing for the defence of the German political commonwealth. Instead, after the geopolitical revolution of 1815, Prussia was cast willy-nilly as the champion of the national cause. The old Germany was never intended to be a *Machtstaat*, but the new Germany would have to be one.

# NOTES AND REFERENCES

Abbreviations used in the Notes and References and Bibliographical Essay:

AHR      *American Historical Review*
CEH      *Central European History*
GG       *Geschichte und Gesellschaft*
GH       *German History*
HJ       *Historical Journal*
HZ       *Historische Zeitschrift*
JMH      *Journal of Modern History*
PCRE     *Proceedings of the Consortium on Revolutionary Europe*
PP       *Past and Present*
ZFHF     *Zeitschrift für Historische Forschung*

## 1 Introduction

1. Quoted in Alexander von Hase, 'Das konservative Europa in Bedrängnis: zur Krise des Gleichgewichtspublizisten Friedrich von Gentz (1805–1809)', *Saeculum*, 29 (1978), 393.
2. Quoted in Klaus Deppermann, 'Der preußische Absolutismus und der Adel: eine Auseinandersetzung mit der marxistischen Absolutismustheorie', *Geschichte und Gesellschaft*, 8 (1982), 546.
3. See T. C. W. Blanning, 'The death and transfiguration of Prussia', *Historical Journal*, 29 (1986), 458–9.
4. See Thomas Nipperdey, 'Probleme der Modernisierung', *Saeculum*, 30 (1979), 292 *et passim*; Hartmut Kaelble, Horst Matzerath, Hermann-Josef Rupieper, Peter Steinbach, Heinrich Volkmann, *Problem der Modernisierung in Deutschland. Sozialhistorische Studien zum 19. und 20. Jahrhundert* (Opladen, 1978), 6–7; Hans-Ulrich Wehler, 'Max Webers Klassentheorie und die neuere Sozialgeschichte', in Wehler, *Aus der Geschichte lernen? Essays* (Munich, 1988), 155 *et passim*.
5. For an introduction to the *Sonderweg* see David Blackbourn and Geoff Eley, *The Peculiarities of German History: bourgeois society and politics in nineteenth-century Germany* (Oxford, 1984).
6. Paradigmatic: Hans-Ulrich Wehler, *Deutsche Gesellschaftsgeschichte. Vol. I. Vom Feudalismus des alten Reiches bis zur defensiven Modernisierung der Reformära 1700–1815* (Munich, 1987), especially 347–550.
7. See Lothar Gall's critique of Wehler's *Gesellschaftsgeschichte*: 'Deutsche Gesel-

lschaftsgeschichte', *Historische Zeitschrift*, 248 (1989), 365–75; and Gall (ed.), *Vom alten zum neuen Bürgertum. Die mitteleuropäische Stadt im Umbruch, 1780–1820*, HZ *Beiheft* 14 (Munich, 1990), esp. 2–3, 7.

8. Cited in Barbara Vogel, *Allgemeine Gewerbefreiheit. Die Reformpolitik des preußischen Staatskanzlers Hardenberg (1810–1820)* (Göttingen, 1983), 12–13.

## 2   Germany before the French Invasion, 1779–92

1. Cited in T. C. W. Blanning, 'Empire and state in Germany, 1648–1848', *German History*, 12 (1994), 225.

2. John Gagliardo, *Reich and Nation: The Holy Roman Empire as idea and reality, 1763–1806* (Bloomington, IN, 1980), 3.

3. Karl Otmar von Aretin, *Heiliges römisches Reich 1776–1806. Reichsverfassung und Staatssouveränität*, 2 vols (Wiesbaden, 1967).

4. Charles Ingrao, *The Hessian Mercenary State: ideas, institutions and reform under Frederick II, 1760–1785* (Cambridge, 1987), 2.

5. See Hans Jürgen Jüngling, *Reichsstädtische Herrschaft und bäuerlicher Protest. Der Konflikt zwischen der Reichsstadt Schwäbisch Gmünd und ihrem Landgebiet (1775–1792)* (Schwäbisch Gmünd, 1989).

6. See the figures in Jürgen Kocka, *Weder Stand noch Klasse. Unterschichten um 1800* (Bonn, 1990), 53.

7. Cited in Silke Göttsch, 'Widerständigkeit leibeigener Untertanen auf schleswig-holsteinischen Gütern im 18 Jahrhundert', in Jan Peters (ed.), *Gutsherrschaft als soziales Modell Beiheft 18 Historische Zeitschrift* (Munich, 1995), 368.

8. See Werner Trossbach, *Bauern. 1648–1806* (Munich, 1993), 12–16.

9. See Edgar Melton, '*Gutsherrschaft* in East-Elbian Germany and Lithuania, 1500–1800: a critique of the model', *Central European History*, 21 (1988), 315–49.

10. Helmuth Feigl, 'Die Auswirkungen der theresianisch-josephinischen Reformgesetzgebung auf die ländliche Sozialstruktur Österreichs', in Richard Plaschka and Grete Klingenstein (eds), *Österreich im Europa der Aufklärung. Kontinuität und Zäsur in Europa zur Zeit Maria Theresias un Josephs II* (Vienna, 1985), 46.

11. Edgar Melton, 'The decline of Prussian *Gutsherrschaft* and the rise of the Junker as rural patron, 1750–1806', *German History*, 12 (1994), 337.

12. Wilfrid Reininghaus, *Gewerbe in der frühen Neuzeit* (Munich, 1990), 71–2.

13. Troßbach, *Bauern*, 22–5.

14. Bernd Roeck, *Lebenswelt und Kultur des Bürgers* (Munich, 1991), 14.

15. Christine Vanja, 'Zwischen Verdrängung und Expansion, Kontrolle und Befreiung – Frauenarbeit im 18. Jahrhundert im deutschsprachigem Raum', *Vierteljahresschrift für Sozial- und -Wirtschaftsgeschichte*, 79 (1992), 460–1.

16. Troßbach, *Bauern*, 88–90.

17. Claudia Ulbrich in Peters (ed.), *Gutsherrschaft als soziales Modell*, 359–64.

18. David Warren Sabean, *Property, production and family in Neckarhausen, 1700–1870* (Cambridge, 1990), 223–46.
19. Peter Borscheid, 'Jugend und Alter. Zum Verhältnis der Generationen zwischen den Revolutionen 1789–1918', *Archiv für Sozialgeschichte*, 30 (1990), 2.
20. See Richard van Dülmen, *Theater des Schreckens. Gerichtspraxis und Strafrituale in der frühen Neuzeit* (Munich, 1985).
21. Friedrich Lenger, *Sozialgeschichte der deutsche Handwerker seit 1800* (Frankfurt, 1988), 13–14.
22. See Norbert Finzsch, *Obrigkeit und Unterschichten: zur Geschichte der rheinischen Unterschichten gegen Ende des 18. und zu Beginn des 19. Jahrhunderts* (Stuttgart, 1990).
23. Sylvia Paletschek, 'Adelige und bürgerliche Frauen (1770–1870)', in Elizabeth Fehrenbach (ed.), *Adel und Bürgertum in Deutschland, 1770–1848* (Munich, 1994), 169.
24. Schulamit Volkov, *Die Juden in Deutschland, 1780–1918* (Munich, 1994), 4.
25. Peter Blickle, *Unruhen in der ständischen Gesellschaft, 1300–1800* (Munich, 1988), 97.
26. Otto Ulbricht, 'The debate about foundling hospitals in eighteenth-century Germany: infanticide, illegitimacy and infant mortality rates', *Central European History*, 18 (1985), 168.
27. Ernst Schubert, *Arme Leute, Bettler und Gauner im Franken des 18. Jahrhunderts* (Neustadt, 1983), 248–9.
28. See Josef Mooser, *Ländliche Klassengesellschaft, 1770–1848. Bauern und Unterschichten, Landwirtschaft und Gewerbe im östlichen Westfalen* (Göttingen, 1984).
29. See Diedrich Saalfeld, 'Ländliche Bevölkerung und Landwirtschaft Deutschlands am Vorabend der Französischen Revolution', *Zeitschrift für Agrargeschichte und Agrarsoziologie*, 37 (1989), 106.
30. Kocka, *Unterschichten um 1800*, 202.
31. Hanna Schissler, 'Die Junker. Zur Sozialgeschichte und historischen Bedeutung der agrarischen Elite in Preußen', in Hans-Ulrich Wehler and H. J. Puhle (eds), *Preußen im Rückblick*, Sonderheft 6 Geschichte und Gesellschaft (Göttingen, 1980), 97; Heinz Reif, *Westfälischer Adel 1770–1860. Vom Herrschaftsstand zur regionalen Elite* (Göttingen, 1979).
32. Wolfgang Neugebauer, *Politischer Wandel im Osten. Ost- und Westpreußen von den alten Ständen zum Konstitutionalismus* (Stuttgart, 1992).
33. Clemens Zimmermann, 'Bäuerlicher Traditionalismus und agrarischer Fortschritt in der frühen Neuzeit', in Peters (ed.), *Gutsherrschaft als soziales Modell*, 228–38.
34. Troßbach, *Bauern*, 67.
35. Troßbach, *Bauern*, 63.
36. Christoph Dipper, 'Landwirtschaft und ländliche Gesellschaft um 1800', in Helmut Berding and Hans-Peter Ullmann (eds), *Deutschland zwischen Revolution und Restauration* (Königsstein, 1981), 291.
37. Saalfeld, 'Ländliche Bevölkerung', 106.
38. Quoted in Wilhelm Bleek, *Von der Kameralsbildung zum Juristenprivilege. Studium, Prüfung und Ausbildung der höheren Beamten des allgemeinen Verwaltungsdienstes in Deutschland im 18. und 19. Jahrhundert* (Göttingen, 1985), 61.
39. Ulrike Müller-Weil, *Absolutismus und Außenpolitik in Preußen. Ein Beitrag zur Strukturgeschichte des preußischen Absolutismus* (Stuttgart, 1992), 233.

40. Harm Klueting, *Die Lehre von der Macht der Staaten. Das außenpolitische Machtproblem in der 'politischen Wissenschaft' und in der praktischen Politik im achtzehnten Jahrhundert* (Berlin, 1986), 155, 253.

41. Contra Franz Szabo, 'Prince Kaunitz and the balance of power', *International History Review*, 1 (1979), 399–408. See now Franz Szabo, *Kaunitz and Enlightened Absolutism, 1753–1780* (Cambridge, 1994); Klueting, *Die Lehre von der Macht der Staaten*, 182–4.

42. See Otto Hintze, 'Staatenbildung und Verfassungsentwicklung. Eine historisch-politische Studie', in Otto Hintze, *Staat und Verfassung: Gesammelte Abhandlungen zur allgemeine Verfassungsgeschichte*, ed. Gerhard Oestreich, intro. Fritz Hartung (Göttingen, 1962), 49.

43. Cited in Günther Birtsch, 'Zur sozialen und politischen Rolle des deutschen vornehmlich preußischen Adels am Ende des 18. Jahrhundert', in Rudolf Vierhaus (ed.), *Der Adel vor der Revolution. Zur sozialen und politischen Funktion des Adels im vorrevolutionären Europa* (Göttingen, 1971), 87.

44. D. E. Schremmer, 'Taxation and public finance: Britain, France and Germany', in Peter Mathias and Sidney Pollard (eds), *The Cambridge Economic History of Europe Vol. VIII, The industrial economies: the development of economic and social policies* (Cambridge, 1989).

45. See the classic account by Otto Büsch, *Militärsystem und Sozialleben im alten Preußen 1737–1807. Die Anfänge der sozialen Militarisierung der preussisch-deutschen Gesellschaft* (Berlin, 1962).

46. Manfred Messerschmitt, 'Preußens Militär in seinem gesellschaftlichen Umfeld', in Puhle (ed.), *Preußen im Rückblick, passim*.

47. Hanna Schissler, 'Germany: the social and political power of the Prussian Junkers', in Martin Blinkhorn and Ralph Gibson (eds), *Landownership and Power in Modern Europe* (London, 1991), 103.

48. Hermann Wellenreuther, 'Forschungen zur Geschichte der Arbeiter in Deutschland, England und Nordamerika im 18. Jahrhundert: Der Arbeitsmarkt', in Klaus Tenfelde (ed.), *Arbeiter und Arbeiterbewegung im Vergleich. Berichte zur internationalen historischen Forschung* (Munich, 1986), 84.

49. Wilhelm Naudé, 'Die brandenburgisch-preußische Getreidehandelspolitik von 1713-1806', in [Schmoller's] *Jahrbuch für Gesetzgebung, Verwaltung und Volkswirtschaft im deutschen Reiche*, 29 (1905), 161–90; August Skalweit, *Die Getreidehandelspolitik und Kriegsmagazinverwaltung Preußens, 1756–1806* (Berlin, 1936).

50. Richard van Dülmen, *Frauen vor Gericht: Kindsmord in der frühen Neuzeit* (Frankfurt, 1991); Ann Taylor Allen, *Feminism and motherhood in Germany, 1800–1914* (New Brunswick, NJ, 1991), 19 on 'biopolitics'.

51. Rudolf von Thadden, 'Kirche im Schatten des Staates. Zur Problematik der evangelischen Kirche in der preußischen Geschichte', in Puhle and Wehler (eds), *Preußen im Rückblick*, 146–75.

52. Brendan Simms, *The Impact of Napoleon: Prussian high politics, foreign policy and the crisis of the executive, 1797–1806* (Cambridge, 1997), 35–41.

53. Hans Rosenberg, *Bureaucracy, Aristocracy and Autocracy: the Prussian experience 1660–1815* (Cambridge, MA, 1958).

54. Ibid., *passim*, and Eckhart Kehr, 'Zur Genesis der preußischen Bürokratie und des Rechtsstaats', in *Der Primat der Innenpolitik. Gesammelte Aufsätze zur preußisch-*

deutschen Sozialgeschichte im 19. und 20. Jahrhundert, ed. Hans-Ulrich Wehler (Berlin, 1975), 31–52.

55. W. L. Dorn, 'The Prussian bureaucracy in the eighteenth century', Political Science Quarterly, 47 (1932), 261.

56. Jürg Zimmermann, 'Militärverwaltung und Heeresaufbringung in Oesterreich bis 1806', in Militärgeschichtliches Forschungsamt (ed.), Deutsche Militärgeschichte in sechs Bänden, 1648–1939, I (Munich, 1983) 111.

57. Contra Ingrao, The Hessian Mercenary State, 6–7.

58. See Maiken Umbach, 'Franz of Anhalt-Dessau and England: the Wörlitz landscape garden and anti-Prussian politics in the late Enlightenment', (Ph.D. thesis, University of Cambridge, 1996), 283, for a critique of Ingrao.

59. See most recently Peter Wilson, War, State and Society in Württemberg, 1677–1793 (Cambridge, 1995).

60. Volker Press, 'Landtage im Alten Reich und im Deutschen Bund. Voraussetzungen ständischer und konstuitutioneller Entwicklungen 1750–1830', in Zeitschrift für Württembergische Landesgeschichte, 39 (1980), 103.

61. Karl Otmar von Aretin, Bayerns Weg zum souveränen Staat. Landstände und konstitutionelle Monarchie, 1714–1818 (Munich, 1976), 60.

62. Aretin, Bayerns, 31; Gabriele Haug-Moritz, Württembergischer Ständekonflikt und deutscher Dualismus. Ein Beitrag zur Geschichte des Reichsverbandes in der Mitte des 18. Jahrhunderts (Stuttgart, 1992).

63. Erwin Hölzle, Das alte Recht und die Revolution. Geschichte Württembergs in der Revolutionszeit, 1789–1805 (Munich, 1931), 22.

64. Ingrao, The Hessian Mercenary State, 9 et passim. But see also Peter K. Taylor, Indentured to liberty: peasant life and the Hessian military state, 1688–1815 (Ithaca, NY, 1994).

65. Ingrao, The Hessian Mercenary State, 212.

66. Keith Tribe, 'Cameralism and the science of government', JMH, 56 (1984), passim; James Allen Vann, 'On the nature of German reform: a commentary', Proceedings of the Consortium on Revolutionary Europe (PCRE), 1981, 95.

67. Andreas Gestrich, Absolutismus und Öffentlichkeit. Politische Kommunikation in Deutschland zu Beginn des 18. Jahrhunderts (Göttingen, 1994).

68. See Jürgen Habermas, Strukturwandel der Öffentlichkeit: Untersuchungen zu einer Kategorie der bürgerlichen Gesellschaft (Neuwied, 1962).

69. Daniel Moran, Toward the Century of Words. Johann Cotta and the politics of the public realm in Germany (1795–1832) (Berkeley, Los Angeles, and Oxford, 1990), 4–5.

70. Werner Schneiders, 'Die philosophie des aufgeklärten Absolutismus. Zum Verhältnis von Philosophie und Politik, nicht nur im 18. Jahrhundert', in Hans Erich Bödeker and Ulrich Herrmann (eds.), Aufklärung als Politisierung-Politisierung der Aufklärung (Hamburg, 1987), 33; Horst Möller, Vernunft und Kritik. Deutsche Aufklärung im 17. und 18. Jahrhundert (Frankfurt, 1986), 281–3.

71. Gestrich, Absolutismus und Öffentlichkeit, passim.

72. James Allen Vann, 'On the nature of German reform', PCRE, 93. Contra Peter Gay, The Enlightenment: an interpretation, 2 vols (New York, 1966–9).

73. Joachim Whaley, 'The ideal of youth in late eighteenth-century Germany', in Mark Roseman (ed.), Generations in conflict: youth revolt and generation formation in Germany 1770–1968 (Cambridge, 1995) 55.

74. Ibid., 62.

75. Richard van Dülmen, *The Society of the Enlightenment: the rise of the middle class and Enlightenment culture in Germany* (Cambridge, 1992), 115–17.
76. Horst Möller, 'Aufklärung und Adel', in Fehrenbach (ed.), *Adel und Bürgertum*, 1.
77. I owe this phrase to Maiken Umbach, 'Franz von Anhalt-Dessau', 48.
78. Immanuel Kant, 'An answer to the question: what is Enlightenment?', in Hans Reiss (ed.), *Kant's Political Writings* (Cambridge, 1970), 54.
79. T. C. W. Blanning, 'Frederick the Great and enlightened absolutism', in H. M. Scott (ed.), *Enlightened Absolutism: reform and reformers in later eighteenth-century Europe* (Basingstoke, 1990), 286
80. Paradigmatic: Marc Raeff, *The Well-ordered Police State: social and institutional change through law in the Germanies and Russia 1600–1800* (New Haven, 1983).
81. Derek Beales, 'The false Joseph II', *Historical Journal*, 18 (1975).
82. Klueting, *Die Lehre von der Macht der Staaten*, 159.
83. Ibid., 219.
84. Joseph Karniel, *Die Toleranzpolitik Kaiser Josephs II* (Gerlingen, 1985), 243.
85. *Pace* John Breuilly, 'State-building, modernization and liberalism from the late eighteenth century to unification: German peculiarities', *European History Quarterly*, 22 (1992), 260.
86. Quoted in T. C. W. Blanning, *Joseph II* (London, 1994), 76.
87. John Komlos, *Nutrition and Economic Development in the Eighteenth-century Habsburg Monarchy* (Princeton, NJ, 1989), 125.
88. Komlos, *Nutrition and Economic Development*, 127.
89. Klueting, *Lehre von der Macht der Staaten*, 248.
90. Feigl, 'Auswirkungen', 51.
91. W. R. Lee, 'Tax structure and economic growth in Germany (1750–1850)', *Journal of European Economic History*, 4 (1975), 158.
92. Clemens Zimmermann, *Reformen in der bäuerlichen Gesellschaft. Studien zum aufgeklärten Absolutismus in der Markgrafschaft Baden* (Ostfildern, 1983), 7; Helen P. Liebel, *Enlightened Bureaucracy versus Enlightened Despotism in Baden, 1750–1792* (Philadelphia, 1965).
93. Zimmermann, 'Bäuerlicher Traditionalismus und agrarischer Fortschritt', 229–31.
94. Stefan Brakensiek, 'Agrarian individualism in north-western Germany', *German History*, 12 (1994), 149.
95. Feigl, 'Auswirkungen', 56.
96. Blanning, *Joseph II*, 58.
97. David Good, *The Economic Rise of the Habsburg Empire: 1750–1914* (Berkeley, CA, 1984), 34–5.
98. Henry E. Strakosch, *State Absolutism and the Rule of Law: the struggle for the codification of civil law in Austria 1753–1811* (Sydney, 1967), 152–63.
99. Gustav Otruba, 'Staatshaushalt und Staatsschuld unter Maria Theresia und Joseph II', in Plaschka and Klingenstein (eds), *Österreich im Europa der Aufklärung*, 211.
100. Ibid., 213.
101. See Roman Rozdolsky, *Untertan und Staat in Galizien. Die Reformen unter Maria Theresia und Joseph II* edited by Ralph Melville (Mainz, 1992).
102. Ibid., XX.

103. Otruba, 'Staatshaushalt und Staatsschuld', 214.
104. Blanning, *Joseph II*, 65.
105. Zimmermann, 'Militärverwaltung und Militäraufbringung in Oesterreich', 114.
106. Rozdolsky, *Untertan und Staat in Galizien*, xxii.
107. Ernst Wangermann, 'Preußen und die revolutionären Bewegungen in Ungarn und den österreichischen Niederlanden zur Zeit der Französischen Revolution', in Otto Büsch and Monika Neugebauer-Wölk (eds), *Preußen und die revolutionäre Herausforderung seit 1789* (Berlin, 1991), 83.
108. Andreas Schulz, *Herrschaft durch Verwaltung. Die Rheinbundreformen in Hessen-Darmstadt unter Napoleon (1803–1815)* (Stuttgart, 1991), 21.
109. Aretin, *Bayern*, 116.
110. Quoted in Karl Otmar von Aretin, 'Deutschland und die französische Revolution', in Aretin and Karl Härter (eds), *Revolution und konservatives Beharren. Das alte Reich und die Französische Revolution* (Mainz, 1990), 13.
111. Aretin, *Bayern*, 14–15; Wilson, *War, State and Society in Württemberg*, 8 *et passim*.
112. Alexander von Witzleben, *Staatsfinanznot und sozialer Wandel. Eine finanzsoziologische Analyse der preußischen Reformzeit zu Beginn des 19. Jahrhunderts* (Stuttgart and Wiesbaden, 1995), 61–7; Schremmer, *passim*.
113. Rainer Wohlfeil, *Vom stehenden Heer des Absolutismus zur allgemeinen Wehrpflicht (1789–1814)* Handbuch zur deutschen Militärgeschichte 1648–1939 (Frankfurt am Main, 1964), 87.
114. Cited in Eberhard Weis, 'Enlightenment and absolutism in the Holy Roman Empire: thoughts on enlightened absolutism in Germany', *JMH*, 58 (1986), 185.
115. Cited in Wohlfeil, *Vom stehenden Heer des Absolutismus*, 99.
116. Dennis Showalter, 'Hubertusburg [*sic*] to Auerstädt: the Prussian army in decline', *German History*, 12 (1994), 318–19.
117. See Wolfgang Ruppert, *Bürgerlicher Wandel. Studien zur Herausbildung einer nationalen deutschen Kultur im 18. Jahrhundert* (Frankfurt and New York, 1981).
118. Ingrao, *The Hessian Mercenary State*, 139.
119. Blanning, *Joseph II*, 205.
120. Feigl, 'Auswirkungen', 57.
121. Christopher Clark, *The Politics of Conversion: missionary Protestantism and the Jews in Prussia 1728–1941* (Oxford, 1995), 44.
122. Quoted Liebel, *Enlightened Bureaucracy versus Enlightened Despotism in Baden*, 32.
123. Cited in Rainer Erb and Werner Bergmann, *Die Nachtseite der Judenemanzipation. Der Widerstand gegen die Integration der Juden in Deutschland, 1780–1860* (Berlin, 1989), 21.
124. Rudolf Vierhaus, *Germany in the Age of Absolutism*, trans. Jonathan Knudsen (Cambridge, 1988), 89.
125. Eckhard Buddruss, 'Die Deutschlandpolitik der Französischen Revolution zwischen Traditionen und revolutionärem Bruch', in Aretin and Härter (eds), *Deutschland und die Französische Revolution*, 147.
126. Cited in Charles Ingrao, 'Habsburg Strategy and Geopolitics during the Eighteenth Century', in Gunther Rothenberg, Béla Kiraly and Peter Sugar (eds), *East Central European Society and War in the Pre-revolutionary Eighteenth Century* (Boulder, CO, 1982), 58.

127. Cited in Klueting, *Die Lehre von der Macht der Staaten*, 178–9.
128. Cited in Klueting, *Die Lehre von der Macht der Staaten*, 222.
129. Klueting, *Die Lehre von der Macht der Staaten*, 178.
130. Hamish Scott, 'Aping the great powers: Frederick the Great and the defence of Prussia's international position, 1763–1786', *German History*, 12 (1994), 287.
131. Klueting, *Die Lehre von der Macht der Staaten*, 232–3.
132. Cited in Blanning, *Joseph II*, 135.
133. Ibid., 132
134. Haug-Moritz, *Württembergischer Ständekonflikt und deutscher Dualismus*, 169.
135. Peter Burg, *Die deutsche Trias in Idee und Wirklichkeit. Vom alten Reich zum deutschen Zollverein* (Wiesbaden und Stuttgart, 1989), 10.
136. Cited in Claus Scharf, *Katharina II, Deutschland und die Deutschen* (Mainz, 1995), 369.
137. Hölzle, *Das alte Recht und die Revolution*, 64.
138. Blanning, *Joseph II*, 150.
139. Pace Haug-Moritz, *Württembergischer Ständekonflikt und deutscher Dualismus*, passim.
140. Wehler, *Gesellschaftsgeschichte*, I, 48.

## 3 The Impact of the French Wars, 1792–1815

1. Hölzle, *Das alte Recht und die Revolution*, 99.
2. T. C. W. Blanning, *The French Revolutionary Wars* (London, 1996).
3. Cited in Eckhard Buddruss, *Die französische Deutschlandpolitik, 1756–1789* (Mainz, 1995), 149.
4. Cited in Dominique Bourel, 'Zwischen Abwehr und Neutralität. Preußen und die Französische Revolution 1789 bis 1795/1795 bis 1803/6', in Neugebauer-Wölk and Büsch (eds), *Preußen und die revolutionäre Herausforderung*, 47.
5. Quoted in G. P. Gooch, *Germany and the French Revolution* (London, 1920), 393–4.
6. Quoted in Gooch, *Germany and the French Revolution*, 509–10.
7. Horst Möller, 'Der Primat der Aussenpolitik: Preussen und die Französische Revolution', in Jürgen Voss (ed.), *Deutschland und die französische Revolution* (Munich, 1983), 65–81.
8. Helmut Reinalter, 'Einwirkungen der Französischen Revolution auf die Innen- und Außenpolitik des Kaiserhofes in Wien', in Reinalter, *Die Französische Revolution und Mitteleuropa. Erscheinungsformen und Wirkungen des Jakobinismus. Seine Gesellschaftheorien und politischen Vorstellungen* (Frankfurt am Main, 1988), 97.
9. Ibid., 102.
10. T.C.W. Blanning, *The Origins of the French Revolutionary Wars* (London, 1986).
11. See Kurt Heidrich, *Preussen im Kampfe gegen die französische Revolution bis zur Zweiten Teilung Polens* (Stuttgart and Berlin, 1908).
12. See Marcelle Adler-Bresse, *Sièyes et le monde allemande* (Lille and Paris, 1977).

13. Cited in Max Braubach, 'Frankreichs Rheinlandpolitik im Zeitalter der Französischen Revolution', *Archiv für Politik und Geschichte*, 5 (1927), 175.
14. Buddruss, *Französische Deutschlandpolitik, passim*.
15. Braubach, 'Frankreichs Rheinlandpolitik', 180.
16. Eckhard Buddruss, 'Die Deutschlandpolitik der Französischen Revolution zwischen Traditionen und revolutionärem Bruch', in Karl Otmar von Aretin and Karl Härter (eds), *Revolution und konservatives Beharren. Das alte Reich und die Französische Revolution* (Mainz, 1990), 49 *et passim*.
17. On Bavaria see Aretin, *Bayern*, 142.
18. Cited in Hölzle, *Das alte Recht und die Revolution*, 243.
19. Cited in Wolf Gruner, 'Der deutsche Bund und die europäische Friedensordnung', in Helmut Rumpler (ed.), *Deutscher Bund und deutsche Frage, 1815–1866. Europäische Ordnung, deutsche Politik und gesellschaftlicher Wandel im Zeitalter der bürgerlich-nationalen Emanzipation* (Munich, 1990), 242.
20. Quoted in Mathias Bernath, 'Die auswärtige Politik Nassaus 1805–1812. Ein Beitrag zur Geschichte des Rheinbundes und den politischen Ideen am Mittelrhein zur Zeit Napoleons', *Nassauische Annalen*, 63 (1952), 110. See also on further fears of polonization, Kraehe, *Metternich's German Policy*, I, 23.
21. Hölzle, *Das alte Recht und die Revolution*, 131.
22. Cited in Heinz Duchhardt, *Protestantisches Kaisertum und altes Reich. Die Diskussion über die Konfession des Kaisers in Politik, Publizistik, und Staatsrecht* (Wiesbaden, 1977), 313.
23. Waclav Dlugoborski, 'Volksbewegungen im preußisch-polnischen Grenzraum während der Französischen Revolution 1789 bis 1794', in Büsch and Neugebauer-Wölk (eds), *Preußen und die revolutionäre Herausforderung*, 155.
24. Aretin, *Heiliges römisches Reich*, 370 *et passim*; contra Karl Roider, *Baron Thugut and Austria's response to the French Revolution* (Princeton, NJ, 1987).
25. Reinalter, 'Einwirkungen der französischen Revolution', 112–13.
26. Roider, *Thugut and Austria's Response to the French Revolution*, p. xix *et passim*.
27. Johann Eustach von Schlitz zu Görtz, *Memoiren eines deutschen Staatsmannes aus den Jahren 1788–1816* (Leipzig, 1833), 184.
28. Quoted in Kraehe, *Metternich's German policy*, I, 22.
29. Quoted in Aretin, *Heiliges römisches Reich*, 349.
30. Heinz Duchhardt, *Protestantisches Kaisertum und altes Reich. Die Diskussion über die Konfession des Kaisers in Politik, Publizistik und Staatsrecht* (Wiesbaden, 1977).
31. See Simms, *The Impact of Napoleon, passim* for the background to this.
32. Blanning, 'The French Revolution and the modernisation of Germany', *CEH*, 22 (1989), 116.
33. Cited Bernath, 'Auswärtige Politik Nassaus', 133.
34. Ibid., 133.
35. Cited ibid., 129; similar sentiment: 120.
36. Hölzle, *Das alte Recht und die Revolution*, 329–30.
37. Cited in Eva Kell, 'Die Frankfurter Union (1803–1806). Eine Fürstenassoziation zur verfassungsmäßigen Selbsterhaltung der kleineren weltlichen Adelsherrschaften', *ZFHF*, 18 (1991), 76.
38. Enno Kraehe, 'Foreign policy and the nationalities problem in the Habsburg monarchy, 1800–1867', *Austrian History Yearbook*, 3 (1967), 4.

39. Duchhardt, *Protestantisches Kaisertum*, 315; Roider, *Thugut and Austria's response to the French Revolution*, 385.

40. Aretin, *Heiliges römisches Reich*, 370.

41. See Brendan Simms, *The Impact of Napoleon: Prussian high politics, foreign policy and executive reform, 1797–1806* (Cambridge, 1997), 101–5.

42. Ingrao, 'Habsburg geopolitics', 63.

43. Kraehe, *Metternich's German Policy*, I, 29.

44. Uta Krüger-Löwenstein, *Russland, Frankreich und das Reich, 1801–1803* (Wiesbaden, 1972); Ulrike Eich, *Russland und Europa: Studien zur russischen Deutschlandpolitik in der Zeit des Wiener Kongresses* (Cologne and Vienna, 1986).

45. T. M. Islamov, 'Österreich und Russland. Zusammenarbeit und Gegensatz am Ende des 18. und zu Beginn des 19. Jahrhunderts', in Anna M. Drabek, Walter Leitsch and Richard Plaschka (eds), *Russland und Österreich zur Zeit der napoleonischen Kriege* (Vienna, 1989), 51.

46. Harald Heppner, 'Der österreichisch-russische Gegensatz in Südosteuropa im Zeitalter Napoleons', in Drabek, Leitsch and Plaschka (eds), *Russland und Oesterreich*, 88.

47. Re Austria: Kraehe, *Metternich's German Policy*, I, 29; Prussia: see Simms, *Impact of Napoleon*, 104.

48. Wehler, *Deutsche Gesellschaftsgeschichte*, I, 353–62; Volker Press, 'Warum gab es keine deutsche Revolution? Deutschland und das revolutionäre Frankreich, 1789–1815', in Dieter Langewiesche (ed.), *Revolution und Krieg. Zur Dynamik historischen Wandels seit dem 18. Jahrhundert* (Paderborn, 1989), 67–85.

49. Gooch, Vierhaus, Wehler.

50. See Karl Otmar von Aretin, *Der aufgeklärte Absolutismus* (Cologne, 1967).

51. As cited in Paul Bailleu (ed.), *Preussen und Frankreich 1795–1807* (Leipzig, 1881), vol. I, 505.

52. Karl Wegert, *German Radicals Confront the Common People: revolutionary politics and popular politics, 1789–1849* (Mainz, 1992), 13.

53. T. C. W. Blanning, *Reform and Revolution in Mainz 1743–1803* (Cambridge, 1974); T. C. W. Blanning, 'The German Jacobins and the French Revolution', *HJ*, 23 (1980), 988; T.C.W. Blanning, *The French Revolution in Germany: occupation and resistance in the Rhineland, 1792–1802* (Oxford, 1983).

54. See Reinalter, 'Einwirkungen der Französischen Revolution', 106.

55. Paul Nolte, 'Republikanismus, Revolten und Reformen. Reaktionen auf die Französische Revolution in Deutschland 1789–1820', in Manfred Hettling (ed.), *Revolution in Deutschland? 1789–1989* (Göttingen, 1991), 15.

56. Blickle, *Unruhen*, 100.

57. Klaus Müller, 'Städtische Unruhen im Rheinland des späten 18. Jahrhunderts. Ein Beitrag zur rheinischen Reaktion auf die Französische Revolution', *Rheinische Vierteljahresblätter*, 54 (1990), 184.

58. Wegert, *German Radicals Confront the Common People*, 69 *et passim*.

59. Werner Troßbach, *Bauern 1648–1806* (Munich, 1993), 87; Wegert, *German Radicals Confront the Common People*, 70.

60. Dipper, 'Landwirtschaft und ländliche Gesellschaft um 1800', in Ullmann and Berding (eds), *Deutschland zwischen Revolution und Restauration*, 292.

61. Kocka, *Unterschichten um 1800*, 193, 218.

62. Albert Eßer, 'Die Lohn-Preis-Entwicklung für landwirtschaftliche Arbeiter in Deutschland, England und Nordamerika im 18. Jahrhundert', in Tenfelde (ed.), *Arbeiter und Arbeiterbewegung im Vergleich*, 106–8; Skalweit, *Getreidehandelspolitik Preussens*, 199–200.

63. Reinalter, 'Auswirkungen der Französischen Revolution', 96; Lenger, *Deutsche Handwerker*, 18.

64. Ingrid Mittenzwei, *Preußen nach dem Siebenjährigen Krieg* (Berlin, 1979), 100, 241–2 *et passim*

65. Rudolf Vierhaus, 'Die Revolution als Gegenstand der geistigen Auseinadersetzung in Deutschland, 1789–1830', in Roger Dufraisse and Elizabeth Müller-Lückner (eds), *Revolution und Gegenrevolution, 1789–1830. Zur geistigen Auseinandersetzung in Frankreich und Deutschland* (Berlin, 1991), 257.

66. Rudolf Vierhaus, '"Sie und nicht wir." Deutsche Urteile über den Ausbruch der französischen Revolution', in Vierhaus, *Deutschland im 18. Jahrhundert: Politische Verfassung, Soziales Gefüge, Geistige Bewegungen* (Göttingen, 1987), 215.

67. Cited in Vierhaus, 'Die Revolution als Gegenstand der geistigen Auseinandersetzung', in Dufraisse and Müller-Lückner (eds), *Revolution und Gegenrevolution*, 252.

68. Horst Möller, 'Preußische Aufklärungsgesellschaften und Revolutionserfahrung', in Büsch and Neugebauer-Wölk (eds), *Preußen und die revolutionäre Herausforderung*, 114.

69. Reinalter, 'Einwirkungen der Französischen Revolution', *passim*.

70. Möller, 'Preußische Aufklärungsgesellschaften', 113–14.

71. Quoted in Gooch, *Germany and the French Revolution*, 72.

72. Eberhard Weis, 'Die außenpolitischen Reaktionen der Deutschen Staaten auf die französische Hegemoniepolitik: zwischen Anpassung und Widerstand', in Karl Otmar Aretin and Gerhard A. Ritter (eds), *Historismus und moderne Geschichtswissenschaft. Europa zwischen Revolution und Restauration 1797–1815* (Wiesbaden, 1987), 188.

73. Liebel, *Enlightened Government in Baden*, 17; Berdahl, *Politics of the Prussian Nobility*, 105.

74. Press, 'Landstände im alten Reich und Bund', 109–10.

75. Hölzle, *Das alte Recht und die Revolution*, 19.

76. Ibid., 22.

77. Ibid., 102.

78. Ibid., 128.

79. Ibid., 105.

80. Ibid., 276.

81. Ibid., 210.

82. Ibid., 145, 244 *passim*.

83. Ibid.: re France: 128; re Prussia: 326.

84. Ibid., 225.

85. Ibid., 259–67.

86. Ibid., 152.

87. Eberhard Weis, 'Bayern und Frankreich in der Zeit des Konsulats und des ersten Empire (1799–1815)', *HZ*, 237 (1983), 566.

88. Weis, 'Bayern und Frankreich', 568.

89. Gooch, *Germany and the French Revolution*, 516.
90. Wehler, *Deutsche Gesellschaftsgeschichte*, I, 531.
91. Gagliardo, *Reich and Nation*, 283.
92. For a spirited defence of the *Reich's* performance in the Revolutionary Wars see Karl Härter, *Reichstag und Revolution, 1789–1806. Die Auseinandersetzung des immerwährenden Reichstags zu Regensburg mit den Auswirkungen der Französischen Revolution auf das alte Reich* (Göttingen, 1992).
93. Blanning, *French Revolution in Germany*, 20.
94. T. C. W. Blanning, 'The French Revolution and the modernisation of Germany', *CEH*, 22 (1989), 110.
95. Wohlfeil, *Vom stehenden Heer des Absolutismus zur allgemeinen Wehrpflicht*, 106.
96. Otto Hintze, 'Preußische Reformbestrebungen vor 1806', in Gerhard Oestreich (ed.), *Regierung und Verwaltung. Gesammelte Abhandlungen zur Staats-, Rechts-, und Sozialgeschichte* (Göttingen, 1967), 504–29. See also Simms, *Impact of Napoleon*, 115–27.
97. Cited in Simms, *Impact of Napoleon*, 127.
98. See Berdahl, *Politics of the Prussian Nobility*, 102–3.
99. Cited in Johannes Ziekursch, *Hundert Jahre schlesischer Agrargeschichte. Vom Hubertusburger Frieden bis zum Abschluß der Bauernbefreiung* (Breslau, 1915), 272.
100. Cited in Wohlfeil, *Vom stehenden Heer des Absolutismus zur allgemeinen Wehrpflicht*, 105.
101. Cited in Colmar von der Goltz, *Von Roßbach bis Jena und Auerstädt: ein Beitrag zur Geschichte des preußischen Heeres* (Berlin, 1906), 543–9.
102. Werner Gembruch, 'Krieg und Heerwesen im politischen Denken des Freiherrn vom Stein', in *Staat und Heer. Ausgewählte historische Studien zum ancien régime, zur Französischen Revolution und zu den Befreiungskriegen* (Berlin, 1990), 520, 547.
103. Mathew Levinger, 'Imagining a nation: the constitutional question in Prussia, 1806–1815', (unpublished D.Phil. dissertation, University of Chicago, 1992), 25–6. Some of Levinger's arguments are more accessible in 'Hardenberg, Wittgenstein and the constitutional question in Prussia, 1815–1822', *German History*, 8 (1990), 260 *et passim*.
104. Neugebauer, *Politischer Wandel im Osten*, 87, 487.
105. See Dietz Bering, *Der Name als Stigma*.
106. *Pace* Schissler, 'Junkers', 102.
107. Klaus Vetter, 'Der brandenburgische Adel und der Beginn der bürgerlichen Umwälzung in Deutschland', in Armgard von Reden-Dohna and Ralph Melville (eds), *Der Adel an der Schwelle des bürgerlichen Zeitalters, 1780–1860* (Stuttgart, 1988), 301.
108. Cited in Wohlfeil, *Vom stehenden Heer des Absolutismus zur allgemeinen Wehrpflicht*, 144.
109. Vetter, 'Der brandenburgische Adel und der Beginn der bürgerlichen Umwälzung in Deutschland', 289 and 298.
110. Schissler, *Preussische Agrargesellschaft im Wandel*.
111. Karl Roider, 'The Habsburg foreign ministry and political reform', *CEH*, 22 (1989), 162–3, 172.
112. Volker Press, 'Das "Droit d'Epaves" des Kaisers von Österreich. Finanzkrise

und Stabilisierungspolitik zwischen Luneviller und Preßburger Frieden', in Helmut Berding (ed.), *Napoleonische Herrschaft und Modernisierung*, Geschichte und Gesellschaft, Beiheft 6/4 (1980), 559.

113. Zimmermann, 'Militärverwaltung und Heeresaufbringung in Oesterreich bis 1806', 126.

114. Roider, 'Habsburg foreign ministry and political reform', 177.

115. Zimmermann, 'Militärverwaltung und Heeresaufbringung in Oesterreich bis 1806', 126.

116. Weis, *Montgelas*, 266 (Bavaria); Bernd Wunder, 'Rolle und Struktur staatlicher Bürokratie in Frankreich und Deutschland', in Berding, François and Ullmann (eds), *Deutschland und Frankreich im Zeitalter der Französichen Revolution*, 145, 151 (Baden); Wolfgang Jäger, *Staatsbildung und Reformpolitik. Politische Modernisierung im Herzogtum Nassau zwischen Französischer Revolution und Restauration* (Wiesbaden, 1993), 265–6.

117. Cited in Karl Wegert, 'The genesis of youthful radicalism: Hesse-Nassau, 1806–1819', *CEH* 10 (1977), 186.

118. Weis, *Montgelas*, 266ff; Weis, 'Bayern und Frankreich in der Zeit des Konsulats', 567.

119. Hölzle, *Das alte Reich*, 295.

120. Elisabeth Fehrenbach, *Vom ancien régime zum Wiener Kongress* (Munich, 1993), 83.

121. Wunder, 'Rolle und Struktur staatlicher Bürokratie', 146–7; Schulz, *Herrschaft durch Verwaltung*, 228; Hölzle, *Das alte Recht*, 304.

122. Jäger, *Staatsbildung und Reformpolitik*, 49.

123. Weis, 'Bayern und Frankreich in der Zeit des Konsulats', 592.

124. Helmut Berding, 'Der Gesellschaftsgedanke Napoleons und seine Auswirkungen im rheinbündischen Deutschland: ein Verrat der Revolution?', in Berding and Müller-Lickner (eds), *Revolution und Gegenrevolution*, 116.

125. Wolfgang von Hippel, 'Napoleonische Herrschaft und Agrarreform in den deutschen Mittelstaaten 1800–1815', in Berding and Ullmann (eds), *Deutschland zwischen Revolution und Restauration*, 301.

126. John Breuilly, 'State-building, modernization and liberalism from the late eighteenth century to unification: German peculiarities', *European History Quarterly*, 22 (1992), 268.

127. Hölzle, *Das alte Recht und die Revolution*, introduction.

128. Press, 'Landstände im alten Reich und Bund', 114.

129. Hans-Peter Ullmann, *Staatsschulden und Reformpolitik. Die Entstehung moderner öffentlicher Schulden in Bayern und Baden, 1780–1820* (Göttingen, 1986), 25 *passim*.

130. Hans-Peter Ullmann, 'The Emergence of Modern Public Debts in Bavaria and Baden between 1780 and 1820', in Peter-Christian Witt (ed.), *Wealth and Taxation in Central Europe: the history and sociology of public finance* (Leamington Spa, Hamburg, New York, 1987), 71.

131. Schulz, *Herrschaft durch Verwaltung*, 260.

132. For a less positive view see Bernd Sösemann (ed.), *Gemeingeist und Bürgersinn. Die preußischen Reformen*, Sonderheft: Forschungen zur brandenburgisch-preußischen Geschichte Neue Folge 2 (Berlin, 1993).

133. Frank-Michael Kuhlemann, *Modernisierung und Disziplinierung. Sozialgeschichte des preußischen Volksschulwesens, 1794–1872* (Göttingen, 1992), 356–7.
134. Fehrenbach, *Vom ancien régime zum Wiener Kongress*, 80.
135. Hölzle, *Das alte Recht und die Revolution*, 24–7.
136. Cited in Fehrenbach, *Vom ancien régime zum Wiener Kongress*, 85.
137. Cited in Erwin Hölzle, *Württemberg im Zeitalter Napoleons und der Deutschen Erhebung. Eine deutsche Geschichte der Wendezeit im einzelstaatlichen Raum* (Stuttgart, 1937), II, 30.
138. Whaley, 'The ideal of youth in late-eighteenth-century Germany', 53.
139. See Heiner Wilharm, 'Rückzugsgefecht der Aufklärung?', *Archiv für Sozialgeschichte*, 29 (1989), 424.
140. Ruppert, *Bürgerlicher Wandel*, 137–8.
141. Cited in Hans-Dietrich Schultz, '"Mittellage" und "Mitteleuropa" in der Diskussion der Geographen seit dem Beginn des 19. Jahrhunderts', *Geschichte und Gesellschaft*, 15 (1989), 251.
142. Cited in Hölzle, *Das alte Recht und die Revolution*, 273.
143. Cited in Hobsbawm, *Nations and Nationalism*, 21.
144. Erich Pelzer, 'Sprachpolitik und Propaganda in Strassburg während der Französischen Revolution', in Aretin and Härter (eds), *Revolution und konservatives Beharren*, 47.
145. Pelzer, 'Sprachpolitik', 55, 52–3.
146. Michael Jeismann, *Das Vaterland der Feinde. Studien zum nationalen Feindbegriff und Selbstverständnis in Deutschland und Frankreich 1792–1918* (Stuttgart, 1992), 16,21,76 *et passim*.
147. See Blanning, *French Revolution in Germany*.
148. Cited in Helmut Bock, 'Reform und revolution. Zur Einordnung des preußischen Reformministeriums Stein in den Kampf zwischen Fortschritt und Reaktion', in Gustav Seeber and Karl-Heinz Noack (eds), *Preußen in der deutschen Geschichte nach 1789* (Berlin, 1983), 72.
149. Levinger, 'Imagining a nation', 15–16.
150. See Dieter Düding, *Organisierter gesellschaftlicher Nationalismus Deutschland (1808–1847). Bedeutung und Funktion der Turner- und Sängervereine für die deutsche nationalbewegung* (Munich, 1984).
151. Kraehe, *Metternich's German Policy*, I, 63.
152. See Walter C. Langsam, *The Napoleonic Wars and Nationalism in Austria* (New York, 1930).
153. Cited in Kraehe, 'Foreign policy and the nationalities problem', 6.
154. Kraehe, *Metternich's German Policy*, I, 135.
155. Ibid., 166.
156. Heppner, 'Der österreich-russische Gegensatz', 90.
157. Kraehe, *Metternich's German Policy*, I, 293.
158. Cited in Michael Rowe, 'German civil administrators and the politics of the Napoleonic state in the Department of the Roer, 1798–1815', (Ph.D. thesis, University of Cambridge, 1996).
159. Contra Michael V. Leggière, 'Soldiers or serfs? The role of the Prussian Landwehr in the campaign of 1815', *PCRE* (1994), 65.
160. Aretin, *Bayern*, 120–1.

## 4  The Old Politics and the New Nation, 1815–39

1. See Wolf Gruner, 'Die deutschen Einzelstaaten und der Deutsche Bund. Zum Problem der "nationalen" Integration in der Frühgeschichte des Deutschen Bundes am Beispiel Bayerns und der süddeutschen Staaten', in Andreas Kraus (ed.), *Land und Reich, Stamm und Nation. Probleme und Perspektiven bayerischer Geschichte. Festgabe für Max Spindler zum 90. Geburtstag* (Munich, 1984), 27

2. Cited in Bertrand Michael Buchmann, *Militär-Diplomatie-Politik. Österreich und Europa 1815 bis 1835* (Berne, Frankfurt and Paris, 1991), 43–4.

3. General Radetzky, 'Militärische Beurteilung der Lage Österreichs, Januar 1828', in Count Radetzky, *Denkschriften militärisch-politischen Inhalts aus dem handschriftlichen Nachlaß des k.k. österreichischen Feldmarschalls Grafen Radetzky* (Stuttgart and Augsburg, 1858), 424–5.

4. Gruner, 'Die deutschen Einzelstaaten und der Deutsche Bund', 27.

5. Cited in Wolf Gruner, 'Der Deutsche Bund und die europäische Friedensordnung', in Helmut Rumpler (ed.), *Deutscher Bund und deutsche Frage, 1815–1866* (Munich, 1990), 248.

6. Enno Kraehe, 'Foreign policy and the nationality problem in the Habsburg monarchy, 1800–1867', *Austrian History Yearbook*, 3 (1967), 14.

7. R. D. Billinger, *Metternich and the German Question: state rights and federal duties 1820–1834* (London, 1991), 20, 12; Billinger, 'The German Confederation: Metternich's school for nationalism for the German princes', *PCRE* (1980), 174.

8. Hellmut Seier, 'Zur Frage der militärischen Exekutive in der Konzeption des Deutschen Bundes', in Johannes Kunisch (ed.), *Staatsverfassung und Heeresverfassung in der europäischen Geschichte der frühen Neuzeit* (Berlin, 1986), 418.

9. Gruner, 'Der Deutsche Bund und die europäische Friedensordnung', 255

10. Ibid., 247.

11. Lawrence J. Baack, *Christian Bernstorff and Prussia: diplomacy and reform conservatism, 1818–1832* (New Brunswick, NJ, 1980), 75.

12. Cited in Wolfgang Heuser, *Kein Krieg in Europa. Die Rolle Preußens im Kreis der europäischen Mächte bei der Entstehung des belgischen Staates (1830–1839)* (Pfaffenweiler, 1992), 60.

13. Burg, *Die Deutsche Trias*, 158, 116.

14. Cited in Baack, *Bernstorff and Prussia*, 46.

15. Wilhelm Treue, *Wirtschafts- und Technik-Geschichte Preussens* (Berlin and New York, 1984), 293.

16. David T. Murphy, 'Prussian aims for the *Zollverein*, 1828–1833', *Historian*, 53 (1991), 287, 291 *et passim*.

17. Cited in Baack, *Bernstorff and Prussia*, 123.

18. Billinger, *Metternich and the German Question*, 36.

19. Cited in Baack, *Bernstorff and Prussia*, 126.

20. Cited in Buchmann, *Militär-Diplomatie-Politik*, 335.

21. Baack, *Bernstorff and Prussia*, 167.

22. Heuser, *Kein Krieg in Europa*, 77.

23. Peter Burg, 'Die französische Politik gegenüber Föderationen und Föderationsplänen deutscher Klein- und Mittelstaaten, 1830–1833', in

Raymond Poidevin and Hans-Otto Sieburg (eds), *Aspects des relations franco-alle-mandes 1830–1848* (Metz, 1978), 54.
24. Baack, *Bernstorff and Prussia*, 190.
25. Jürgen Angelow, *Von Wien nach Königgrätz*. *Die Sicherheitspolitik des deutschen Bundes im europäischen Gleichgewicht 1815–1866* (Munich, 1996), 81.
26. Baack, *Bernstorff and Prussia*, 265.
27. Cited in Angelow, *Von Wien nach Königgrätz*, 63.
28. Moran, *Towards a Century of Words*, 231; Burg, *Die Deutsche Trias*, 228.
29. Burg, 'Die französische Politik gegenüber Föderationen', 26.
30. Baack, *Bernstorff and Prussia*, 271.
31. Berdahl, *The Politics of the Prussian Nobility*, 202.
32. Aretin, *Bayern*, 264.
33. Quoted in Eckhard Trox, *Militärischer Konservativismus*. *Kriegervereine und Militärpartei in Preussen zwischen 1815 und 1848/49* (Stuttgart, 1990), 37.
34. Quoted in Clark, *The Politics of Conversion*, 127.
35. Rudolf Buchner, 'Der Durchbruch des modernen Nationalismus in Deutschland', in *Festgabe dargebracht Harold Steinacker zur Vollendung des 80. Lebensjahres* (Munich, 1955), 311.
36. Reinhart Koselleck, *Preußen zwischen Reform und Revolution. Allgemeines Landrecht, Verwaltung und soziale Bewegung von 1791 bis 1848* (Stuttgart, 1967), *passim*. But see also Hermann Beck, *The Origins of the Authoritarian Welfare State in Prussia: conservatives, bureaucracy and the social question, 1815–1870* (Ann Arbor, MI, 1995).
37. Wehler, *Deutsche Gesellschaftsgeschichte*, II, 330.
38. Ibid., 332.
39. Cited in Herbert Obenaus, *Anfänge des Parlamentarismus in Preussen 1848* (Düsseldorf, 1984), 190, 125.
40. Ibid., 124.
41. Cited in Alfons von Klinkowström, *Aus Metternich's nachgelassenen Papieren* (Vienna, 1881), [Metternich, *Papieren*, III], 67. In same vein see Metternich, *Papieren*, IV, 604.
42. Cited in Buchmann, *Militär-Diplomatie-Politik*, 339.
43. Radetzky, *Denkschriften*, 428.
44. Brandt, *Neoabsolutismus*, 5.
45. Buchmann, *Militär-Diplomatie-Politik*, 168.
46. Brandt, *Neoabsolutismus*, 25; 88.
47. Metternich, *Papieren*, III, 69.
48. Cited in Buchmann, *Militär-Diplomatie-Politik*, 43–4.
49. Ibid., 145.
50. Brandt, *Neoabsolutismus*, 21.
51. Ronald E. Coons, 'Kübeck and the Pre-revolutionary Origins of Austrian Neo-Absolutism', in Ferenc Glatz and Ralph Melville (eds), *Gesellschaft, Politik, und Verwaltung in der Habsburgermonarchie, 1830–1918* (Stuttgart, 1987), 65–74.
52. Metternich to the emperor, 27 Nov. 1817, *Papieren*, III, 68.
53. Radetzky, *Denkschriften*, 446–7.
54. Ibid., 450–1.
55. Cited in O.-H. Brandt (ed.), *Metternich's Denkwürdigkeiten* (Munich, 1926), 9.
56. Coons, 'Kübeck and the Origins of Neo-Absolutism', 62.
57. Metternich to the emperor, 27 Nov. 1817, *Papieren*, III, 68.

58. Buchmann, *Militär-Diplomatie-Politik*, 157–67.
59. Eberhard Büssem, *Die Karlsbader Beschlüsse von 1819* (Hildesheim, 1974), 88; Baack, *Bernstorff and Prussia*, 49.
60. Metternich, *Papieren*, III, 171.
61. Baack, *Bernstorff and Prussia*, 53.
62. Aretin, *Bayern*, 134, 205.
63. Ibid., 224.
64. Loyd E. Lee, 'The German Confederation and the consolidation of state power in the South German states, 1815–1848', *PCRE* (1985), 332–9.
65. See Wolfgang Hartdwig, 'Strukturmerkmale und Entwicklungstendenzen des Vereinswesens in Deutschland 1789–1848', in Otto Dann (ed.), *Vereinswesen und bürgerliche Gesellschaft in Deutschland*, Historische Zeitschrift Beiheft 9, Neue Folge (Munich, 1984).
66. On Berthold Auerbach see Anita Bunyan, ''Volksliteratur' und nationale Identität. Zu kritischen Schriften Berthold Auerbachs', in Martina Lauster (ed.), *Deutschland und der europäische Zeitgeist. Kosmopolitische Dimensionen in der Literatur des Vormärz* (Bielefeld, 1994), 63–89.
67. Moran, *Towards the Century of Words, passim*.
68. Angelow, *Von Wien nach Königgrätz*, 87.
69. Manfred Meyer, *Freiheit und Macht. Studien zum Nationalismus süddeutscher, insbesondere badischer Liberaler 1830–1848* (Frankfurt, 1994), 117–30, 132–3, 137.
70. Quoted in Moran, *Towards the Century of Words*, 270.
71. David Hansemann, *Preußen und Frankreich. Staatswirtschaftlich und politisch unter vorzüglicher Berücksichtigung der Rheinprovinz* (Leipzig, 1834, reprinted 1975), 195.
72. Ibid., 197.
73. Meyer, *Freiheit und Macht*, 69.
74. Jeffry Diefendorf, *Businessmen and Politics in the Rhineland, 1789–1834* (Princeton, NJ, 1980), 5.
75. Cited in Wienfort, *Monarchie in der bürgerlichen Gesellschaft*, 173.
76. Clark, *Politics of Conversion*, 216.
77. Christopher Clark, 'Confessional policy and the limits of state action: Frederick William III and the Prussian church union, 1817–1840', *HJ*, 39 (1996), 985–1004.
78. See R. J. W. Evans, 'The Habsburgs and the Hungarian problem, 1790–1848', *Transactions of the Royal Historical Society*, 39 (1989), 45, for a more positive view.
79. Lorant Tilkovszky, 'Adelige Opposition und der Bauernaufstand in Ungarn und der Wiener Hof, 1831–32', in Glatz and Melville (eds), *Gesellschaft, Politik, und Verwaltung*, 30–2.
80. Kraehe, 'Foreign policy and the nationality problem in the Habsburg monarchy', 16, 19.
81. Cited in Jiri Koralka, *Tschechen im Habsburgerreich und in Europa, 1815–1914. Sozialgeschichtliche Zusammenhänge der neuzeitlichen Nationsbildung und der Nationalitätenfrage in den böhmischen Ländern* (Munich, 1991), 54.
82. Cited in Heuser, *Kein Krieg in Europa*, 93.
83. Koralka, *Tschechen im Habsburgerreich*, 31.
84. Cited in Arthur Haas, 'Austria before the Revolution: the beginning of the internal breakdown', *PCRE* (1986), 370.

85. J. Feldman, 'The Polish Provinces of Austria and Prussia after 1815; the springtime of the nations', in W. F. Reddaway et al. (eds), *The Cambridge History of Poland. From Augustus II to Pilsudski*, vol. II (Cambridge, 1951), 339.

86. See, for example, Lawrence J. Flockherzie, 'State-building and nation-building in the 'Third Germany': Saxony after the Congress Of Vienna', *Central European History*, 24 (1991), 268–92.

87. Otto Vossler, *Die Revolution von 1848 in Deutschland* (Frankfurt, 1967), 39.

88. John W. Cranston, 'The German Confederation and an end to innocence, 1815-1821', *PCRE* (1985), 351.

89. Enno E. Krahe, 'Austria, Russia and the German Confederation, 1813–1820', in Rumpler (ed.), *Deutscher Bund und deutsche Frage*, 278

90. Wehler, *Deutsche Gesellschaftsgeschichte*, II, 412.

91. Ibid., 568.

92. Rainer Erb and Werner Bergmann, *Die Nachtseite der Judenemanzipation. Der Widerstand gegen die Integration der Juden in Deutschland, 1780–1860* (Berlin, 1989), 249, 251.

93. Clark, *Conversion*, 94–6.

94. Volkov, *Juden in Deutschland*, 20.

95. Wegert, *Common Man*, 109.

96. Ibid., 116.

97. Baack, *Bernstorff and Prussia*, 234.

98. Ibid., 243.

99. Hardtwig Brandt, *Parlamentarismus in Württemberg, 1819–1870. Anatomie eines deutschen Landtags* (Düsseldorf, 1987), 424.

100. Brandt, *Parlamentarismus in Württemberg*, 100, 372 *et passim*.

101. Baack, *Bernstorff and Prussia*, 332.

102. Friedrich Meinecke, *Das Leben des Generalfeldmarschalls Hermann von Boyen* (Suttgart, 1899), II, 437; see also Heuser, *Kein Krieg in Europa*, 127.

103. Wehler, *Deutsche Gesellschaftsgeschichte*, II, 547.

104. See David Warren Sabean, *Property, Production and Family in Neckarhausen, 1700–1870* (Cambridge, 1991); see also Robert Lee, 'Family and 'Modernisation': the peasant family and social change in nineteenth-century Bavaria', in Evans and Lee (eds), *The German Family*, 84–119, *passim*.

105. Arthur E. Imhof, 'Women, family and death: excess mortality of women in [*sic*] child-bearing age in four communities in nineteenth-century Germany', in Evans and Lee, *The German Family*, 153.

106. See especially Catherine M. Prelinger, 'Prelude to consciousness. Amalie Sieveking and the female association for the care of the poor and the sick', in John C. Fout (ed.), *German Women in the Nineteenth Century: a social history* (New York and London, 1984), 118–32. See also Frevert, *Women in German History*, 71; Allen, *Feminism and Motherhood in Germany*, 57.

107. Karin Hausen, 'Family and role-division: the polarisation of sexual stereotypes in the nineteenth century – an aspect of the dissociation of work and family life', in Evans and Lee, *The German Family*, 54–5.

108. Volker Press, 'Adel im 19. Jahrhundert. Die Führungsschichten Alteuropas im bürgerlich-bürokratischen Zeitalter', in Armgard von Reden-Dohna and Ralph Melville (eds), *Der Adel an der Schwelle des bürgerlichen Zeitalters, 1780–1860* (Stuttgart, 1988), 5.

109. See Berdahl, *Politics of the Prussian Nobility*.
110. See Berdahl, *Politics of the Prussian Nobility*; Hanna Schissler, *Preussische Agrargesellschaft im Wandel: Wirtschaftliche, gesellschaftliche und politicshe Transform-ationsprozesse von 1763 bis 1847* (Göttingen, 1978).
111. Edgar Melton, 'The decline of Prussian *Gutsherrschaft* and the rise of the Junker as rural patron, 1750–1806', *German History*, 12 (1994), 341.
112. Jerome Blum, 'The condition of the European peasantry on the eve of eman-cipation', *JMH*, 46 (1974), 396.
113. See Press, 'Adel im 19. Jahrhundert', 6.
114. Aretin, *Bayern*, 229,
115. Rosenberg, *Bureaucracy, Aristocracy and Autocracy*.
116. Cited in Wilhelm Bleek, *Von der Kameralausbildung zum Juristenprivileg, Studium, Prüfung und Ausbildung der höheren Beamten des allgemeinen Verwaltungsdienstes in Deutschland im 18. und 19. Jahrhundert* (Göttingen, 1985), 43.
117. Lenore O'Boyle, 'The problem of an excess of educated men in western Europe, 1800–1850', *JMH*, 42 (1970), 471–95.
118. Treue, *Wirtschafts- und Technikgeschichte Preussens*, 361.
119. Nachum Gross, 'Austria-Hungary in the World Economy', in John Komlos (ed.), *Economic Development in the Habsburg Monarchy in the Nineteenth Century: essays* (Boulder, CO, 1983), 11.
120. Metternich to Kübeck, 20 Oct. 1841, Vienna, Metternich, *Papieren*, VI, 534.
121. Treue, *Wirtschafts- und Technikgeschichte Preussens*, 333.
122. See Richard J. Bazillion, 'State bureaucracy and the modernization process in the Kingdom of Saxony, 1830–1861', *German History*, 13 (1995), 308.
123. Treue, *Wirtschafts- und Technikgeschichte Preussens*, 291.
124. Hubert Kiesewetter, 'Economic Preconditions for Germany's Nation-build-ing in the Nineteenth Century', in Hagen Schulze (ed.), *Nation-building in Central Europe* (Leamington Spa, Hamburg and New York, 1987), 95.
125. Richard Tilly, 'The Take-off in Germany', in Erich Angermann and Marie-Luise Frings (eds), *Oceans Apart? Comparing Germany and the United States* (Stuttgart, 1981), 47.
126. Wolfgang Radtke, *Die preußische Seehandlung zwischen Staat und Wirtschaft in der Frühphase der Industrialierung* (Berlin, 1981), 1.
127. Richard H. Tilly, *Vom Zollverein zum Industriestaat. Die wirtschaftlich-soziale Entwicklung Deutschlands 1834–1914* (Munich, 1990), 213ff.
128. Cited in Sheehan, *German History*, 432.
129. Wehler, *Aus der Geschichte lernen?*, 171.
130. Treue, *Wirtschafts- und Technikgeschichte Preussens*, 316–17.
131. Ibid., 350.
132. See Peter Marschalck, 'The Age of Demographic Transition: mortality and fertility', in Klaus J. Bade (ed.), *Population, Labour and Migration in 19th- and 20th-century Germany* (Leamington Spa, Hamburg and New York, 1987), 20.
133. For a useful discussion of pauperism see Frederick D. Marquardt, '*Pauperismus* in Germany during the *Vormärz*', *CEH*, 2 (1969), 77–88.
134. Abel, *Massenarmut*, 327–8.
135. Cited in Hermann Beck, 'State and society in pre-March Prussia: the weavers' uprising, the bureaucracy, and the association for the welfare of workers', *CEH*, 25 (1992), 304.

136. Thomas Küster, *Alte Armut und neues Bürgertum: öffentliche und private Fürsorge in Münster von der Ära Fürstenberg bis zum Ersten Weltkrieg (1756–1914)* (Münster, 1995), 127–9, 201.

137. Rogers Brubaker, *Citizenship and Nationhood in France and Germany* (Cambridge, MA, 1992), 51.

138. Andreas Fahrmeir, 'Ausländer in Deutschland 1815–1866. Zur Gesetzgebung und Praxis von "Fremdenpolizey" in den hessischen Staaten', (MA dissertation, University of Frankfurt, 1994).

139. Reinhard Doerries, 'German Transatlantic Migration from the Early Nineteenth Century to the Outbreak of World War II', in Bade (ed.), *Population, Labour and Migration*, 121.

140. Cited in Hermann Beck, 'Conservatives and the Social Question in Nineteenth-century Prussia', in Larry Eugene Jones (ed.), *Between Reform, Reaction and Resistance: studies in the history of German conservatism from 1789–1945* (Providence, RI, and Oxford, 1993), 77.

141. Wolfgang Hardtwig, 'Krise der Universität, studentische Reformbewegung (1750–1819) und die Sozialisation der jugendlichen deutschen Bildungsschicht. Aufriß eines Forschungsproblemes', *Geschichte und Gesellschaft*, 11 (1985), 159.

142. Wehler, *Aus der Geschichte lernen?*, 164.

143. Bernd Wunder, 'Adel und Bürokratie im Großherzogtum Baden', in Elisabeth Fehrenbach (ed.), *Adel und Bürgertum in Deutschland 1770–1848* (Munich, 1994), 67.

144. Press, 'Adel im 19. Jahrhundert', 17.

145. This is the general anti-revisionist tendency of Fehrenbach (ed.), *Adel und Bürgertum in Deutschland, 1780–1848*.

146. For the nuances particularly of South German liberalism see Lothar Gall, *Bürgertum in Deutschland* (Berlin, 1989); and 'Liberalismus und "bürgerliche Gesellschaft". Zu Charakter und Entwicklung der liberalen Bewegung in Deutschland', *Historische Zeitschrift*, 220 (1975), 324–56.

147. See Mack Walker, *German Home Towns: community, state and general estate, 1648–1871* (Ithaca, NY, 1971).

148. See James Sheehan, 'Liberalism and society in Germany, 1815–1848', *JMH*, 45 (1973), 598.

149. Paul Nolte, *Gemeindebürgertum und Liberalismus in Baden 1800–1850. Tradition-Radikalismus-Republik* (Göttingen, 1993), 420, 424.

150. 'Denkschrift von D. Hansemann über Preußens Lage und Politik', Aachen, 31 Dec. 1830, in Joseph Hansen (ed.), *Rheinische Briefe und Akten zur Geschichte der politischen Bewegung, 1830–1850* (Essen, 1919), I, 70.

151. Beck, 'State and society in pre-March Prussia', 304.

152. Dieter Langewiesche, 'Die deutsche Revolution von 1848/49 und die vorrevolutionäre Gesellschaft: Forschungsstand und Forschungsperspektiven, Teil II', *Archiv für Sozialgeschichte*, 31 (1991), 336.

153. Cited in Sheehan, *German History*, 451.

## 5   The State versus the Nation, 1839–50

1. Irmline Veit-Brause, *Die deutsch-französische Krise von 1840* (Cologne, 1967), 12–14 *et passim*; Horst Lademacher, 'Frankreich, Preussen und die belgische Frage in der Juli-Monarchie', in Poidevin and Sieburg (eds), *Aspects des relations franco-allemandes*, 60.
2. Sylvia Krauss, *Die politischen Beziehungen zwischen Bayern und Frankreich, 1814/1815–1840* (Munich, 1987), 381–3.
3. See Rudolf Buchner, 'Der Durchbruch des modernen Nationalismus in Deutschland', in *Festgabe dargebracht Harold Steinacker zur Vollendung des 80. Lebensjahres* (Munich, 1955), 322.
4. Veit-Brause, *Deutsch-französische Krise*, 25; Gary Cox, 'The crisis of 1840 in the continuum of French strategic planning', *PCRE*, 17 (1987), 561–72.
5. 'Denkschrift von D. Hansemann über Preußens Lage und Politik, August/September 1840', [Hansemann, 1840], 217; again: 265, 267.
6. See Simms, *Impact of Napoleon*, 101.
7. Metternich to Frederick William IV, 9 Oct. 1840, Vienna, in Prince R. Mettenich-Winneburg (ed.), *Aus Metternichs nachgelassenen Papieren* (Vienna, 1884) [Metternich, *Papieren*, VI], 467–8.
8. Harm-Hinrich Brandt, *Der österreichischer Neoabsolutismus: Staatsfinanzen und Politik, 1848–1860*, 2 vols (Göttingen, 1978), 103 *et passim*.
9. Krauss, *Politischen Beziehungen zwischen Bayern und Frankreich*, 394, and Jürgen Angelow, *Von Wien nach Königgrätz. Die Sicherheitspolitik des Deutschen Bundes im europäischen Gleichgewicht, 1815–1866* (Munich, 1996), 121.
10. R. D. Billinger, 'They sing the best songs badly: Metternich, Frederick William IV, and the German Confederation during the war scare of 1840–41', in Rumpler (ed.), *Deutscher Bund und Deutsche Frage*, 110–11; also Werner, *Bavaria in the German Confederation*, 199.
11. Billinger, 'They sing the best songs badly', 97.
12. Loyd Lee, '1840, the confederation and German military reform', *PCRE* (1987), 582.
13. Hansemann, 1830, 76.
14. Ibid., 71.
15. Hansemann, 1840, 265.
16. Hansemann, 1830, 71.
17. Manfred Meyer, *Freiheit und Macht. Studien zum Nationalismus süddeutscher insbesondere badischer Liberaler 1830–1848* (Frankfurt, 1994), 178, 198–9, 201–2.
18. Heinrich von Gagern to Hans Christian von Gagern, 17 Mar. 1845, Mosheim, in Paul Wentzcke and Wolfgang Klötzer (eds), *Deutscher Liberalismus im Vormärz. Heinrich von Gagern. Briefe und Reden 1815–1848* [Gagern, *Briefe*] (Göttingen, Berlin and Frankfurt am Main, 1959), 289.
19. Karl Biedermann, 'Die Fortschritte des nationalen Prinzips in Deutschland', cited in Hans Fenske (ed.), *Vormärz und Revolution, 1840–1849* (Darmstadt, 1976), 58.
20. Dieter Langewiesche, *Liberalismus in Deutschland* (Frankfurt, 1988), 32.
21. Christian Bansa to Heinrich von Gagern, 9 Jan. 1842, Gießen, in Gagern, *Briefe*, 247.
22. Manfred Püschner, 'Die Rheinkrise von 1840/41 und die anti-feudale

Oppositionsbewegung', in Helmut Bleiber (ed.), *Bourgeoisie und bürgerliche Umwälzung in Deutschland, 1789–1871* (Berlin, 1977), 122, 125.

23. Gagern, 29 Jan. 31, in Gagern, *Briefe*, 92; see also similar sentiments in Hansemann, 1830, 72.
24. Obenaus, *Anfänge des Parlamentarismus in Preußen*, 726.
25. David Hansemann, *Preußen und Frankreich. Staatswirtschaftlich und politisch unter vorzüglicher Berücksichtigung der Rheinzprovinz* (Leipzig, 1834), 218–21.
26. Hansemann, 1830, 17–18.
27. Ibid., 1830, 19.
28. Hansemann, 1840, 217.
29. Cited in Püschner, 'Rheinkrise und anti-feudale Oppositionsbewegung', 125.
30. Hansemann, 1830, 22–5, 28, 67 *et passim*; Monika Wienfort, *Monarchie in der bürgerlichen Gesellschaft. Deutschland und England von 1640 bis 1848* (Göttingen, 1993). 181; 1834 memorandum, 218–19, 221, 245, etc.
31. Angelow, *Von Wien nach Königgrätz*, 114.
32. Ibid., 115; Helmut Seier, 'Zur Frage der militärischen Exekutive in der Konzeption des Deutschen Bundes', in Johannes Kunisch and Barbara Stollberg-Rillinger (eds), *Staatsverfassung und Heeresverfassung in der europäischen Geschichte der frühen Neuzeit* (Berlin, 1986), 437, Sontheim on importance of Austria.
33. Paul Hassell, *Josef Maria von Radowitz, I. 1797–1848* (Berlin, 1905), 404.
34. Buchner, 'Der Durchbruch des modernen Nationalismus', 314–18.
35. David E. Barclay, *Frederick William IV and the Prussian Monarchy, 1840–1861* (Oxford, 1995), 189.
36. Billinger, 'They sing the best songs badly', 109.
37. Hassell, *Radowitz*, 311.
38. Buchner, 'Der Durchbruch des modernen Nationalismus', 322.
39. Dieter Düding, *Organisierter gesellschaftlicher Nationalismus in Deutschland (1808–1847). Bedutung und Funktion der Turner-und Sängervereine für die deutsche nationalbewegung* (Munich, 1984), 214.
40. Barclay, *Frederick William IV*, 41.
41. Hassell, *Radowitz*, 295.
42. Angelow, *Von Wien nach Königgrätz*, 130
43. Heinrich to Hans Christian von Gagern, 11 Jan 1845, p. 286.
44. Metternich to Canitz, 22 Aug 46, Königswart, in Metternich, *Papieren*, VII, 257.
45. Harald Müller, *Im Widerstreit von Interventionsstrategie und Anpassungszwang. Die Außenpolitik Oesterreichs und Preußens zwischen dem Wiener Kongreß 1814/15 und der Februarrevolution, 1848*, 2 vols (Berlin, 1990), II, 484–5, 495–6.
46. Harald Müller, 'Der Blick über die deutschen Grenzen. Zu den Forderungen der bürgerlichen Opposition in Preußen nach außenpolitischer Einflußnahme am Vorabend und während des ersten Preußischen Vereinigten Landtags von 1847', *Jahrbuch für Geschichte*, 32 (1985), 213.
47. Harald Müller, 'Zu den außenpolitischen Zielvorstellungen der gemäßigten Liberalen am Vorabend und im Verlauf der bürgerlich-demokratischen Revolution von 1848/49 am Beispiel der "Deutschen Zeitung"', in Bleiber (ed.), *Bourgeoisie und bürgerliche Umwälzung*, 233.
48. Müller, 'Der Blick über die Deutschen Grenzen', 219.
49. Müller, 'Deutsche Zeitung', 236–8.

50. Ibid., 237.
51. Müller, *Widerstreit*, I 10, 59, II, 665.
52. Cited in Geoffrey Wawro, *The Austro-Prussian War: Austria's war with Prussia and Italy in 1866* (Cambridge, 1996), 31.
53. Hassell, *Radowitz*, 424.
54. Wolfgang Keul, *Die Bundesmilitärkommission (1819–1866) als politisches Gremium. Ein Beitrag zur Geschichte des Deutschen Bundes* (Frankfurt, 1977), 225–6.
55. Eduard Bleich (ed.), *Der erste Vereinigte Landtag in Berlin 1847. Dritter Theil Verhandlungen nach den stenographischen Berichten 19. Mai bis 11 Juni* (Berlin, 1847), I, 226.
56. Bleich (ed.), *Der erste Vereinigte Landtag*, III, 1510–11.
57. Ibid., 1467, also 1454.
58. Ibid., 1506.
59. Müller, 'Der Blick über die deutschen Grenzen', 205, 212, Müller, *Widenstreit*, II, 453; Bleich debates, *Der erste Vereinigte Landtag*, II, 914, 927, III, 1287.
60. See also Bleich, *Der erste Vereinigte Landtag*, I, 11ff.
61. Lee, '1840, the Confederation and military reform', 582.
62. Ibid., 581–2.
63. Speech of Heinrich von Gagern to Landtag of Hesse-Darmstadt, 25 July 1831, in Gagern, *Briefe*, 149–50.
64. Harald Müller, 'Der Widerhall auf den Schweizer Sonderbundskrieg 1847 in den Staaten des Deutschen Bundes', 230, 234.
65. Metternich's thoughts on Hungary, late 1844, Metternich, *Papieren*, VII, p. 51.
66. Arthur G. Haas, 'Continuing calm or continuing calamity: Metternich's perceptions of revolutionary danger in Austrian Italy', *PCRE*, (1989), 620, *passim*.
67. Metternich to Schwarzenberg, 26 June 1849, Richmond, in Metternich, *Papieren*, VIII, p. 481.
68. Brandt, *Neoabsolutismus*, 88.
69. Haas, 'Metternich's perceptions of revolutionary danger in Italy', 622–3.
70. Brandt, *Neoabsolutismus*, 145–51.
71. Jürgen Bergmann, 'Oekonomische Vorraussetzungen der Revolution von 1848. Zur Krise von 1845 bis 1848 in Deutschland', in Hans-Ulrich Wehler (ed.), *200 Jahre amerikanische Revolution und moderne Geschichtsforschung* (Göttingen, 1976), 285.
72. Jonathan Sperber, *Rhineland Radicals: the democratic movement and the revolution of 1848-1849* (Princeton, NJ, 1991),
73. Evans, 'Habsburgs and Hungary', 41.
74. Arnost Klima, 'The Bourgeois Revolution of 1848–49 in Central Europe', in Roy Porter and Mikulas Teich (eds), *Revolution in History* (Cambridge, 1986), 78, 89.
75. See Langewiesche, *Liberalismus*.
76. See Franz J. Bauer, *Bürgerwege und Bürgerwelten: familienbiographische Untersuchungen zum deutschen Bürgertum im 19. Jahrhundert* (Göttingen, 1991), 140–4.
77. Müller, 'Deutsche Zeitung', 234.
78. Erb and Bergmann, *Nachtseite der Judenemanzipation*, 253.
79. Stefan Rohrbacher, *Antijüdische Ausschreitungen in Vormärz und Revolution (1815–1848/49)* (Berlin, 1993).

80. Reinhard Rürup, *Emanzipation und Antisemitismus* (Göttingen, 1975), *passim*.
81. Clark, *Politics of Conversion*, 160.
82. For a strong argument that the countryside did not withdraw see Sperber, *Rhineland Radicals*, and Dieter Langewiesche, 'Die deutsche Revolution von 1848/49 und die vorrevolutionäre Gesellschaft: Forschungsstand und Forschungsperspektiven, Teil II', *Archiv für Sozialgeschichte*, 31 (1991), 412.
83. Barclay, *Frederick William IV*, 171.
84. See Eckhard Trox, *Militärischer Konservativismus. Kriegervereine und 'Militärpartei' in Preußen zwischen 1815 und 1848/49* (Stuttgart, 1990).
85. Wienfort, *Monarchie*, 193, 203, *et passim*.
86. See Mooser, *Ländliche Klassengesellschaft*.
87. Karl-Egon Lönne, *Politischer Katholismus im 19. und 20. Jahrhundert* (Frankfurt am Main, 1986), 110.
88. See the exhaustive study of Heinrich Best, *Die Männer von Bildung und Besitz. Struktur und Handeln parlamentarischer Führungsgruppen in Deutschland und Frankreich 1848/49* (Düsseldorf, 1990), 466–9.
89. Angelow, *Von Wien nach Königgrätz*, 149.
90. Angelow, *Von Wien nach Königgrätz*, 151.
91. Loyd Lee, 'People's army or princely armies: the German revolution of 1848–49', *PCRE*, (1989), 650.
92. Eckhard Trox, *Militärischer Konservativismus: Kriegervereine und Militärpartei in Preussen zwischen 1815 und 1848/49* (Stuttgart, 1990), 234.
93. Barclay, *Frederick William IV*, 162.
94. Langewiesche, 'Die deutsche Revolution von 1848/49 und die vorrevolutionäre Gesellschaft', 379.
95. Wollstein, *Das Großdeutschland der Paulskirche*, 249.
96. Stanley Z. Pech, *The Czech Revolution of 1848* (Chapel Hill, NC, 1969), 334–5.
97. Ibid., 337.
98. Günter Wollstein, *Das 'Großdeutschland' der Paulskirche. Nationale Ziele der bürgerlichen Revolution 1848/49* (Düsseldorf, 1977), 212.
99. Feldman, *Cambridge History of Poland*, 358.
100. Wollstein, *Das Großdeutschland der Paulskirche*, 130–5.
101. Ibid., 122.
102. Müller, 'Deutsche Zeitung', 249.
103. Ibid., 254–5.
104. Ibid., 245.
105. See Ralph C. Canevali, 'The "false French alarm": revolutionary panic in Baden, 1848', in *CEH*, 18 (1985), esp. 120, 130, 134.
106. Angelow, *Von Wien nach Königsgrätz*, 133–4.
107. Werner, *Bavaria in the German Confederation*, 205.
108. Felix Rachfahl, *Deutschland, König Friedrich Wilhelm III und die Berliner Märzrevolution* (Halle, 1901), 76, 138–9; Werner, *Bavaria in the German Confederation*, 215.
109. See W. E. Mosse, *The European Powers and the German Question, 1848–1871. With special reference to England and Russia* (Cambridge, 1958): Günther Gillessen, *Lord Palmerston und die Einigung Deutschlands. Die englische Politik von der Paulskirche bis zu den Dresdener Konferenzen 1848–1851* (Lübeck, 1961), esp. 149.

110. Mosse, *The European Powers and the German Question*, 31.
111. Gillessen, *Lord Palmerston und die Einigung Deutschlands*, 152; Mosse, *The European Powers and the German Question*, 18–19.
112. Radowitz memorandum, 20 Nov. 1847, in Hassel, *Radowitz*, 461.
113. Rachfahl, *Deutschland, König Friedrich Wilhelm III und die Berliner Märzrevolution*, 63.
114. Radowitz memorandum, 28 Feb. 1848, in Hassel, *Radowitz*, 483.
115. Rachfahl, *Deutschland, König Friedrich Wilhelm III und die Berliner Märzrevolution*, 115.
116. Ibid., 82.
117. Ibid., 99–100.
118. Barclay, *Frederick William IV*, 146.
119. Angelow, *Von Wien nach Königsgrätz*, 135.
120. Cited Rachfahl, *Deutschland, König Friedrich Wilhelm III und die Berliner Märzrevolution*, 36.
121. Lawrence Sondhaus, 'Schwarzenberg, Austria and the German Question, 1848-1851', *International History Review*, 13 (1991), 6; Roy A. Austensen, 'Metternich, Austria, and the German Question, 1848–51', *International History Review*, 13 (1991), 22.
122. Kraehe, 'Foreign policy and the nationality problem', 27.
123. Angelow, *Von Wien nach Königsgrätz*, 161.
124. Offenburg demands of Democrats, 10 Sept. 1847, in Ernst Rudolf Huber (ed.), *Dokumente zur deutschen Verfassungsgeschichte*, I (Stuttgart, 1957), 262.
125. Cited in Huber (ed.), *Dokumente, I*, 269.
126. Wollstein, *Das Großdeutschland der Paulskirche*, 31.
127. Heppenheim programme of Liberals, 10 Oct. 1847, in Huber (ed.), *Dokumente, I*, 262–3.
128. Wollstein, *Das Großdeutschland der Paulskirche*, 40.
129. Ibid., 295. On the initial determination of German Liberals to include Austria see 284.
130. See Adolf M. Birke, 'German Catholics and the Quest for National Unity', in Hagen Schulze (ed.), *Nation-building in central Europe* (Leamington Spa, Hamburg and New York, 1987), 57.
131. Langewiesche, *Liberalismus*, 54.
132. Wollstein, *Das Großdeutschland der Paulskirche*, 124; Vorparlament: Huber (ed.), *Dokumente, I*, 271.
133. Müller, 'Deutsche Zeitung', 242.
134. Hobsbawm, *Nations and Nationalism*, 31; Jiri Koralka, *Tschechen im Habsburgerreich und in Europa, 1815–1914. Sozialgeschichtliche Zusammenhänge der neuzeitlichen Nationsbildung und der Nationalitätenfrage in den böhmischen Ländern* (Munich, 1991), 39.
135. Müller, 'Deutsche Zeitung', 241; Wollstein, *Das Großdeutschland der Paulskirche*, 217.
136. Pech, *The Czech Revolution*, 178.
137. Ibid., 185.
138. Cited in Koralka, *Tschechen im Habsburgerreich und Europa*, 175.
139. Schmidt, 'Internationale Stellung', 35–9.
140. Cited in Müller, 'Deutsche Zeitung', 247.

141. Cited in Wollstein, *Das Großdeutschland der Paulskirche*, 316.
142. Wollstein, *Das Großdeutschland der Paulskirche*, 110.
143. Müller, 'Deutsche Zeitung', 258.
144. Cited in Felix Gilbert, *Johann Gustav Droysen und die preussisch-deutsche Frage* (Munich and Berlin, 1931), 121–2.
145. Cited in Wollstein, *Das Großdeutschland der Paulskirche*, 335.

## 6  Conclusion

1. Cited in Austensen, 'Metternich, Austria and the German question', 1848–1851', 27.
2. Quoted in Wollstein, *Das Großdeutschland der Paulskirche*, 241.
3. Quoted in Lenger, *Sozialgeschichte der deutschen Handwerker*, 88.
4. W. R. Lee, 'Tax structure and economic growth in Germany (1750–1850)', *Journal of Economic History*, 4 (1975), 155.
5. D. E. Schremmer, 'Taxation and Public Finance: Britain, France and Germany', in Peter Mathias and Sidney Pollard (eds), *The Cambridge Economic History of Europe*. Vol. VIII. *The Industrial Economies: the development of economic and social policies* (Cambridge, 1989), 419.
6. Quoted in the *Frankfurter Allgemeine Zeitung*, 19 Jan. 96.
7. Peter Gray, *The Irish Famine. New Horizons* (London, 1995).
8. Püschner, 'Rheinkrise und feudale Oppositionsbewegung', 115.
9. Oscar Pechel quoted in Detlef Döring, 'Neue Beiträge zur Geschichte der Bildungs- und Forschungsinstitutionen vom ausgehenden 18. bis zum 20. Jahrhundert', *Archiv für Sozialgeschichte*, 32 (1992), 451.
10. Cited in T. C. W. Blanning, 'The death and transfiguration of Prussia', *Historical Journal*, 29 (1986), 444.

# BIBLIOGRAPHICAL ESSAY

By far and away the best detailed general histories of Germany in this period are James J. Sheehan, *German History, 1770–1866* (Oxford, 1989) and Thomas Nipperdey, *Germany from Napoleon to Bismarck, 1800–1866*, (trans. Daniel Nolan, Dublin, 1995). Both volumes are a little weak on Austria and the general Habsburg context, which may be supplemented by R. J. W Evans, 'The Habsburgs and the Hungarian problem, 1790–1848', in *Transactions of the Royal Historical Society*, 39 (1989), 41–62, and R. J. W. Evans, 'The Habsburg monarchy and Bohemia, 1526–1848', in Mark Greengrass (ed.), *Conquest and Coalescence* (London, 1991). The essential international context is set out in Paul Schroeder's magisterial *The Transformation of European Politics, 1763–1848* (Oxford, 1994).

General themes are well covered in R. J. Evans and W. R. Lee, *The German Family: essays on the social history of the family in nineteenth- and twentieth-century Germany* (London, 1981); R. J. Evans and W. R. Lee (eds), *The German Peasantry: conflict and community in rural society from the eighteenth to the twentieth centuries* (London, 1986); David Blackbourn and R. J. Evans (eds), *The German Bourgeoisie: essays on the social history of the German middle class from the late eighteenth to the early twentieth century* (London and New York, 1991); Charles E. McClelland, *State, Society and University in Germany, 1700–1914* (Cambridge, 1980); Ute Frevert, *Women in German History: from bourgeois emancipation to sexual liberation* (New York, Oxford and Munich, 1988); Lynn Abrams and Elizabeth Harvey, *Gender Relations in German History: power, agency and experience from the sixteenth to the twentieth century* (London, 1997); David Good, *The Economic Rise of the Habsburg Empire, 1750–1914* (Berkeley, CA, 1984); Mark Roseman (ed.), *Generations in Conflict: youth revolt and generation formation in Germany, 1770–1968* (Cambridge, 1995); D. E. Schremmer, 'Taxation and Public Finance: Britain, France and Germany', in Peter Mathias and Sidney Pollard (eds), *The Cambridge Economic History of Europe. Vol. VIII. The Industrial Economies: the development of economic and social policies* (Cambridge, 1989), 315–494; W. R. Lee, 'Tax structure and economic growth in Germany, 1750–1850', *Journal of Economic History*, 4 (1975), 153–78; Geoffrey Cocks and Konrad Jarausch (eds), *The German Professions, 1800–1950* (New York, 1990); and the invaluable series edited by Anthony Nicholls, Werner Pöls and Gerhard A. Ritter, *German Historical Perspectives*, which provides syntheses of recent German-language research on specialist areas: Klaus J. Bade (ed.), *Population, Labour and Migration in 19th- and 20th- Century Europe*, Peter-Christian Witt (ed.), *Wealth and Taxation in Central Europe: the history and sociology of public finance*, and Hagen Schulze (ed.), *Nation-building in Central Europe* (see below).

Jewish issues are particularly well-covered: Jacob Katz, *Out of the Ghetto: the social background of Jewish emancipation, 1770–1870* (Cambridge, MA, 1974); Paul Lawrence Rose, *Revolutionary Anti-Semitism in Germany from Kant to Wagner* (Princeton, NJ, 1990); C. M. Clark, *The Politics of Conversion: missionary protestantism and the Jews in Prussia, 1728–1941* (Oxford, 1995); David Sorkin, *The Transformation of German Jewry, 1780–1840* (New York, 1987); Werner E. Mosse, 'From "Schutzjuden" to "Deutsche Staatsbürger Jüdischen Glaubens": the long and bumpy road of Jewish emancipation in Germany', in Pierre Birnbaum and Ira Katznelson (eds), *Paths of Emancipation: Jews, states and citizenship* (Princeton, NJ, 1995), 59–93; Reinhard Rürup, 'The tortuous and thorny path to legal equality: "Jew laws" and emancipatory legislation in Germany from the late eighteenth century', *Leo Baeck Institute Yearbook*, 31 (1986), 3–33.

Finally, John Breuilly 'State-building, modernization and liberalism from the late eighteenth century to unification: German peculiarities', *European History Quarterly*, 22 (1992), 257–84, and T. C. W. Blanning, 'Empire and state in Germany, 1648–1848', *German History*, 12 (1994), 220–36, are both very stimulating on new literature and old problems.

A good general introduction to eighteenth-century Germany is still T. C. W. Blanning, 'Prologue: The "German Problem" in the Eighteenth Century', in idem, *Reform and Revolution in Mainz, 1743–1803* (Cambridge, 1974), 1–38.

The best general book on the *Reich* is still John G. Gagliardo, *The Holy Roman Empire as idea and reality, 1763–1806* (Bloomington, IN, and London, 1980). It should be supplemented by the very useful articles in Supplement 4 (1986) of the *Journal of Modern History*, especially those by James Allen Vann ('New directions for study of the Old *Reich*') and Karl Otmar von Aretin ('Russia as guarantor power of the imperial constitution under Catherine II'). A good discussion of the role of the estates in the empire can be found in Peter H. Wilson, *War, State and Society in Württemberg, 1677–1793* (Cambridge, 1995). Mack Walker, *Johann Jakob Moser and the Holy Roman Empire of the German Nation* (Chapel Hill, NC, 1981) is very useful on the vibrant imperial reform debate.

An excellent general introduction to society and economy in eighteenth-century Germany can be found in Sheilagh Ogilvie (ed.), *Germany: a new social and economic history, 1630–1800*, vol. II (London, 1996); this includes coverage of all the recent German-language research. John Theibault, 'Toward a new socio-cultural history of the rural world of early modern Germany', *CEH*, 24 (1991), 304–24, is a useful discussion of the methodological approaches to rural Germany before 1800. Mack Walker, *German Home Towns: community, state, general estate, 1648–1871* (Ithaca, NY, 1971) is a classic on urban life.

For more detail on the interminable proto-industrialization debate see: Peter Kriedtke, Hans Medick und Jürgen Schlumbohm, *Industrialization before Industrialization: rural industry in the genesis of capitalism* (Cambridge, 1981); D. C. Coleman, 'Proto-industrialisation: a concept too many?', *Economic History Review*, 36 (1983) 435–48; P. Kriedtke et al., 'Proto-industrialisation revisited: demography, social structure, and modern domestic industry', *Continuity and Change*, 8 (1993) 217–52; M. German, 'Proto-industrialisation in an urban environment: Vienna, 1750–1857', *Continuity and Change*, 8 (1993) 281–320; Sheilagh Ogilvie and Markus German (eds), *European Proto-industrialisation* (Cambridge, 1996).

On population see: Arthur Imhof, *Life Expectancies in Germany from the 17th to the 19th century* (also in German) (1990); John Knodel, *Demographic Behaviour in the Past: a study of fourteen German village populations in the eighteenth and nineteenth centuries* (1988). John Komlos, *Nutrition and Development: an anthropometric history of the eighteenth century Habsburg monarchy* (Princeton, NJ, 1989) should be read in conjunction with Hans-Joachim Voth, 'Height, nutrition and labour: recasting the "Austrian model"', *Journal of Interdisciplinary History*, 25 (1995), 627–36 and the subsequent debate in that journal. Steven Lawrence Hochstadt, 'Migration in pre-industrial Germany', *CEH*, 16 (1983), 195–224 is useful on migration; Hans Fenske, 'International migration: Germany in the eighteenth century', *CEH*, 4 (1980), 332–47, is focused on the period before 1780, but none the less provides an interesting introduction to the phenomena of migration and *Peuplierungspolitik*.

On deviance, women and the poor see: Isabel Hull, *Sexuality, State and Civil Society in Germany, 1700–1815* (Ithaca, NY, and London, 1996); Otto Ulbricht, 'The debate about foundling hospitals in eighteenth-century Germany: infanticide, illegitimacy and infant mortality rates', *Central European History*, 18 (1985), 211–56; Peter Petschauer, *The Education of Women in Eighteenth-century Germany* (Lewiston, New York, 1989); Lesley Sharpe, 'Theodor Gottlieb von Hippel: Argumentative strategies in the debate on the rights of women', in Dario Castiglione and Lesley Sharpe (eds), *Shifting the Boundaries: transformations of the languages of public and private in the eighteenth century* (Exeter, 1995); and the recent case study by Karl Wegert, *Popular Culture, Crime and Social Control in Eighteenth-century Württemberg* (Stuttgart, 1994).

A good introduction to peasants and nobles can be found in H. M. Scott (ed.), *The European Nobilities in the Seventeenth and Eighteenth Centuries*, vol. 2 (London and New York, 1995), especially the article by Edgar Melton 'The Prussian Junkers, 1600–1786', which summarizes his considerable and innovative *oeuvre* on the *Junkers*. A rather bleak view of the Prussian Junkers is taken by Hanna Schissler, 'The Social and Political Power of the Prussian Junkers', in Martin Blinkhorn and Ralph Gibson (eds), *Landownership and Power in Modern Europe* (London, 1991), 99–110. See also F. L. Carsten, *A History of the Prussian Junkers* (Aldershot, 1989); and R. M. Berdahl, *The Politics of the Prussian Nobility: the development of a conservative ideology 1770–1848* (Princeton, NJ, 1988). There are no recent comparable works on Austria. Roman Rosdolsky, 'On the nature of peasant serfdom in central and eastern Europe', *Journal of Central European Affairs*, 12 (1952–3), 128–39, concentrates on the Habsburg lands. Peasants in the Third Germany are discussed in Helmut Gabel and Winfried Schulze, 'Peasant Resistance and Politicization in Germany in the Eighteenth Century', in Eckhart Hellmuth (ed.), *The Transformation of Political Culture. England and Germany in the late eighteenth century* (Oxford, 1990) and Stefan Brakensiek, 'Agrarian individualism in north-western Germany', *German History*, 12 (1994). Useful general studies are: Wilhelm Abel, *Agricultural Fluctuation in Europe*

(London, 1980), 158–220; and Jerome Blum, 'The condition of the European peas-antry on the eve of emancipation', *Journal of Modern History*, 46 (1974), 395–424. There is also much relevant detail in Jerome Blum, *The End of the Old Order in Rural Europe* (Princeton, NJ, 1978).

A good place to start on Enlightened Reform Absolutism is Hamish Scott (ed.), *Enlightened Absolutism: reform and reformers in later eighteenth century Europe* (Basingstoke and London, 1990), especially the articles by H. M. Scott (on the Habsburg monarchy), R. J. W. Evans (on Hungary), Charles Ingrao (on the smaller German states) and T. C. W. Blanning (on Prussia). Marc Raeff, 'The well-ordered police state and the development of modernity in seventeenth and eighteenth century Europe: an attempt at a comparative approach', *AHR*, 80 (1975), 1221–43 and Keith Tribe, 'Cameralism and the science of government', *JMH*, 56 (1984), 263–84, are useful studies of reforming methods and motivations. Mary Fulbrook, *Piety and Politics: religion and the rise of absolutism in England, Württemberg and Prussia* (Cambridge, 1983) examines the complex links between religion and absolutism. Useful case studies are: Charles Ingrao, *The Hessian Mercenary State: ideas, institutions and reform under Frederick II 1760–1785* (Cambridge, 1987); T. C. W. Blanning, *Joseph II* (London, 1994); Derek Beales, *Joseph II: in the shadow of Maria Theresa 1741–1780* (Cambridge, 1987); James van Horn Melton, *Absolutism and the Eighteenth-century Origins of Compulsory Schooling in Prussia and Austria* (Cambridge, 1988); J. Komlos, 'Institutional change under pressure: enlightened government policy in the 18th century Habsburg monarchy', *Journal of European Economic History*, 15 (1986), 427–82.

The German Enlightenment is best approached at first via the articles by Joachim Whaley and T. C. W. Blanning in Roy Porter and Mikulas Teich (eds), *The Enlightenment in its National Contexts* (Cambridge, 1981). A useful antidote to the common notion of the 'unpolitical German' can be found in Fania Oz-Salzberger, *Translating the Enlightenment. Scottish civic discourse in eighteenth-century Germany* (Oxford, 1995). Jürgen Habermas, *The Structural Transformation of the Public Sphere* (Cambridge, 1989) is now available in translation. On the 'public sphere' and the emergence of a literary market see in general: Albert Ward, *Book Production, Fiction and the German Reading Public, 1740–1800* (London, 1974); Daniel Moran, *Towards the Century of Words: Johann Cotta and the politics of the public realm in Germany, 1795–1832* (Berkeley, Los Angeles and Oxford, 1990); Reinhart Koselleck, *Critique and Crisis: enlightenment and the pathologies of modern society* (Oxford, 1988); and Craig Calhoun (ed.), *Habermas and the Public Sphere* (Cambridge, MA, and London, 1992); Immanuel Kant's famous 'An answer to the question: what is enlightenment?' can be found in Hans Reiss (ed.), *Kant's Political Writings* (Cambridge, 1970), 54–60. Also useful are: Richard van Dülmen, *The Society of the Enlightenment: the rise of the middle class and enlightenment culture in Germany* (Cambridge, 1992); H. B. Nisbet, 'Was ist Aufklärung? The concept of enlightenment in 18th century Germany', *Journal of European Studies*, 12 (1982), 77–95.

International relations before 1792 are well covered by Schroeder, *Transformation of European Politics*. For the various external pressures on Austria see Karl Roider, *Austria's Eastern Question 1700–1790* (Princeton, NJ, 1982); H. M. Scott, 'Aping the great powers: Frederick the Great and the defence of Prussia's international position', *GH*, 12 (1994), 286–307 is an excellent discussion of Prussian security dilemmas. Charles Ingrao, 'Habsburg strategy and geopolitics during the 18th century', in *East Central European Society and War in the pre-Revolutionary 18th Century*, ed. B. Kiraly, Peter Sugar and G. Rothenburg (New York, 1982), stops short of 1780 but provides invaluable background on Austrian preoccupations.

The (non-)Revolutionary decade in Germany is the preserve of T. C. W. Blanning: *Reform and Revolution in Mainz 1743–1803* (Cambridge, 1974), Part 3: Germany and the French Revolution; T. C. W. Blanning, *The French Revolution in Germany* (Oxford, 1983); T. C. W. Blanning, 'The French revolution and the modernisation of Germany', *Central European History*, 22/2 (1989); T. C. W. Blanning, 'German Jacobins and the French Revolution', *Historical Journal*, 23/4 (1980). Still useful, especially on literary responses to the French Revolution is G. P. Gooch, *Germany and the French Revolution* (London, 1920, reprint 1965). See also: Janet Polasky, *Revolution in Brussels 1787–1793* (London, 1987); Horst Dippel, *Germany and the American Revolution 1770–1800* (Chapel Hill, NC, 1977); K. H. Wegert, *German Radicals Confront the Common People: revolutionary politics and popular politics, 1789–1849* (Mainz, 1992); Kinley Brauer and William E. Wright (eds), *Austria in the Age of the French Revolution* (Minneapolis, 1990). Ernst Wangermann, *From Joseph II to the Jacobin Trials: government policy and public opinion in the Habsburg dominions in the period of the French Revolution* (Oxford, 1959) is typical of the vast literature exaggerating the role of German Jacobins.

The initial diplomatic response to French expansionism is covered in: T. C. W. Blanning, *The Origins of the French Revolutionary Wars* (London, 1986) and T. C. W. Blanning, *The French Revolutionary Wars* (London, 1996). Karl Roider, *Baron Thugut and Austria's response to the French Revolution* (Princeton, NJ, 1987) attempts to rehabilitate Thugut and Austrian policy. Brendan Simms, *The Impact of Napoleon: Prussian high politics, foreign policy and executive reform, 1797–1806* (Cambridge, 1997) discusses Prussian responses.

There is no recent synthesis on the Prussian, *Rheinbund* and Austrian reforms. A good discussion of pre-reform in Prussia is Otto Hintze, 'Prussian Reform Movements before 1806', in *The Historical Essays of Otto Hintze*, ed. Felix Gilbert (New York, 1975). Individual aspects of the Prussian reform movement are covered by: Marion Gray, 'Schroetter, Schön and Society: aristocratic liberalism versus middle-class liberalism in Prussia, 1808', *Central European History*, 6 (1973); and Peter Paret, *Yorck and the Era of Reform in Prussia, 1807–1815* (Princeton, NJ, 1966). Mathew Levinger, 'Hardenberg, Wittgenstein, and the constitutional question in Prussia, 1815–22', *German History*, 8 (1990), 257–77, makes a strong case that political reform was intended to enhance not subvert the monarchy. The philosophical background to some of the reforms is set out in Wilhelm von Humboldt, *The Limits of State Action* (Cambridge, 1969) edited by John Burrow. Karl A. Roider, 'The Habsburg foreign ministry and political reform, 1801–1805', *CEH*, 22 (1989), 160–82 is somewhat broader than its title suggests. Austrian military reform is covered in Gunther Rothenberg, *Napoleon's Great Adversaries: the Archduke Charles and the Austrian Army, 1792–1814* (Bloomington, IN, 1982). The articles by Barbara Anderson (Nassau), Loyd E. Lee (Baden) and Lawrence J. Flockherzie (Saxony) in 'Symposium: state building in the "Third Germany"', *CEH*, 24 (1991), are useful introductions to the *Rheinbund* reforms and their consequences. A good introduction to fiscal reform in the Third Germany is Hans-Peter Ullmann, 'The emergence of modern public debts in Bavaria and Baden between 1780 and 1820', in Peter-Christian Witt (ed.), *Wealth and Taxation in Central Europe: the history and sociology of public finance* (Leamington Spa, Hamburg and New York, 1987), 63–80.

An indispensable introduction to German nationalism is Hagen Schulze, *The Course of German Nationalism: from Frederick the Great to Bismarck, 1763–1867* (Cambridge, 1991). This may be supplemented by: Michael Hughes, *Nationalism and Society. Germany 1800–1945* (London, 1988); John Breuilly (ed.), *The State of Germany: the national idea in the making, unmaking and remaking of a modern nation-state* (London, 1992); and Robert M. Berdahl, 'New thoughts on German nationalism', *American Historical Review*, 77/1 (1972) 65–80. W. C. Langsam, *The Napoleonic Wars and German Nationalism in Austria* (New York, 1930) investigates the neglected phenomenon of Austrian-led nationalism in 1809.

The liberation of Germany is covered by: Hans A. Schmitt, 'Stein, Alexander and the crusade against Napoleon', *JMH*, 31 (1959); and Enno Kraehe, *Metternich's German policy. Vol. I. The contest with Napoleon* (Princeton, NJ, 1963), which is crucial to an understanding of the impact of Russia.

Interstate relations after 1815 and the German Confederation are discussed in R. D. Billinger, *Metternich and the German Question: state rights and federal duties 1820–1834* (London, 1991). Austrian policy is surveyed in F. R. Bridge, *The Habsburg Monarchy among the Great Powers, 1815–1918* (Providence, RI, and Oxford, 1990) and Barbara Jelavich, *The Habsburg Empire in European Affairs, 1814–1918* (Chicago, 1969). Prussian policy is well covered in Lawrence J. Baack, *Christian Bernstorff and Prussia: diplomacy and reform conservatism, 1818–1832* (New Brunswick, NJ, 1980). The role of Bavaria is discussed in George S. Werner, *Bavaria in the German Confederation, 1820–1848* (London, 1977). Also worth a look are Robert D. Billinger, 'The war scare of 1831 and Prussian-South German plans for the end of Austrian dominance in Germany', *Central European History*, 9 (1976), 203–19 and David T. Murphy, 'Prussian aims for the Zollverein, 1828–1833', *The Historian*, 53 (1991), 285–302. Enno Kraehe, 'Foreign policy and the nationalities problem in the Habsburg monarchy, 1800–1867', *Austrian History Yearbook* 3/3 (1967), 3–36 is a very useful discussion of the 'national' dimension in Austria.

Society and politics in Germany after 1815 are historiographically extremely well served. The growth of the national movement is described in Hagen Schulze (ed.), *Nation-building in Central Europe* (Leamington Spa, 1987), especially the article by Dieter Düding on associations. James J. Sheehan, *German Liberalism in the Nineteenth Century* (Chicago, 1978) remains the classic account of German liberalism in some of its permutations and ambiguities. German conservatism is discussed in Klaus Epstein, *The Genesis of German Conservatism* (Princeton, NJ, 1966); Andreas Fahrmeir's review article, 'Recent books on the ambiguities of German conservatism and nationalism', *HJ*, 39 (1996), 813–21 is also useful. A good short introduction to nineteenth-century German bureaucracy is Erich Angermann, 'Germany's "Peculiar institution"': the *Beamtentum*', in Erich Angermann and Marie-Luise Frings (eds), *Oceans Apart? Comparing Germany and the United States* (Stuttgart, 1981), 77–101. Despite its brevity Jonathan Sperber, 'State and civil society in Prussia: thoughts on a new edition of Reinhart Koselleck's *Preußen zwischen Reform und Revolution*', *Journal of Modern History*, 57/2 (1985), 278–96 is an excellent introduction to Prussia before 1848. The most recent work on the Prussian bureaucracy is Hermann Beck, *The Origins of the Authoritarian Welfare State in Prussia: conservatives, bureaucracy and the social question, 1815–1870* (Ann Arbor, MI, 1995). Alf Lüdtke, *Police and State in Prussia, 1815–1850* (Cambridge, 1989) is methodologically ambitious and claims that the Prussian bureaucracy was as brutal as the society it had to deal with.

Also of interest on state and society before 1848 are: Eric Dorn Brose, *The Politics of Technological Change in Prussia: out of the shadow of antiquity, 1809–1848* (Princeton, NJ, 1993); Kenneth Barkin, 'Social control and the Volksschule in Vormärz Prussia', *Central European History*, 16 (1983), 31–52; Karl A. Schleunes, *Schooling and Society: the politics of education in Prussia and Bavaria* (Oxford, New York and Munich, 1989); Arleen Marcia Turner, *Science, Medicine and the State in Germany: the case of Baden, 1815–1871* (New York and Oxford, 1993) discusses the links between science and liberalism; David Blackbourn, 'Between resignation and volatility: the German petite bourgeoisie in the nineteenth century', in G. Crossick and H.-G. Haupt (eds), *Shopkeepers and Master Artisans in nineteenth-century Europe* (London and New York, 1984), 35–61; Richard Bazillion, 'State bureaucracy and the modernization process in the Kingdom of Saxony, 1830–1861', *GH*, 13 (1995), 305–25; Rolland F. Lutz, 'The German revolutionary student movement 1819–1833', *Central European History*, 4 (1970), 215–41; Gary Stark, 'The ideology of the German Burschenschaft generation', *European Studies Review*, 8 (1978); Dagmar Herzog, *Intimacy and Exclusion: religious politics in pre-revolutionary Baden* (Princeton, NJ, 1996); John C. Fout (ed.), *German Women in the Nineteenth Century: a social history* (New York and London, 1984); and Richard Tilly, 'Popular disorders in nineteenth-century Germany: a preliminary survey', *Journal of Social History*, 4 (1970), 1–40.

Broader Austrian preoccupations are covered in: D. E. Emerson, *Metternich and the Political Police: security and subversion in the Habsburg monarchy, 1815–1830* (The Hague, 1968); George Barany, *Stephen Szechenyi and the Awakening of Hungarian Nationalism, 1791–1841* (Princeton, NJ, 1968); Egon Radvany, *Metternich's Projects for Reform in Austria* (The Hague, 1971).

Essential on the German working class – or lack of it – before 1850 is Jürgen Kocka, 'Problems of working class formation in Germany: the early years, 1800–1875', in Ira Katznelson and Aristide Zolberg (eds), *Working-class Formation: nineteenth-century patterns in western Europe and the United States* (Princeton, NJ, 1986), 279–351, which provides both a summary of his own extensive writings and recent German research. On population see Klaus J. Bade (ed.), *Population, Labour and Migration in 19th and 20th century Germany* (Leamington Spa, 1987), especially the articles by Peter Marschalck (population), Dieter Langewiesche and Friedrich Lenger (internal migration) and Reinhard Doerries (emigration). A useful introduction to 'pauperism' is Frederick D. Marquardt, '*Pauperismus* in Germany during the *Vormärz*', *CEH*, 2 (1969), 77–88. Recent research is tackled in Dirk Hoeder and Jörg Nagler (eds), *People in Transit: German migrations in comparative perspective, 1820–1930* (Cambridge, 1995).

Economy and industry are discussed briefly in W. R. Lee, 'Economic development and the state in nineteenth-century Germany', *Economic History Review*, 41 (1988), 346–67; Richard Tilly, 'Germany', and David Good, 'Austria-Hungary', in Richard Sylla and Gianni Toniolo (eds), *Patterns of European Industrialisation: the nineteenth century* (London, 1991), 175–96, 218–47. More detailed accounts are to be found in W. R. Lee (ed.) *German Industry and German Industrialisation* (London, 1991); F. Tipton, *Regional Variations in the Economic Development of Germany during the Nineteenth Century* (Middletown, T, 1976); David F. Good, *The economic rise of the Habsburg empire, 1750–1914* (Berkeley, Los Angeles and London, 1984); and John Komlos, *The Habsburg Monarchy as a Customs Union: economic development in the nineteenth century* (Princeton, NJ, 1983).

Unfortunately, there are very few works on the liberal nationalist public sphere and the growing fiscal-political crisis in Austria and Prussia after 1840. The introduction by Harm-Hinrich Brandt, 'Public finances of neo-absolutism in Austria in the 1850s: integration and modernisation', in Witt (ed.), *Wealth and Taxation*, 81–110, is indispensable for an understanding of the crisis in Austria. Alan Kahan, 'Liberalism and *Realpolitik* in Prussia, 1830–52: the case of David Hansemann', *German History*, 9 (1991), 280–307, is weak on liberal geopolitics. Loyd E. Lee, 'Confederation and German military reform', *Proceedings of the Consortium on Revolutionary Europe* [PCRE], (1987), 573–86, is a useful account of the effects of the Rhine Crisis.

The approach of 1848 is well-captured in Manfred Gailus, 'Food riots in Germany in the late 1840s', *Past and Present*, 145 (1994), 157–93. A readily accessible Marxist account, though lacking in the hard-headed *Realpolitik* of the original Marx and Engels, is Arnost Klima, 'The Bourgeois Revolution of 1848–49 in Central Europe', in Roy Porter and Mikulas Teich (eds), *Revolution in History* (Cambridge, 1986), 74–100. David Barclay's *Frederick William IV and the Prussian Monarchy, 1840–1861* (Oxford, 1995) is an excellent account of the role of the Prussian king during the revolution of 1848–9. Events in the Habsburg Empire are described in: Istvan Deak, *The Lawful Revolution: Louis Kossuth and the Hungarians, 1848–1849* (New York, 1979); Alan Sked, *The Survival of the Habsburg Empire: Radetzky, the Imperial army and the class war 1848* (London, 1979); R. J. Rath, *The Viennese Revolution of 1848* (New York, 1969); and Stanley Z. Pech, *The Czech Revolution of 1848* (Chapel Hill, NC, 1969). The divide between Liberals and Democrats is charted in: P. H. Noyes, *Organization and Revolution: working-class associations in the German revolutions of 1848–9* (Princeton, NJ, 1966); and Lenore O'Boyle, 'The Democratic left in Germany, 1848', *Journal of Modern History*, 33 (1961) 374–83. Jewish issues are addressed by W. E. Mosse, A. Paucker and R. Rürup (eds), *Revolution and Evolution: 1848 in German-Jewish history* (Tübingen, 1981), and most recently by James F. Harris, *The*

*People Speak! Anti-semitism and emancipation in nineteenth-century Bavaria* (Ann Arbor, MI, 1994). Finally, an introduction to the crucial diplomatic context can be found in W. E. Mosse, *The European Powers and the German Question, 1848–1871: with special reference to England and Russia* (Cambridge, 1958).

# INDEX